T0304307

FORCED SAVING

Mandating Private Retirement Incomes

Population ageing, combined with electoral pressure for smaller government, is inevitably leading to increased action to reform retirement provision policy to place much greater reliance on self-provision for the elderly. This development is bringing into ever sharper focus the need for research directed at exploring the links between private retirement provision and public sector policies and institutions. This book offers an analysis of pension policy from an economic perspective. It begins with an overview of the problem of population ageing around the world, and then provides a framework within which policy responses may be consistently assessed.

Hazel Bateman is a Senior Lecturer in Economics at the University of New South Wales, Sydney.

Geoffrey Kingston is an Associate Professor of Economics at the University of New South Wales, Sydney.

John Piggott is a Professor of Economics at the University of New South Wales, Sydney.

to Elizabeth, Nicholas and Thomas

Grace

and

Claire and Andrew

FORCED SAVING

Mandating Private Retirement Incomes

HAZEL BATEMAN
University of New South Wales

GEOFFREY KINGSTON
University of New South Wales

JOHN PIGGOTT
University of New South Wales

CAMBRIDGE
UNIVERSITY PRESS

CAMBRIDGE UNIVERSITY PRESS
Cambridge, New York, Melbourne, Madrid, Cape Town,
Singapore, São Paulo, Delhi, Mexico City

Cambridge University Press
The Edinburgh Building, Cambridge CB2 8RU, UK

Published in the United States of America by Cambridge University Press, New York

www.cambridge.org
Information on this title: www.cambridge.org/9780521481625

First published 2001

A catalogue record for this publication is available from the British Library

National Library of Australia Cataloguing in Publication Data
Bateman, Hazel.
Forced saving: mandating private retirement incomes
Bibliography.
Includes index.
ISBN 0 521 48162 7.
ISBN 0 521 48471 5.
1. Retirement income – Australia. 2. Saving and investment
– Australia. 3. Pensions – Government policy – Australia.
4. Pension trusts – Australia. I. Piggott, John, 1947– .
II. Kingston, Geoffrey H., 1950– . III. Title.
331.2520994

ISBN 978-0-521-48162-5 Hardback
ISBN 978-0-521-48471-8 Paperback

Contents

Preface and acknowledgments

This book had its origins in the observation that Australian retirement provision policies were quite different from those prevailing in most developed countries. By 1993 we had become aware that the Australian superannuation guarantee was an example of a distinct policy paradigm that was becoming increasingly prominent in the international policy debate. These policies pose a series of interesting and important research questions, spanning both finance and economics, on which analysis of the Australian experience might help to shed some light. As a result, a book seemed a sensible initiative. Had we known then that it would take eight years to complete, we might have had second thoughts.

Along the way, we have had help from many quarters. A steady stream of research assistants and associates toiled diligently and competently on our behalf, among them (in chronological order of association) Andrew Formica, Gina Wu, Suzy Casimiro and Deirdre Frost. Matthew Williams deserves special mention. He worked with us for the last 18 months, and acted as a hands-on editor through a number of drafts of the book, as well as providing research support. In addition to his excellent research and drafting skills, his patience and good humour were frequently important ingredients in the final stages of the book's completion.

Among our graduate research students, Suzanne Doyle and Sachi Purcal deserve special acknowledgment. We are particularly grateful to Suzanne for agreeing to the incorporation of joint research into Chapter 5 of the book. Sachi was (and is) an invaluable source of knowledge, particularly on the actuarial aspects of our work.

Financial support was forthcoming from a total of four Australian Research Council grants. One of these was a collaboration with AMP Ltd. We are grateful to these organisations for their support.

The final manuscript has benefited greatly from the comments of colleagues. Olivia Mitchell read the entire manuscript, and offered extensive comments, which resulted in major changes; Estelle James, Owen Covick and Carol White read several chapters and gave valuable advice. Individual chapters were read by Robert Palacios, Salvador Valdes-Prieto and Edward Whitehouse. Both Robin Derricourt and Peter Debus, commissioning editors of CUP Australia over the duration of the contract, encouraged, cajoled and remained courteous throughout. Edward Caruso, the copyeditor assigned to us, saved us from many ambiguities and considerably improved the final product. We are grateful to them all.

Finally, our families deserve a special salute for their understanding and forbearance through the long period during which the book was brought to fruition.

Tables

Figures

CHAPTER 1

Introduction

Pension policy has become one of the more volatile areas of economic reform in recent years. The onset of demographic transition, in developing and developed economies alike, has combined with concerns about the efficiency effects of a large public sector, to generate a search for pension reform options that reduce the legal responsibility of governments to provide financial support for the retired. Many countries around the world have recently undertaken reform, are in the middle of the reform process, or are actively debating reform options (see, for example, Kalisch and Aman 1998, Schwarz and Demirgüç-Kunt 1999 and Disney 2000).

A natural policy response to population ageing is to find ways to increase self-provision for retirement. This normally involves some minimum compulsory retirement saving, either by employees or their employers. Such schemes have been advocated by the World Bank (for example, *Averting the Old Age Crisis* (World Bank 1994a)) and have been adopted in a number of countries. Australia and Switzerland are among the developed nations to adopt mandatory policies, while among developing economies, Chile has the most mature system. More than a dozen countries, mostly from Latin America and the transition economies of central Europe, have either mandated private retirement provision or have stated their intention to reform their pension policies along these lines (see Palacios and Pallarès-Miralles 2000 for a complete list). Further, a number of developed countries have either reformed their pension systems in this direction (for example, the United Kingdom) or have debated doing so (the United States). Rarely has a novel policy design spread so swiftly across disparate nations.

The retirement policies operating in these countries all entail private-sector management of mandatory second-pillar retirement

1

accumulations. These are mainly of the defined contribution (DC), or accumulation type.

In spite of this rapid proliferation, there have been few attempts to systematically analyse the economic implications of the design and implementation of mandatory privately based retirement saving policies. This book attempts to partially fill this gap. Taking Australia as a benchmark case, but with appeal to general argument and to international experience, we examine the components of retirement policy, which must fit together to successfully deliver mandatory private retirement provision.

Impetus for reform

Most developed countries have more or less compulsory pay as you go (PAYG) retirement income provision. The central feature of this type of scheme is that tax payments by the currently working generation finance transfers to the currently retired. These entitlements are typically linked to the employment history of the retired worker. With balanced growth, this perpetual debt arrangement can be made equitable between generations, except that the first retired generation experiences a windfall gain, to be paid for by subsequent generations. Assuming that the efficiency implications of the perverse incentives set up by such an unfunded scheme are negligible, and insofar as bequest motives are weak, it is welfare-improving. When people are myopic (as well as disinclined to leave bequests) this welfare improvement will be all the greater. These characteristics of unfunded social security systems have made them popular with electorates in most countries where government contracts can be trusted.

Figure 1.1 dramatically illustrates the important role this paradigm plays in retirement policy throughout the world. Half of the 130 mandatory pension plans represented in Figure 1.1 are traditional PAYG

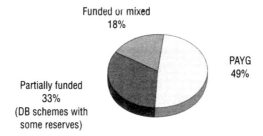

Figure 1.1 Mandatory pension plans in the world
Source: Palacios and Pallarès-Miralles (2000), Figure 3.4, p. 14

Table 1.1 Net pension liabilities and net public debt (% of GDP)

	Net public debt, 1994	Net pension liability, 1995–2050	Combined net debt liability
Major industrial countries	57.2	60.0	117.2
United States	63.3	25.7	89.0
Japan	33.2	106.8	140.0
Germany	52.5	110.7	163.2
France	42.4	113.6	156.0
Italy	112.9	75.5	188.4
United Kingdom	37.7	4.6	42.3
Canada	71.6	67.8	139.4
Sweden	54.5	20.4	74.9

Source: Chand and Jaeger (1996), Table 8

defined-benefit (DB) schemes, while another third are DB schemes with some reserves (partially funded). These reserves typically cover only a fraction of total pension liabilities. Reserves are transitory. In most of these countries the funds will start to dissipate as the scheme matures and population ageing takes its toll. The funded category includes provident funds like those in Singapore, India and Malaysia, as well as the multi-pillar schemes where one part of the mandatory system is a privately managed and fully funded scheme.

The ageing of the baby-boomers presents special problems for compulsory, unfunded PAYG retirement schemes. While currently a large working population is supporting a relatively small, retired population, the opposite will be true in another generation. This has implications not only for the aged, but for the economy as a whole. PAYG social security schemes seemed to be excellent policies when they were first introduced, and would have worked well enough if demographic equilibrium had been maintained, but population ageing has put intolerable strain on the early promises that were made.

Future liabilities are expected to be very large. Table 1.1 shows that among the major industrial countries, the current ratio of government debt to GDP stands at about 60%, and adding in future pension liabilities to 2050 adds another 60%. The position is worse in Japan, Germany and France, where net pension liabilities are around 110% of GDP (Chand and Jaeger 1996). On their own, these estimates carry with them serious implications for future saving and investment performance.

Seen from this perspective, the appeal of policies designed to have each generation provide to a greater extent for its own retirement is

Table 1.2 World population by region, 1990 and 2050 (millions)

	1990	2050	Change	% change
Africa	627	1999	1372	219
Latin America and Caribbean	435	804	370	85
Northern America	281	374	94	33
East And South-East Asia	1788	2644	856	48
South Asia	1185	2484	1299	110
Central and Western Asia	200	509	309	154
Europe	723	721	−2	0
Oceania	27	42	15	56
Total	5266	9578	4312	82

Source: World Bank (1994b)

understandable. Many developed nations are now looking to reform their social security systems with a shift towards self-provision and 'privatisation'. Demographics provide a major motivation for reform and are described further below.

In addition, the emphasis on market forces in aiding development and growth that emerged during the 1980s, and the associated thrust to curb centralised government inefficiency, were important factors in promoting the privatisation of pension policy. The trend towards smaller government has seen mandating replace provision as governments seek to meet the preferences of their constituents in this regard. This has been particularly true in Latin America, where corrupt PAYG schemes had become commonplace.

Demographics in more detail

Any discussion of global demographics should begin with a portrayal of overall magnitudes. Table 1.2 reports population estimates for the world's major regions, as they were in 1990, along with projections for 2050. The world's population is projected to increase rapidly over the next two generations, and this increase is even more marked among developing countries.

Of greater importance in the present context, however, is growth in the 'old' population, and again this transition is more dramatic in the developing countries. As the World Bank pointed out:

> Because of the broad diffusion of medical knowledge and declining fertility, developing countries are aging much faster than the industrial countries did … As a result, developing countries will have 'old' demographic profiles at

Table 1.3 Percentage of population aged 65 or more, by income and regional groupings, and selected countries

	1990	2010	2030	2050
High-income economies	13.0	16.3	23.6	25.3
Upper middle-income economies	5.5	7.0	11.6	16.9
Lower middle-income economies	6.3	7.4	10.9	15.2
Low-income economies	4.6	5.5	9.0	13.1
Africa	3.0	3.2	4.4	7.5
East Africa	*3.0*	*2.8*	*3.7*	*6.2*
West Africa	*2.7*	*3.0*	*3.9*	*6.7*
North Africa	*3.6*	*4.3*	*7.5*	*12.7*
Americas	7.8	8.8	14.6	18.9
Latin America and the Caribbean	*4.8*	*6.2*	*10.9*	*17.0*
Chile	*6.0*	*8.1*	*14.3*	*18.8*
Northern America	*12.4*	*13.6*	*21.9*	*22.9*
Asia	5.1	6.5	10.7	15.6
East And South-East Asia	*5.7*	*7.8*	*13.4*	*18.4*
South Asia	*4.2*	*5.2*	*8.1*	*13.2*
Central Asia	*5.6*	*6.4*	*10.7*	*15.4*
Western Asia	*3.7*	*4.5*	*7.0*	*11.2*
Europe	12.7	16.1	22.5	24.7
Switzerland	*15.0*	*19.1*	*27.5*	*27.2*
Oceania	8.9	10.3	15.9	19.1
Australia	*10.7*	*12.6*	*20.3*	*23.5*

Source: World Bank (1994b)

much lower levels of per capita income than the industrial nations. (World Bank 1994a, p. 1)

In Table 1.3 we reproduce World Bank estimates and projections of the proportion of people aged 65 years or older, in 1990, and for selected future years for the next two generations, to 2050, by major income and regional groupings. While the expected proportion of people over 65 doubles in high-income countries, it more than doubles in Africa, and in Asia, a region that currently accounts for more than half the world's population, it triples. Table 1.3 also reports separately the demographic projections for Australia, Chile and Switzerland.

Figure 1.2 translates these proportionate projections into numbers. Again, the dramatic aged population increase in the Asian region, and to a lesser extent Africa and Latin America, is emphasised, through the combination of rapid overall population growth, and large increases in the percentages of the population aged 65 and over.

The importance of this observation lies in the extent to which demographic transition is projected to increase the burden of the aged on the working population. This is best illustrated by reporting changes in the aged dependency ratio, defined here as the ratio of the number of people aged 65 and older to the number of people aged between 15 and 65.

The ratio attempts to provide a rough and ready index of the proportionate burden that the aged will place on working members of the population. In the Australian case, it is predicted to nearly double, from 16% in 1990 to 30% in 2030; the corresponding figures for the OECD are 18.2%, moving to 31.2%.

These projections amply demonstrate the existence and magnitude of the transition that will be visited upon economies across the world in the next half century. However, they also mask three important features of population ageing (World Bank 1994a). First, chronological age must be distinguished from functional age – it may be quite common for someone aged 55 to be working in Japan, but much less common to find a 55-year-old working in Afghanistan. Further, the statistics reported make no reference to gender – yet old age means quite different things to women and to men. Typically, women live longer than men, and marry men older than themselves. They are therefore much more likely to end up living alone. Finally, about one elderly (over 60) person in four is 'very old' – over 75, and of these,

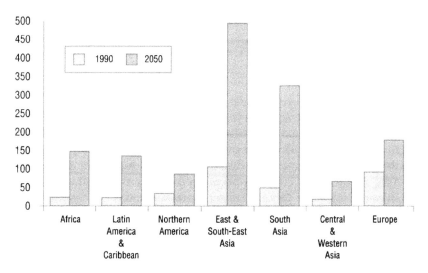

Figure 1.2 Population aged 65 and over, by region (millions)
Source: World Bank (1994b)

about two-thirds are women. The 'very old' are usually in a very different economic position than the old – their life savings may have run out, their children may already be classified as 'old', and their health needs are likely to be much greater and much more expensive.

This demographic transition raises a number of issues revolving around provision of services for the aged. As we get older, our command over resources is less flexible, our productivity declines, and our health service requirements escalate. One way of thinking of this is that we need insurance to cover our old age. This insurance, however provided, is expensive. In economies that are developing rapidly as well as ageing, the cost will be particularly high by historical norms. This is because:

- traditional family support for the aged is likely to be less secure when there are fewer children for each family
- expectations concerning living standards are likely to be linked to community standards, which will be increasing fast
- medical technology is likely to advance rapidly, especially for the aged, and this will be more expensive than in the past.

It is easy to demonstrate that such insurance will not be provided efficiently, and in some cases may not be provided at all, in unregulated voluntary markets.

A taxonomy of retirement provision policies

Many countries have attempted to formulate policies to redress the shortcomings of private markets in this area, but governments have responded in different ways to the retirement income provision needs of the elderly. It is conventional, in discussing these, to identify three 'pillars' of retirement support, although the definitions of the pillars themselves are not yet standardised. In our usage, the first pillar is thought of as a safety net, which allows recipients to avoid abject poverty. This sometimes takes the form of a minimum social security pension to workers, contingent on a minimum number of years of contributions, as in the United States or Chile. Alternatively, it may be available to the poorest sections of the aged community, regardless of age or employment history, as in Australia. The second pillar is a compulsory earnings or employment-related participation pillar for workers. This is often publicly provided, as in much of North America and continental Europe (see Figure 1.1), and need not be funded. Alternatively, it may be a mandatory system of saving, privately organised as in Australia and Chile, or publicly organised through national provident funds such as in Singapore.[1] The third pillar comprises voluntary saving. This may be linked to employment; for example, the 401(k) plans in the United

States. Often, it is a concessional long-term saving vehicle, such as the United Kingdom Peps (Personal Equity Participation Scheme). As well, non–tax-preferred voluntary saving is included here.

Figure 1.3 offers a schema of these three pillars, along with a simple menu of policy choices for each component. At the cost of some oversimplification, most formal retirement provision policies can be characterised using this schema. For example, safety net payments may be universal, in the sense of not means-tested, as in the United States, or targeted, as in Australia. The compulsory employment-related component can be provided by central government, as in Japan, mandated through a public authority, as in Singapore, or through the private sector, as in Chile and Australia. Voluntary saving for retirement can be facilitated through various tax-preferred channels, such as individual retirement accounts (IRAs) and registered retirement saving plans (RRSPs) in the United States and Canada, or they can be confined to occupational pension schemes, as in Australia.

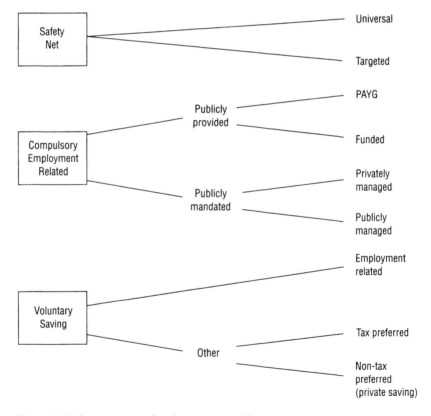

Figure 1.3 Components of retirement provision

These elements can be combined in various ways. In Chile, for example, a minimum pension, set at about 25% of average earnings, is guaranteed to workers who have contributed for at least 20 years; the contribution period covers the previous PAYG system, as well as the current private mandate. A low level of welfare payment (about 15% of average earnings) is offered to others without significant resources. While the welfare transfer is means-tested over all resources, from whatever source, the minimum pension is available to all whose pension entitlements would otherwise fall below some stipulated level – the pension guarantee is not affected by non-pension income or assets. In Australia, by contrast, these two first-pillar functions are folded into a single 'age pension'. Fairly comprehensive income and assets means tests apply, with tapering. Those entitled to a full pension receive about 25% of average earnings, regardless of employment history (these policies are summarised in Appendices 1 and 2).

Rationale for retirement income policy

The economic rationale for government intervention in retirement provision was first systematically articulated by Diamond (1977). In an insightful and prescient article, he identified the major reasons for a retirement social security program as redistribution, market failure, paternalism (particularly related to inadequate saving for retirement) and administrative efficiency in social insurance delivery.

He points to both the intra- and intergenerational aspects of redistribution, and the importance of a life-cycle perspective in thinking about this question. Market failures include adverse selection[2] in the life annuity market, and the absence of adequate inflation insurance, in financial asset markets generally and in annuity markets in particular. He emphasised risk associated with the length of working life as one that private markets would find difficult to insure against.

Working largely with aggregate data, he also anticipated the more recent finding that many people systematically undersave for their own retirement. Among much survey evidence accumulated since to suggest that people undersave for their retirement is the study by Bernheim and Scholz (1993) who find that households whose heads are well educated save systematically in line with conventional consumption smoothing, but that others do not. This is the major basis for the paternalistic element in his rationale.

A further example of market failure, not emphasised by Diamond but developed since, relates to the social allocation of risk. Various writers, for example, Gordon and Varian (1988), have emphasised the intergenerational risk-sharing function of social security, building on the idea that private markets will not be able to allocate risk efficiently between generations that are alive and those that are unborn. Indeed, Gordon and Varian argued that risk-sharing rather than redistribution as such best accounts for the timing of the introduction of the US Social Security program. More generally, efficient allocation of retirement risks between live cohorts of different ages will be difficult to achieve.

Diamond had in mind a program that was publicly provided and in some sense funded. Growing unfunded government social security liabilities and the related current thrust of retirement policy towards privately based mandation have led to further development of his line of argument. We consider these further below.

Responding to problems in the private market for saving

Retirement provision policy typically embraces more than just publicly provided income support of the elderly poor, or a minimum guarantee for retired workers. Workers confront an income profile throughout their life cycle that is far different than their preferred consumption profile because for perhaps a third of their adult lives, during their retirement years, their labour earnings are close to zero, while their consumption requirements remain nearly the same. Retirement provision policies are ideally designed to deliver adequate income replacement during retirement. For most workers, the financial requirements for adequate replacement exceed those offered by the social welfare safety net.

Of course, voluntary life-cycle saving can, and perhaps should, smooth consumption throughout the life cycle.[3] But in practice this is a complicated calculation for individuals to make. Apart from anything else, the magnitudes involved are startling for someone young, even with modest assumptions about inflation and real wage growth, and standard planned retirement and longevity. For example, we have calculated that in Australia, a single male on average weekly earnings wanting to privately fund his retirement over 35 years of employment would have to accumulate over $A1 million in order to retire with an income that is equivalent to 65 per cent of his pre-retirement income.[4]

As well, however, life events that are central to the retirement provision decision are uncertain in their effect. Planned retirement age may be altered by illness or retrenchment. Longevity is difficult to predict. Rates of return on broad asset classes can vary considerably from historical norms, and for quite long time periods. And inflation is difficult to predict more than a few years out, which is a problem when you are saving over a working life of several decades, and then arranging retirement income to cover a further two decades or more.

The various uncertainties mentioned above could be adequately resolved by insuring against the associated risk. For example, the purchase of a life annuity with periodic payments indexed for inflation would insure against longevity and inflation risk. However, the private market for such insurance is very weak. While financial risk may be diversified, it is expensive to insure against poor market performance. Voluntary private life annuity markets are thin worldwide, and appear not to offer actuarially fair prices to the full population. This is partly because of adverse selection.

Also, private financial insurance against early retirement will be very expensive, where offered at all, because the existence of such insurance may increase the propensity of the insured to retire early, or that of his or her employer to retrench him or her before the expected retirement date.

Finally, the existence of government policies may themselves discourage adequate voluntary life-cycle saving. Because it taxes the return on saving, the income tax strikes at saving twice, but consumption only once. This effectively raises the price of future consumption relative to current consumption. For example, $1 earned today attracts income tax before it can be spent. By contrast, $1 saved today in a bank, for use in 30 years time, attracts income tax now, along with earnings tax over the investment period. Even more important, the existence of support for the aged through the social welfare safety net induces those who are not poor to nevertheless save less than they otherwise would for retirement, and instead rely partly on this benefit.

Alternative reform strategies

Any descriptive assessment of worldwide trends in pension reform, such as the studies cited above, reveals a wide variety of policy responses. These can be usefully divided into 'parametric'[5] and structural reforms.[6]

Parametric reform

In a typical OECD-type unfunded PAYG plan it is possible to institute reform of a kind by simply altering the values of one or more key parameters. The critical parameters are the number of beneficiaries, the number of contributing workers, the contribution rate, and the value of the benefit. These can be altered in various ways. For example, an increase in the eligibility age will reduce the number of beneficiaries and may increase the number of contributing workers. The number of beneficiaries may also be reduced by altering survivorship provisions or vesting periods. The number of contributing workers may also be increased by, for example, cutting back on disability benefits. Contribution rates may be increased; benefits may be reduced through a number of mechanisms. A popular device is the modification of indexation provisions.

Any change of this kind is of course politically difficult, since in one way or another, each change involves a default of a government promise. From an economic point of view it is necessary to factor in behavioural response to legislated change of this kind before conclusions can be drawn about fiscal impact. For example, while observation suggests that the modal retirement age in developed economies is conditioned by eligibility age, this may not follow if eligibility age is increased significantly.

A special kind of parametric reform is one in which the parameters are set by appeal to broader considerations of actuarial fairness. Such a reform has recently been enacted by Sweden. In the Swedish case, retirement benefits are indexed to life expectancy for successive cohorts of retirees; thus as individuals live longer, annual benefits will be lower for a given retirement age (Sundén 2000). If properly formulated and implemented, such reforms will ensure avoidance of the fiscal shortfalls currently being experienced by and projected for conventional PAYG schemes. But as Disney (2000) points out, in the process these schemes end up failing to address the market failures and equity concerns that motivate public intervention in retirement provision. To take one example, longevity risk is a risk where intergenerational sharing may increase social welfare.

Structural reform

While the term 'structural reform' can be used to describe any change that alters policy design rather than just its parameters, this term is typically used to describe reform involving a transition from reliance from public provision. In most reforms of this kind, the administration of the program is undertaken in the private sector.[7] This kind of reform is the central focus of this book. The best known example is Chile, which reformed its PAYG pension system in 1981. Australia now has a similar structure, the Superannuation Guarantee (SG).

Concern about the size of the public sector in many countries has meant that mandation is replacing provision as a means of ensuring delivery of socially necessary programs without having the cost appear in the government budget. This strategy need not be a success from an economic point of view. In the field of pension reform, however, it has some advantages, which are discussed, along with some reservations, below in 'Pros and cons of mandatory private retirement provision'.

Hybrids

Some countries have sought to combine structural and parametric reform. This usually involves piecemeal reform, in which reduction of government provision is accompanied by increased mandation. The UK experience is perhaps the best example. Other examples are Denmark and The Netherlands, which rely on union agreements with employers to sustain private provision.[8] Disney (2000) argues that the benefit of the UK approach is that it spreads the transition costs of reform more widely than pure structural reform. At the same time, however, reform strategies of this kind are more easily eroded through political opportunism than once-for-all structural reforms.

Structural reform initiatives

In this book, the essential focus is on the implementation and management of mandated privately administered retirement provision policies. But all structures with privately managed second pillars share many of the same challenges in reform and implementation, and some of the benefits, whether privatisation is complete or partial. In this section, we draw on World Bank data to show how widespread is the move towards private mandatory retirement structures.

Table 1.4 provides a list of 22 countries, which have added private mandatory second pillars, or partially privatised part of the old system. Six of the countries on the list are high-income OECD countries, while 10 are Latin American countries (Chile and those that followed its example), and five are former socialist countries; the new system in Hong Kong will begin to operate in the second half of 2000. All of the high-income-country reforms, with the exception of the United Kingdom, involved adding a tier to an existing system or converting a voluntary scheme into a mandatory one. In contrast, all of the Latin American reforms involved a shift from a publicly managed, PAYG scheme to a privately managed, funded scheme. The same is true for Kazakhstan, Poland and Hungary, while Croatia, Romania and Estonia have advanced proposals for reforms along these lines.

Figure 1.4 shows the growth of the number of contributors to a second pillar throughout the world. Beginning with Chile, numbers have risen in the multi-pillar schemes that have spread throughout Latin America, OECD countries and the transition economies of Eastern Europe, such that there are currently almost 80 million workers globally who actively contribute to their own individual retirement savings account. The coverage estimates, of course, conceal the fact that the current level of funded benefits for most members is still very low.

Table 1.4 Countries operating private mandatory second pillars, year 2000

Country	Year second pillar introduced
Argentina	1994
Australia	1988
Bolivia	1997
Chile	1981
Colombia	1994
Costa Rica	legislation introduced 1995
Denmark	1993
El Salvador	1998
Hong Kong	2000
Hungary	1997
Kazakhstan	1997
Latvia	legislation sent to Parliament 1998
Macedonia	–
Mexico	1997
Netherlands, The	1985
Nicaragua	–
Peru	1993
Poland	1998
Sweden	1999
Switzerland	1985
United Kingdom	1988
Uruguay	1996

Source: Adapted from Palacios and Pallarès-Miralles (2000), Table 3.3, p. 20

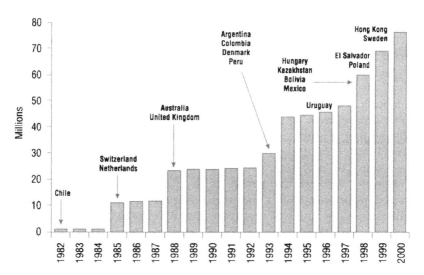

Figure 1.4 Number of contributors to a mandatory private plan
Source: Adapted from Palacios and Pallarès-Miralles (2000), Figure 3.8, p. 21

Table 1.5 Assets of pension funds as percentage of GDP

	1987	1988	1989	1990	1991	1992	1993	1994	1995	1996
Argentina										2.8[3]
Australia	20.4	27.6	32.2	35.7	38.8	43.1	45.4	48.4	52.1	57.9
Chile		16.5		26.5		35.4				44.1[3]
Colombia										1.3[3]
Czech Rep.								0.1	0.2	0.5
Denmark[1]	10.9	10.3	12.2	12.4	12.8	16.6	19.3	18.9	21.1	23.9
Hungary								0.2	0.2	0.2
Mexico										0.2[3]
Netherlands, The	45.5	72.7	81.6	78.4	81.1	72.1	83.5	85.0	86.6	87.3
Peru										2.1[3]
Sweden[2]	33.4	30.9	30.6	31	38.6	29.6	27.1	25.7	30.5	32.6
Switzerland	74.7	64.5	71.3	72.5	75.5	74.7	82.2	86.5	104.0	117.0
United Kingdom	62.3	58.2	65.0	59.7	64.1	58.2	72.4	69.2	73.2	74.7
United States	35.7	36.8	36.3	38.1	48.0	48.2	53.4	50.6	58.9	58.2
Uruguay										1.0[3]

Sources: OECD (1998a), Table 5.1, p. 65; Clare and Connor (1999b), Table A1
1 Includes company pension fund assets from 1995.
2 Including first-pillar assets up to and including 1991.
3 Figures for December 1997.

Nevertheless, it dramatically illustrates the proliferation of mandatory privately managed second pillars.

The associated growth in pension fund assets is documented in Table 1.5. Those countries that moved towards mandatory retirement saving schemes earliest – Chile, Switzerland, The Netherlands, Australia and the United Kingdom – have substantial pension fund cuts – on average, more than 75% of GDP. This compares with 58.2% in the United States, the next highest ratio, and close to zero for many others.

Pros and cons of mandatory private retirement provision

Reform of pension policy is controversial, as evidenced by Orszag and Stiglitz (2001), who specifically challenge blanket advocacy of mandatory private retirement provision as a second pillar. Mandatory public and mandatory private retirement provision can be designed so that they appear similar. Not only is it possible to set up a public PAYG system to mimic a sound private saving plan, at least on an economy-wide basis, but that it is also possible to set up a mandatory private DC policy that mimics a badly run PAYG plan. In practice, however, public pensions are generally unfunded PAYG arrangements that pay defined benefits based on a statutory formula rather than actual contributions. On the other hand, mandatory private retirement saving, as characterised by the arrangements in Chile, Switzerland and Australia, is fully funded with benefits based on defined contributions.

These differences suggest that at least some mandatory private retirement saving can be justified: arguments include improved national saving, political insulation, higher retirement incomes, the development of financial markets, more flexibility in matching investments to individual preferences towards risk, and what we term design diversification. None of these outcomes is guaranteed, but they do seem likely, given the poor design features of many existing PAYG plans.

At the same time, however, mandatory retirement saving policies carry with them some major disadvantages. These include potentially high administration costs, which cut into rates of return and accumulation, and inhibit the role of conventional social security in facilitating the efficient allocation of risk. Private mandatory policies are based on a 'defined-contribution' (DC) or accumulation concept, under which the parameters of the policy focus on the contribution, rather than the payout. This sometimes means that, relative to a defined-benefit (DB)-based policy, insufficient attention is paid to the nature of payouts.

In addition, some of the claimed advantages of private mandation can be offset or nullified through intended or unintended countervailing policies. Important among these is taxation, which can compromise the political insulation that private retirement provision is supposed to deliver. In what follows, we discuss the advantages and disadvantages in turn.

Improving national saving

In recent years there has been concern about declining national savings rates. Neither economic theory nor the relevant empirical studies provide unambiguous results concerning the net impact on aggregate saving of PAYG-financed pensions. However, it is widely believed that funded retirement income arrangements will contribute more to aggregate saving than PAYG arrangements, particularly as the age dependency ratio increases with the ageing of the 'baby-boom' generation (World Bank 1994a, Davis 1995).

Past experience has shown that it is more likely that mandatory private arrangements are fully funded and public schemes will be financed on a PAYG basis.[9] Further, even where the public arrangements are funded, the public or quasi-public trust funds that are built up are vulnerable to political intervention such as compulsory investment in low rate of return assets. Sometimes, they have been used for short-term budgetary purposes.

In other words, private mandatory retirement saving has a greater chance of improving national saving than a PAYG plan since it is much more likely to be funded. At least some fund members are likely to be liquidity constrained, and saving for these individuals will be higher. Further, individuals who are not liquidity constrained but who are aware of the availability of unfunded benefits on retirement may save less than a private mandatory plan implicitly requires.

Political insulation

An important difference between public and private retirement saving is their relative susceptibility to political risk. Diamond (1997) identified the sources of political risk to retirement income provision to include: the granting of excessive benefits to retirees in an immature system, making promises to retirees that cannot be met and over-sensitivity to the state of public finances. He noted that mandatory private retirement saving characterised by the features of full privatisation, full funding, defined contributions and individual accounts has the advantage of complete separation from public finances and therefore the government of the day. In the words of Diamond (1997), mandatory private retirement saving is well insulated from political risks.

On the other hand, of the alternative means of retirement income provision, Diamond considered the traditional public PAYG model – irrespective of any initial intentions to maintain separability from general government finances – to be the most vulnerable to the state of the government budget and therefore provides the least insulation from political risk. This is especially important where political credibility is low, as in some Latin American economies. It is in this context that Chile's mandatory private retirement saving is considered to perform well. It encompasses all the features required to facilitate political insulation and is being used as a prototype for other countries in the region (Diamond 1993, Diamond and Valdes-Prieto 1994). Even in countries where government credibility is high, however, considerable risk is present in public retirement provision because of the very long time spans involved. In the Australian case, for example, the age pension, until recently the main public retirement provision vehicle, has varied between 19% and 26% of average earnings over the last 20 years.

To find evidence of the susceptibility of public PAYG retirement income provision to the state of public finances, one need go no further than to examine the current financing problems facing such schemes in the major OECD economies. Despite pledges to fully fund these programs and keep them separate from government finances, many now exist purely on a PAYG basis, and this is putting considerable strain on public finances as their populations age (see OECD 1998a).

Higher retirement incomes

One of the motivations for the introduction of mandatory private provision – and therefore greater emphasis on the employment-related and private saving pillars – in both Australia and Switzerland has been the desire for higher retirement incomes. Unlike most of the developed world, Australia had never introduced an earnings-related public pension and the voluntary private pension arrangements covered only 40% of employees – mainly public-sector and white-collar workers. The Superannuation Guarantee supplements the first-pillar age pension and voluntary occupational retirement benefits. It promises higher incomes in retirement for all employees. Prior to the introduction of the Superannuation Guarantee the age pension was the only source of retirement income for most retirees.

Similarly, the BVG was introduced in Switzerland in 1985 to increase total retirement incomes. The addition of mandated occupational pensions was designed to increase income replacement in retirement from the 40 per cent achieved under the public pension to around 60 per cent for a retiree with a full working life of 40 years on around average earnings.

Financial market development and innovations

There may be other advantages flowing from mandating private retirement saving. Bodie (see, for example, Bodie 1990a) asserts that the growth of private pensions in the United States has played an important role in the development of new financial products such as zero coupon bonds, collaterised mortgage obligations, guaranteed investment contracts and interest rate futures. He suggests that these developments may not have occurred at all or at a slower pace if public PAYG pensions dominated.[10] These arguments have been expanded in Mitchell and Bodie (2000), who highlight further development and innovations in the form of inflation-linked annuities, survivor bonds, long-term care insurance and reverse annuity mortgages.

Accommodating heterogeneity in preference towards investment risk

Standardised PAYG plans provide benefits that are fully insured against investment risk. It appears plausible that households have a range of preferences towards risk, and certainly, households in different financial or demographic circumstances will desire asset allocations of their financial portfolios with a range of exposures in risks assets.

The major assets of most households approaching or at retirement are their homes and their pension entitlements. Housing has a number of specific asset attributes. While home purchase is an important channel of risky investment, it is an undiversified and illiquid asset. It follows that there may be major efficiency gains in pension reform that provides households with some choice over portfolios. This flexibility is potentially available in DC-type mandatory plans, although it is not always exploited.

Design diversification

Further, some private mandatory retirement saving can be defended by appeal to what might be termed design diversification. Merton et al. (1987) argued that because private mandation offers a different set of risks from a public arrangement, combining public and private provision allows greater risk diversification, and is desirable on these grounds alone.

Administration cost

A frequently cited rationale for public pensions is that they can provide retirement income more efficiently than the private sector. Diamond (1977) pointed to the considerable difference in administrative costs of private and public retirement income provision and concludes that efficiency alone provides strong grounds for the existence of the US Social Security system. He reported 1974 data showing costs of 2% of total payments for the US Social Security program and 17% for the life insurance industry. Valdes-Prieto (1994) reported a similar margin using more recent data for both the United States and Chile, while Mitchell and Zeldes (1996) reported that US Social Security costs were around one-quarter those of private pensions.[11]

However, these raw cost data should be considered in context. It corresponds to the provision of quite different products and in different circumstances. US Social Security is mandatory and involves the provision of both welfare and retirement income insurance, the product is uniform and there is no consumer choice. Further, it is likely that some of the costs of public provision are understated or omitted in these comparisons (Mitchell 1998a).

Social allocation of risk

Finally, we pointed out above that social security provides a mechanism for intergenerational risk-sharing (Hayashi et al. 1996). Second-pillar government-sponsored social security schemes, and to some degree private DB pension plans, provide further channels for such risk-sharing. Retirement provision policy designs that rely on second-pillar DC arrangements thus constrain the efficient social allocation of retirement-related risks. For example, Bohn (1998) using US data found that a social security reform replacing the current scheme with individual accounts would worsen the social allocation of risk. It is not yet clear whether first-pillar arrangements alone provide adequate channels for efficient inter-cohort risk allocation.

Criteria for assessment

Criteria for assessing retirement income policy can be conveniently divided in two parts: those directly relevant to the retiring individual, and those addressing the allocation and distribution of resources in the economy as a whole.

Criteria pertaining to the individual

From the point of view of the individual, it is convenient to think of mandatory private retirement provision as insurance. There are many sources of income uncertainty that a risk-averse individual confronting retirement would like to insure against. In the spirit of Bodie (1990b), we can list the most important:

- *Coverage risk.* This is the statistical risk of a labour force participant falling outside the coverage of the retirement income arrangements.
- *Replacement rate risk.* This is the possibility that the retiree will not have enough income to maintain a reasonable standard of living after retiring, relative to that which he or she enjoyed during pre-retirement years. (The replacement rate is usually defined as the ratio of income in retirement to income prior to retirement.) It is unclear what constitutes an adequate replacement rate or how it should vary across different personal circumstances. Actuaries often recommend 70%, but how this should vary with family size, home ownership, and so on, is not spelt out.
- *Investment risk.* This is the possibility that the amount saved for retirement will be inadequate because the assets in which money is invested perform poorly. This risk is of special importance in the context of private mandatory schemes, because as accumulation

plans they leave this risk squarely in the hands of the contributor. By contrast, DB plans, which are usually the norm for public PAYG pensions, insure against this risk.

- *Longevity risk.* This is the risk that the retiree would exhaust the amount saved for retirement before he or she dies. One way people insure against this risk is by investing in life annuities. In the absence of a policy compelling life annuity purchase, however, adverse selection can seriously limit retirees' effective access to this market. This and related market failures are discussed further below.
- *Inflation risk.* This is the risk of price increases, which erode the purchasing power of lifetime savings.

Criteria pertaining to the whole economy

The conventional public finance criteria for public-policy assessment in an economy-wide context are efficiency, equity and administrative efficacy.

Economic efficiency can potentially be enhanced by public intervention in retirement provision. Second-best responses to price distortion, failure of annuities markets, dynamic inconsistency of preferences and inadequate saving might all, loosely, be considered under this heading.

- *Price distortions.* The main price distortions in relation to retirement income provision are the income tax and the social welfare safety net. The framework for taxation policy is founded upon the concept of income. An income tax makes consumption in retirement more expensive by taxing the return on life-cycle saving. In the absence of tax concessions for retirement saving, households would tend to provide too little for retirement consumption.

  A safety net to provide some economic resources to those with very low levels of income is an essential part of any social welfare system. Therefore a policy that organises saving for retirement income is necessary, in order to minimise exploitation – by those with adequate lifetime economic resources – of the social welfare safety net in their retirement.
- *Market failure.* Markets for financial instruments designed to facilitate a stable retirement income flow are likely to fail in the absence of government intervention. The most important example is that of lifetime annuities. Because insurers cannot distinguish between annuity purchasers with respect to life expectancy, annuity price will be insensitive to this personal characteristic. Those purchasers who do not expect to live very long will find the price too high, and will be driven from the market. This, in turn, leads to further price

increases. This process, leading to adverse selection, is familiar from
health insurance, where, in the absence of policy intervention,
healthy people do not find it worthwhile to purchase insurance. The
surest way of eliminating adverse selection is to make insurance
purchase compulsory for all members of the relevant population.

- *Myopia.* There is some evidence that a significant proportion of
households are short-sighted in lifetime economic planning, and
tend not to provide adequately for their retirement, unless they are
compelled, or given strong incentives to do so. This provides an
example of dynamically inconsistent preferences.

- *Saving.* A further economy-wide criterion is the impact of pension
policy on the saving rate. While this might appropriately be considered under the heading of efficiency, it is sufficiently important in
the present context to warrant a subhead of its own. Demographic
transition may well lead to a decline in the saving rate, as retirees sell
off their assets to finance retirement consumption, and the savings
undertaken by the future working population decline because of
their low numbers.

Equity is also an important criterion in assessing retirement policy
design. Policy should be designed to prevent the mandatory retirement
saving arrangements from being used as a tax shelter for high-income
earners. In addition, intergenerational equity considerations suggest
that over a period of demographic transition, policies should be introduced that ensure that the baby-boomers do not place an undue burden
on subsequent generations when they retire.

The distinction between intra-generational and intergenerational
equity has been emphasised by Kotlikoff (1992), among others. He
pointed out that analysis of a 'tax system's progressivity based on annual
income has misclassified as regressive some of the most progressive
features of [a] fiscal system' (p. 90). He also specifically separates
'generational policy', which addresses the question of how much
each generation will pay in taxes or receive in transfers, and 'distribution policy', which addresses the question of how each generation's
projected lifetime taxes and transfers are spread over its richer
and poorer members. In the present context, where policy reallo-
cates resources over the lifetime of a given consumer, as well as
redistribution within and between cohorts, these distinctions are especially important.

Finally, policy should be designed to be as simple as possible consistent with the criteria tested above, to maintain transparency to the
individual and tractability to the policy-maker. An important consideration is the administrative cost of the policy.

Challenges in private mandatory retirement policy design

Implementation and design of a mandatory private retirement provision policy carries special challenges, beyond those confronting generic retirement policy formulation. Because they are necessarily fully funded, net rates of return are important. Because it is privately administered, governance must be carefully specified and overhead cost must be contained. Because it stems from a defined contribution structure, inter-cohort risk-sharing must receive special attention. And because retirement income streams are to be sold in the private market, adverse selection issues must be addressed.

The structure of the rest of this book is informed by these considerations. Chapter 2 analyses work, saving and retirement from the perspective of an individual who is assumed to be optimising his or her choices over a finite lifetime. Insights from both economic and finance theory are combined with empirical regularities to build a more or less pragmatic picture of how individuals might optimally allocate their time and consumption over the life cycle. The retirement decision itself – perhaps the most important life-cycle-based labour supply and saving choice – is treated explicitly, and health and longevity factors are taken into account. In addition, we consider the implicit contract theory approach to explaining pension provision, and thus attempt to provide an employer perspective on pension provision. Finally, the literature on self-control and retirement saving, analysing the voluntary undersaving for retirement sometimes observed, is reviewed.

In Chapter 3 our focus becomes more specific, as we consider the ways in which pension contributions are mandated and administered, and we try to analyse how the policy choices observed have been arrived at. After a simple treatment of the retirement accumulation process we examine the impact of the institutional frameworks and governance structures within which pension funds operate, and then consider the nature of the pension contributions themselves. A surprisingly long list of choices emerges. Among these are the contribution rate and its specification (gross or net of operating costs, the legally liable agent), coverage (self-employed, the treatment of unemployment spells), contribution floors and ceilings (should the low-paid be compelled to contribute, in spite of the high proportional administration charges they pay; should those on very high salaries have to contribute the same proportion of their salaries as those on average earnings?); and preservation age. The chapter provides a framework for thinking about these aspects of mandated pension provision, and presents evidence on international practice. Issues given more detailed treatment later in the book, such as administration costs and charges, regulation, pension fund governance, and taxation, are to some degree anticipated here.

While Chapter 3 offers an account of the accumulation phase, it does not treat the central question of asset allocation. This is taken up in Chapter 4. A major advantage of a defined-contribution pension scheme is that it provides the potential for exposing retirement savers to the degree of investment risk they prefer. To achieve this, however, effective investment strategies have to be adopted, and portfolio choice must be available to pension fund members. The chapter begins by taking a broad look at asset allocation over the life cycle, and then focuses on investment strategies, including option strategies, that might be adopted by pension funds.

Chapter 5 focuses on payouts. We begin by offering a rationale for mandatory retirement income streams. We then explain the nature of annuities, and examine alternative annuity and quasi-annuity designs. Insurance against not just longevity risk (offered by life annuities), but against investment and inflation risk, is considered, emphasising trade-offs between annuity price and the nature of the insurance implicit in the payouts. We also consider interactions between government retirement income guarantees of various kinds and annuity design. Consumer preference towards these various products is investigated. Specific features of the annuity market, including adverse selection, market structure, and annuity price variation and loadings are explored. We conclude the chapter by drawing out the implications of our analysis for mandatory annuity design.

Chapter 6 examines pension tax design. This is an especially important question in the context of private mandatory retirement saving policies, since one of the major claims to be made for such a paradigm is that it offers insulation from political intervention. This autonomy will be compromised if governments are able to alter taxes applying to pension fund flows: contributions, earnings and benefits. The chapter examines the case for alternative pension tax designs, taking into account both broad criteria of efficiency and equity, and administrative issues in pension tax bases and revenue collection. It provides numerical examples of accumulation and tax collection profiles under alternative tax regimes, and reports international practice. It concludes that a tax regime which exempts contributions and pension fund earnings from the tax base, and taxes benefits under the personal income tax, is probably the best pension tax design.

The final substantive chapter turns to an examination of one of the most intractable issues in pension economics: administrative costs and charges. We begin by offering a metric for standardising the disclosure of charges, emphasising the impact of charges on expected accumulations. The chapter analyses the likely economic impact of alternative charge regimes, and explores the implications of regulations and governance on administrative cost. Empirical evidence is presented in which the administrative charges associated with alternative fund structures in Australia and the Chilean AFPs are compared, along with some broader international experience with administrative charges.

Our concluding Chapter 8 draws together the lessons and findings of the book and makes some suggestions for future research.

Notes

1 This differs from World Bank usage whose classification appears to require that the second pillar be funded.
2 This market failure stems from information asymmetry – the presumption is that the annuity-issuer knows less about the annuitant's life expectancy than he or she does. Two effects – moral hazard and adverse selection – flow from this. *Moral hazard* exists whenever the liability of the insurer is affected by actions of the insured party about which the insurer has incomplete information. *Adverse selection* arises if individuals know their own riskiness but the insurer does not; the possibilities offered are then less efficient than if individually tailored policies could be offered.
3 Consumption smoothing implies that people save during their working life in order to maintain a smooth profile of consumption throughout their life, even if their lifetime income profile is uneven. Underlying this is the assumption that people generally prefer a smooth consumption pattern rather than having 'plenty today and scarcity tomorrow'.
4 Assuming a 3% real rate of return, and retirement at 65. The annual rate of inflation is set at 3% and productivity growth is 1%.
5 Chand and Jaeger (1996) were the first to use this term.
6 Disney (2000) divides reforms into four types: parametric, actuarially fair, clean-break privatisation and partial privatisation. The first two of these retain a strong unfunded component in their second pillar, and are essentially 'parametric' in their approach, even though that term is applied to only one variant. The latter two involve a strong funded component, and encompass structural reform.
7 It is convenient to characterise the provident funds as publicly mandated and publicly administered, although most of these funds hold the bulk of their assets as domestic government bonds. The distinction between these arrangements and public provision thus becomes blurred.
8 Between 1986 and 1992, Australia's Productivity Award Superannuation, the precursor of the Superannuation Guarantee, took this form.
9 Examples of exceptions include the Canadian public pension (C\QPP), which is fully funded, and the Finnish mandatory employer-provided pensions, which are largely PAYG.
10 In Chile, it is generally accepted that the mandating of fully funded private pensions contributed to the development of the financial markets. See Holzmann (1997).

11 Diamond (1996) noted the difficulties in making cost comparisons and
   suggested that the cost differential between the US Social Security system
   and Chile's mandatory private pensions was somewhere in the range 2.5 to
   1 and 12.5 to 1.

CHAPTER 2

Work and Saving Over the Life Cycle

Retirement as a protracted phase of life for ordinary people was a twentieth-century development. Still more recent is the notion of mass retirements financed through the second pillar, without either the family or the State being the main provider of income to retirees. Shopping for life-cycle saving vehicles in the private capital market will represent a novelty for most households. Apart from the trend towards privatised pensions, several familiar factors have combined to raise the stakes for ageing Western workers: the trend for men to retire well before the traditional age of 65, increased life expectancy, and demographic transition that acts to close off the fallback of turning to one's children for support, either directly within the household, or indirectly, via the tax system.

Retirement facts

You are retired to the extent that you have made an irrevocable decision to cease participating in the labour force. A striking feature of work patterns in industrial countries over the course of the twentieth century was the rise of mass retirement on the part of older men. In 1950, for example, 72% of men in the United States aged 65 were in the labour force. By 1985, however, just 30% of this age group remained in the labour force (Quinn 2000).

'Mass Exodus' of Older Men

During the last three decades of the twentieth century, the trend to early male retirement accelerated – a phenomenon described by Merrilees (1982) as a 'mass exodus' of older men from the labour force. Figure

27

2.1 shows the labour force participation rates of men aged 60 to 64, from 1966 until 1998, in selected OECD countries. In the United States, the participation rate of men aged 60 to 64 fell from 79% in 1966 to 55% in 1998. This trend was observed in many other OECD countries; for example, in Australia, between 1966 and 1998, the labour force participation of males in this age group fell more sharply, from 79% to 46%, while in France the older male participation rate in 1998 was less than a quarter of the 1966 figure.

Among the major industrial countries, only Japan seems to have resisted the trend to accelerated early male retirement during the last third of the twentieth century, as Figure 2.1 shows. Yet the specific 'pathways' to early exit from the labour force have varied from one country to the next. In the United States, two major factors were unexpected enhancement of social security benefits together with early retirement incentive programs offered by private employment-related pension plans in that country. In the case of social security, for example, the year 1961 saw benefits become available to men retiring up to three years younger than the 'normal' retirement age of 65. By 1977 benefits paid to men retiring were 51% higher than those paid to their 1968 counterparts. In the United Kingdom there was a similar combination of enhanced public and private pension plans. Austria, Finland and Norway saw rises in the number of people drawing public disability

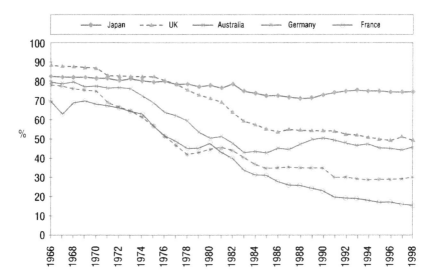

Figure 2.1 Participation rates of men aged 60–64 in selected countries, 1966–98
Source: OECD Labour Force Statistics

benefits. In 1990 more than half of Austrian males aged 55 to 64 were receiving disability benefits.

Data on the average age of retirement of men in 23 OECD countries have been compiled by Blöndal and Scarpetta (1998). Figure 2.2 compares retirement ages in 1960 and 1995. Across most countries the average retirement age of men decreased by around four years during this period. In 1995 Belgian men were retiring on average in their 57th year, compared with their 63rd year in 1960. At the other extreme was Iceland, with an average male retirement age just short of 70. Iceland was the only country in which the average retirement age of men increased between 1960 and 1995, although the decrease in retirement age in Japan was only marginal.

Australian discussions of early retirement focus on relaxations of the means test applying to public pensions, especially veterans' ones, along with a sharp rise in dwelling assets. In 1972, for example, dwelling assets per household stood at $A82 022 (measured in 1996–97 dollars). Two decades later the figure in question was $A140 326, a rise of 71%. Owning your own home is of course a traditional cornerstone of financial planning for a long, comfortable retirement.

Has the trend stabilised?

The final decade of the twentieth century saw preliminary indications that the trend for men to retire early might have levelled out. In the case of the United States, for example, Quinn (2000) identifies the mid-1980s

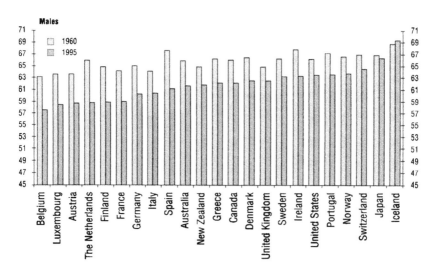

Figure 2.2 Average retirement ages of men in the OECD
Source: Blöndal and Scarpetta (1998), p. 16

as a turning point. Policy has begun to reinforce this change; the 'normal' retirement age for the purpose of calculating social security entitlements is to be gradually escalated, from 65 to 67. Moreover, there were reports (for example, Leckey 1999) that, beginning with the Bank of America in 1985, hundreds of large corporations had switched to 'defined-contribution' or 'cash-balance' plans whereby incentives to early retirement are typically less pronounced than those in traditional 'defined-benefit' plans that tend to encourage early exit by employees with long service (more on pension plan terminology later).

In the case of Australia, a histogram portraying shifts in the pattern of retirement ages during the 1990s showed stabilisation of retirements by men in the 55–64 age group, and a slight decline in the 65-and-over group, although there was a slight increase in retirements in the 45–54 years age group (see Figure 2.3).

In more detail, of the 1 296 000 Australian males who were retired from full-time work in November 1997, 22% retired aged 65 and over, and 53% retired aged 55 to 64. Retirements in these age groups had stabilised. On the other hand, 17% had retired aged 45 to 54. That is, the leading-edge baby-boomers were retiring earlier than had trailing-edge 'children of the Depression'. Finally, 7% of men aged 45 or less had retired, and this trend was unchanged.

The average age of retirement from full-time work was 58. The average age of retirement from both full-time work and part-time work was 59.

Women and the labour force

The last decades of the twentieth century saw increased labour force participation by younger and older women alike, in contrast to falling

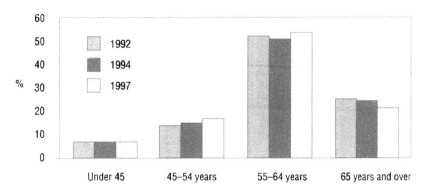

Figure 2.3 Australian men retired from full-time work by age at retirement
Source: Australian Bureau of Statistics (1997a), p. 4

labour force participation among older men. Figure 2.4 shows the patterns of labour force participation among pre-retirement women (those aged between 55 and 59) for selected OECD countries between 1966 and 1998. In all countries the proportion of women in this age group in the labour force increased; in the United States, for example, the participation rate rose from 46% in 1966 to 61% in 1998, and in Australia the rate rose from 26% to 43% over the same period.

What accounted for this difference in retirement behaviour between older men and older women? In the case of Australia, part of the explanation can be found in the rise in female wages relative to male wages during the last decades of the twentieth century. Some relevant facts are set out in Table 2.1 below.

More of the explanation of higher labour force participation by young and old adult women comes from the distinction between the substitution and income effects of higher wages, together with the fact that, within households, adult women tend to be secondary workers (in the paid workforce). The substitution effect of higher wages is to enter the labour force and remain there: 'it's become worthwhile to work outside the home, at least part-time, and to postpone my retirement once in the paid workforce'. This effect seems to have been dominant in the case of female workers.

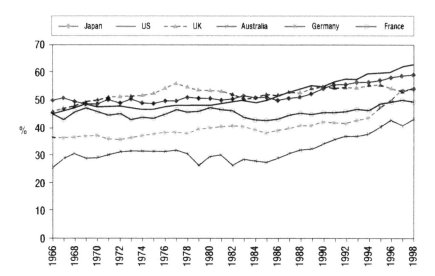

Figure 2.4 Participation rates of women aged 55–59 in selected countries, 1966–98
Source: OECD Labour Force Statistics

Table 2.1 Australian female/male wage
relativities

Average weekly earnings Full-time private-sector adults in non-managerial positions %	
1970	59.1
1975	75.8
1980	75.2
1985	76.8
1990	77.8
1994	82.5

Source: Foster (1996), p. 211

The income effect of higher wages, by contrast, is to retire early: 'my prospective lifetime earnings have risen, so I can afford to bring forward my retirement date'. This effect seems to have been dominant in the case of male workers. Even though men lost ground in relative terms during the second half of the twentieth century, their wages in absolute terms rose strongly, except during the last couple of decades.

Although participation in the labour force by older women has increased, the average age at which women are retiring has fallen over the last 40 years. Again, Blöndal and Scarpetta (1998) provide data on the average age of retirement of women in 23 OECD countries in 1960 and 1995, and this is shown in Figure 2.5.

In 1995 Belgian women were retiring on average at age 54, down from just under age 61 in 1960. Also paralleling Figure 2.2, Icelandic women are at the other extreme, with an average retirement age just short of 67. The smallest decreases in the average retirement age of women occurred in Sweden and Japan.

Moving forward to the 1990s, a histogram portraying the distribution of retirement ages of Australian women who had been in full-time work is shown in Figure 2.6.

Of the 1 918 400 Australian females aged 45 and over who were retired from full-time work in 1997, just 3% retired aged 65 and over; 21% retired aged between 55 and 64, and 22% retired aged between 45 and 54, a percentage not so different from the corresponding male figure of 17%. On the other hand, 54% had retired from full-time work aged less than 45, among which group one-third indicated that marriage had been the reason for leaving full-time work.

The remainder of this chapter discusses work and saving over the life cycle in a more theoretical setting, notably the life-cycle permanent-income hypothesis about the behaviour of consumption and saving.

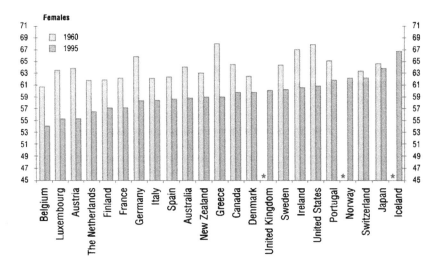

Figure 2.5 Average retirement ages of women in the OECD
Source: Blöndal and Scarpetta (1998), p. 16
* data for 1960 not available

Employee perspective and life-cycle theory

One of the most influential ideas in twentieth-century economics was the *life-cycle permanent-income hypothesis*, according to which households strive to smooth out their consumption through time. However, the twentieth-century fact of mass retirements showed that households do not smooth out their leisure over time. Rather, they prefer to spend one, two or three decades at the end of life engaged in full-time

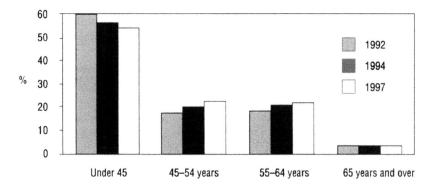

Figure 2.6 Australian women retired from full-time work by age at retirement
Source: Australian Bureau of Statistics (1997a), p. 4

enjoyment of leisure. Theories of endogenous, employee-driven retirement, set in a life-cycle model of consumption and saving, originated during the first half of the 1980s. It is helpful to preface these ideas with a review of the traditional life-cycle model, in which retirement is determined exogenously.

Life-cycle model of consumption and saving

The ideas underlying the traditional life-cycle model can be traced back to the beginning of the twentieth century, to Irving Fisher. One of his mid-century admirers was Milton Friedman, whose 1956 book represented the first systematic tests of the life-cycle permanent-income hypothesis, together with related work by Modigliani and Brumberg (1954). A subsequent influential contribution was made by Feldstein (1976). A new generation of tests was originated by Hall (1978). Discussion of this empirical work can be based on Figure 2.7, which portrays a worker who saves ahead of retirement, and dissaves thereafter, in order to maintain a level consumption profile over the life cycle.

In Figure 2.7 the horizontal axis shows time elapsed since the start of working life. The vertical axis shows three variables: consumption, wage income and 'permanent income'. This latter term was introduced by Milton Friedman. It has been defined subsequently either as the maximum uniform rate of consumption that could be sustained over the life of a household that leaves no bequest (this is the simple approach

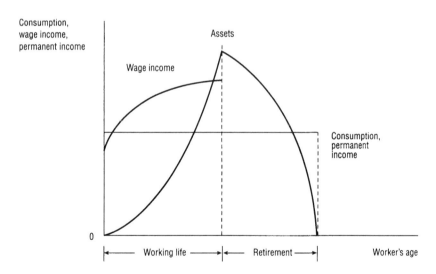

Figure 2.7 Life-cycle permanent-income hypothesis

portrayed by Figure 2.7) or as the level-annuity equivalent of the household's income over its life cycle; that is, the maximum that could be consumed consistent with wealth preservation. The empirical content of the life-cycle permanent-income hypothesis is that, as a consequence of consumption-smoothing behaviour, consumption is proportional to permanent income. Indeed, if the worker leaves no bequest, as is assumed by Figure 2.7, consumption is predicted to equal permanent income.

One complication to the picture presented by Figure 2.7 arises in the case of uncertain lifetimes. Given realistic dispersion of the life-spans of different individuals, the asset profile of retirees becomes convex rather than concave. Another complication arises for realistic degrees of uncertainty concerning wage income. This induces precautionary saving, especially on the part of young households. The implication for Figure 2.7 is a consumption profile that is concave rather than level. See below; see also Gourinchas and Parker (1999).

To recapitulate, the worker saves ahead of retirement, and dissaves after retirement. Some assets, for example those held in pension plans, are *retirement conditioned*; that is, they become available only upon retirement. (This term is due to Burbidge and Robb 1980.) The asset profile portrayed in Figure 2.7 is defined as the assets at each time that would become available if the worker were to retire immediately. Included in such assets is the capitalised value of any retirement-conditioned or age-conditioned pensions. The simple hump shape portrayed in Figure 2.7 evidently does not allow for discontinuities; notably, the 'notches' in typically defined benefit plans arising from the vesting of employer benefits and the attainment of particular ages and employment spans; for example, age 62 in the case of social security in the United States.

A key parameter in life-cycle models, with or without endogenous retirement, is the *coefficient of relative risk aversion*:

Coefficient of relative risk aversion = percentage reduction in marginal utility induced by a 1% rise in consumption.

Marginal utility is the extra felicity engendered by a unit rise in the consumption rate per period.

A high risk averter experiences a large percentage rise in the marginal utility of consumption whenever consumption has fallen by 1%. A low risk averter experiences the opposite. High risk averters strive especially for a dependable living standard. Low risk averters, by contrast, strive especially for a high average living standard. Alas, there are plausible estimates of an 'average' coefficient of relative risk aversion that range all the way from less than one to more than 100. By the end of the twentieth century, researchers were tending to revise their estimates upwards, with numbers such as five becoming viewed as reasonable rather than high (Campbell 2000).

Life-cycle model of retirement

Research by Burbidge and Robb (1980), Fields and Mitchell (1984), Mitchell and Fields (1984), and others extended the life-cycle perma- nent-income hypothesis to the case of endogenous retirement. As usual, the optimum date of retirement is identified by marginal analysis: 'The optimal retirement date R* equates the marginal utility from an addi- tional year of work with the marginal utility of leisure' (Mitchell and Fields 1984, p. 87). Put another way, once retirement assets have reached a sufficient level to support the household for the remainder of its life at something like its pre-existing living standard, it becomes worthwhile no longer to put up with the disutility of work.

An equivalent way of stating the rule for optimum retirement is in terms of *reservation retirement assets*; that is, the minimum level of assets that would induce you to retire immediately. Reservation retirement assets are portrayed as a downward-sloping line in Figure 2.8. (Technical details of the construction of such schedules can be found in Kingston 2000.) Strictly speaking, the simple linear schedule portrayed in Figure 2.8 holds only under log utility and zero time preference. Although its negative slope carries over to more general cases, the schedule changes in shape, from linearity to concavity. The worker's age ranges from the

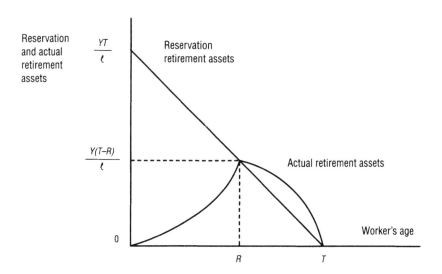

Figure 2.8 Life-cycle model of retirement

labour force entry date O to date of death T. Actual assets have a peak value at the retirement date R, and then dwindle to zero at the death date, assuming no uncertainty about the date of death, and no bequest. Reservation retirement assets depend directly on the worker's wage net of his retirement-conditioned pension, Y, and death date T, and inversely on the disutility of work l. Over the life cycle, consumption (not shown) is level.

Reservation retirement assets are directly related to the worker's wage net of his or her retirement-conditioned pension because that is the opportunity cost of giving up work. Another direct influence is the remaining span of life; the sooner one retires, the longer the time needed to support oneself without a wage. Reservation retirement assets are inversely related to the disutility of work; the more arduous a job, the greater the incentive to retire early. Retirement will occur if and when actual retirement assets hit reservation retirement assets. Actual assets will depend partly on initial assets. Thus, a Rockefeller heir might never enter the labour force in the first place, while an indentured labourer might remain in the labour force until death.

A worker on the verge of retirement will respond to an unanticipated and permanent increase in wages by working longer. As suggested earlier, and in the terminology of Burbidge and Robb (1980) and Fields and Mitchell (1984), there is a pure *substitution effect*. On the other hand, a worker further off retirement has the time needed to accumulate worthwhile additional assets following a wage rise, and that promotes early retirement. In the terminology of the pensions researchers just mentioned, there is in such cases an offsetting *income effect* of wage rises on retirement timing. The case of a dominant income effect is portrayed by Figure 2.9. After Q years in the labour force, the worker receives news of an immediate and permanent rise in net wages, from Y_1 to Y_2. The schedule portraying reservation retirement assets pivots upwards. Whenever there is a wage-related component of retirement assets, for example membership of a typical defined-benefit pension plan, actual retirement assets jump up as well. Irrespective of such assets, saving after time Q could be higher. Given a sufficiently long lead time, together with sufficiently diminishing marginal utility of consumption (that is, sufficiently high risk aversion), retirement timing could be brought forward, from R_1 to R_2

In order to explain the phenomenon of early retirement by older men in the setting of the life-cycle model, it is natural to focus on the possibility of a dominant income effect. However, except in situations where the analyst can identify strong reinforcement from income-linked retirement assets, a permanent wage rise well ahead of retirement is not sufficient to rationalise early retirement. In the context of the life-cycle model of retirement, high risk aversion is needed to explain early retirements in terms of a long-term response to wage rises. Low risk averters, that is people for whom marginal utility from consumption diminishes gradually, will respond to wage rises by retiring later (Kingston 2000).

In short, offsetting income and substitution effects generate a major ambiguity among the predictions generated by the life-cycle model with endogenous retirement (described also by Fields and Mitchell as the 'age-at-retirement' model). Overall, however, the life-cycle model is surprisingly unambiguous in its prediction, as Fields and Mitchell note. They find the following US evidence in support of the life-cycle model of retirement; see also Stock and Wise (1990) and Samwick (1998b):

- Older workers would have added to their income had they deferred retirement; that is, they do not wait until the monetary benefit of another year at work has dwindled to zero.
- Workers with high levels of accrued pension wealth retire earlier than their lower wealth counterparts.
- Degrees of arduousness of different occupations do matter. At least, 'nonpecuniary job attributes may also play a role in retirement' (Fields and Mitchell 1984, p. 129).

That degrees of arduousness do matter is suggested by survey data on retired Australian men (Australian Bureau of Statistics 1997a).

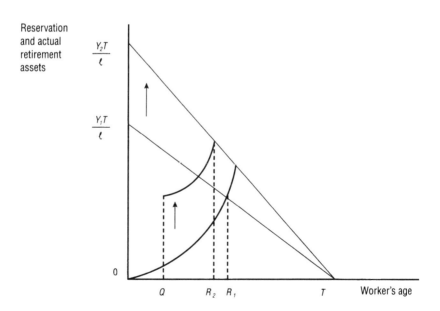

Figure 2.9 Wage rises and early retirements

Among an estimated 107 100 retired managers and administrators, 39% ceased full-time work before age 60. By contrast, among an estimated 142 400 labourers and related workers, 50% ceased full-time work before age 60.

Employer perspective and implicit contracts theory

The preceding section emphasised the simple case of defined-contribution or accumulation pension plans whereby members have specifically allocated investments and accounts. At its most basic, such a plan could consist of a plan to pay off the house by the time of retirement, along with regular saving towards retirement in a bank account. For centuries, however, saving for life-cycle purposes was traditionally associated with a *DB pension plan*: prespecified retirement benefits are promised by a plan 'sponsor'; that is, the employer or the government. Benefits are calculated by reference to years of service, and usually wages as well, often wages in the years immediately preceding retirement. In this way, the employee's pension plan can be designed to perform an income replacement function, provided the employee gives sufficiently long service to the plan sponsor. (Defined-benefit plans are treated from a finance standpoint in Chapter 4.)

Income replacement is one reason that the DB pension plan can suit households conforming to the 'buffer stock model' of consumption and saving (see below), according to which consumption tracks income over long horizons. However, defined benefits can also serve a number of employer/sponsor purposes. First, retirement benefits for short stayers with the enterprise are typically low relative to the employee's contributions. As a result the employee is motivated not to leave the enterprise prematurely; for example, before the costs of on-the-job training can be recouped. Second, retirement benefits are typically linked to salary at retirement. In this way, workers are motivated to get themselves promoted within the enterprise. Third, as the employee's pension (income stream conditional upon retirement) gradually rises up towards the income generated by staying at work, workers characterised by high seniority and low productivity become motivated to retire. Finally, the overall defined-benefit plan typically comes with death and disability insurance cover, so the employee is motivated to undertake hazardous tasks for the enterprise.

On the last point, Nalebuff and Zeckhauser (1985) recall the American Express Company, which established the first formal private pension plan in the United States. Eligibility was conditional not only upon 25 years service and attaining 60 years of age, but incurring a permanent disability while on the job. The company in question owned railway businesses involving hazardous work environments. For this reason, disability insurance helped to motivate employees. Similarly, Costa (1998) recalls the Union army pension program in the United States. Ninety-five per cent of the army were volunteers. Veterans were entitled to about 30% of the income of an unskilled labourer, conditional on total disability as measured by inability to perform manual labour.

By the beginning of the 1990s, about 70% of the financial assets in US private pension plans were in DB plans (Hurd 1990, Sundaresan and Zapatero 1997); in Australia, by contrast, the corresponding figure was only 45%. Hence, the popularity of what Fields and Mitchell (1984) describe as the *implicit contracts model* of the retirement decision, whereby not only does the worker belong to a DB pension plan, but the dominant factors affecting the retirement decision are design features in the pension plan that motivate the worker to retire soon after marginal value product – the worker's contribution to value added by the enterprise – drops below his or her wage rate. According to the implicit contracts model, disutility of work is not a major factor affecting the retirement decision. Rather, retirement occurs if and when the worker has maximised household assets, notably, defined benefits conditional upon having retired.

An appealing feature of the implicit contracts model is that the disutility of work – a subjective parameter – does not have to be measured by the pensions researcher. Yet there are several disadvantages. First, without the disutility of work we only get a theory of employment *separation*, not a theory of exiting the labour force. Strictly speaking, a purely wealth-maximising worker will never retire, so long as there is an employer somewhere who is prepared to hire the worker at a positive wage. Second, there seems to be no broad difference in the retirement patterns of Western countries with and without wide coverage of the labour force by defined-benefit pension plans. For example, Australia has shown a similar trend to early retirement on the part of older men as have northern hemisphere countries distinguished by wide-coverage DB pension plans. Third, even in countries such as the United States, with coverage well in excess of 90%, most assets are nevertheless held outside pension plans. In particular, 33% of household wealth in the United States consists of owner-occupied residential real estate (see Chapter 4). Finally, even in the United States there has been a drift to defined-contribution pension plans, which mesh better with frequent job switching. At a global level the trend is to privatised pensions systems with a DC emphasis.

By the same token, defined-benefit plans have clearly discernible effects at the level of detail. For example, Fields and Mitchell (1984, p. 7) tabulated figures from the US Benefits Amounts Survey showing significant 'notches' whereby 19.7% of the sample retired at age 62, compared to 10.1% at age 61, and 15.1% at age 63. Similarly, retirements at age 65 accounted for 25.5% of the sample, compared to 7.5% at age 64, and 7.8% at age 66. Benefit accrual features of social security have become the standard explanation (see, for example, Gruber and Wise 1999).

Employer influences on retirement ages are not confined to the design of DB plans. For example, Chan and Huff Stevens (1999) found that a 62-year-old man who loses his job has a less than one-third chance of returning to work anytime during the subsequent two years. One possible explanation is 'scarring', whereby an older job loser is perceived by potential employers as having become unproductive.

Health and longevity factors

Simple observation reveals that older workers are influenced by health factors in making their retirement decisions. Equally obvious is that increased life expectancy means increased consumption needs over the life cycle and, therefore, delayed retirement.

Health

Australian survey evidence confirms the importance of health factors. One example is a 1992 survey, by the Australian Bureau of Statistics, of the reasons for 'early' retirement, defined as retirement before age 65 in the case of men, and before age 60 in the case of women. In either case, the most common reason given was 'own ill-health or injury'.

Indirect support for the importance of health comes from international evidence (detailed below) that consumption drops sharply in the wake of retirement, contrary to the life-cycle model. This is consistent with the notion that unanticipated health setbacks bump people off their life-cycle plans for retirement ages and for consumption.

On the other hand, Fields and Mitchell (1984) find a fairly minor role for health setbacks in the US case. Their Analysis of Variance (ANOVA) study of the relative influence of self-reported 'health limitations' and 'economic variables' led to the conclusion that only about one-quarter of the retirement-age decision was explained by the health factor, compared to about three-quarters by economic factors. This finding is consistent with simple observation – if Western men were currently retiring mainly as a consequence of disabilities, then current medical technologies would be producing later retirement, contrary to the facts.

Table 2.2 Longevity and life expectancies for selected countries

		Males		Females	
		% reaching 65	Life expectancy at 65 (years)	% reaching 65	Life expectancy at 65 (years)
Australia	1901–10	48.7	11.3	56.3	12.9
	1994	82.0	15.7	90.0	19.7
United States	1900–02	38.7	11.5	43.2	12.2
	1994	74.8	15.5	85.5	19.0
United Kingdom	1891–1901*	33.1	10.3	39.8	11.3
	1995	80.6	14.6	87.8	18.3
Japan	1899–1903	33.4	10.1	36.7	11.3
	1995	83.3	16.5	91.6	20.9
France	1898–1903	36.0	10.5	42.7	11.5
	1993	76.1	15.9	89.5	20.3
Germany	1910–11	39.5	10.4	46.5	11.0
	1993–95	77.0	14.6	88.4	18.3
Sweden	1901–10	50.0	12.8	54.7	13.7
	1994	83.5	16.0	90.0	19.8
Switzerland	1910–11	40.6	10.2	48.6	10.9
	1994–95	82.0	16.1	90.4	20.2
Chile	1930	24.6	11.2	29.3	12.2
	1996	75.3	15.0	84.9	18.2

* Data for England only.
Source: United Nations *Demographic Yearbook* (except * English Life Tables
No. 6)

Longevity

A commonplace observation is that retirement income provision is
coming under pressure from increased longevity. More people are
surviving to retirement age, and with greater life expectancies at retirement, than was the case in the past. At the beginning of the twentieth
century in Australia, for example, 49% of males and 56% of females
survived to age 65, with subsequent life expectancies of 11 and 13 years
respectively; at the end of the century, by contrast, 82% of males and
90% of females were surviving to age 65, with subsequent life expectancies of 16 and 20 years. Table 2.2 presents longevity and life-expectancy
data at the beginning and end of the 1900s for a number of OECD
countries and for Chile, and shows that these trends were observed
across the board, with at least three-quarters of men surviving to 65, and
subsequently living for 15 or more years, and at least 85% of women
surviving to 65, and living at least 18 years beyond that.

Age–wealth profiles and consumption after retirement

The simple life-cycle model predicts that consumption will be smoothed across different states of nature. In particular, consumption will not drop on the occasion of retirement by, for example, the household head. Rather, assets will be run down in order to support the pre-retirement consumption standard of the household. However, careful research based on UK data by Banks, Blundell and Tanner (1998), on US data by Hurd (1990) and, especially, by Bernheim, Skinner and Weinberg (1997) tells a different story. First, household consumption declines after retirement, even after controlling for such factors as reduced work-related expenses and changes in household composition. Second, household assets tend to rise in the immediate aftermath of retirement. Although assets do eventually decline in advanced old age (Hurd 1990), the overall rate of dissaving is low.

Of these two stylised facts, the latter is easier to rationalise. First, simple observation suggests that the bequest motive is significant. Second, uncertainty of the date of death together with missing markets for actuarially fair life annuities could induce a period of precautionary saving (Hurd 1990), as could uncertainty about returns to risky retirement assets, such as stocks and shares, especially in the case of highly risk-averse households (Merton 1969).

Australians seem to have conformed to the generalisation that dissaving in retirement is surprisingly low (see Figure 2.10).

Baekgaard cautions that the data in Figure 2.10, based as they are on income distribution surveys and household expenditure surveys, are not the longitudinal or panel data that we would ideally want for this sort of exercise. Limited as they are, the data do suggest that assets per person dwindle little or not at all in old households.

The fact of a somewhat discontinuous drop in consumption rates is harder to rationalise. One obvious possibility is that the consumption rate needed for attaining any given utility level declines with advancing age. Another possibility is that retirees have underestimated the assets required to support their pre-retirement living standard (Banks et al. 1990; Bernheim et al. 1997; for a contrary view, see Hurd 1990, p. 617, on the role of unexpected upgrades to social security in boosting US retirement assets during the second half of the twentieth century).

Yet another explanation is unexpected health declines that raise sharply the disutility of effort, thereby precipitating early retirement on a reduced consumption standard. Like uncertain lifetimes, this explanation of consumption discontinuity relies on missing markets. As a consequence of adverse selection and moral hazard, income insurance against health setbacks is not available on actuarially fair terms. (Banks

et al. 1990 canvass the health argument but they lean towards an
alternative argument based on propensities to underestimate the
funds needed in retirement.) Figure 2.11 below spells out the health
argument.

   Disutility of work is initially at level l_1. At age R_2 the worker is initially
on track to retire at expected age R_1. Following an uninsured health
setback, however, disutility of work rises to l_2, which is assumed for
simplicity to be just sufficient to precipitate immediate retirement.
Consumption during an unplanned and uninsured early retirement is
lower than consumption during working years.

Buffer stock saving and consumption before retirement

In tests of the life-cycle permanent-income hypothesis one can distinguish between high-frequency tests, which assess performance of the
hypothesis when time is measured in days, weeks, or quarters, and
low-frequency tests, which assess performance over years or decades.
Following Hall (1978) it became apparent that the empirical performance of the life-cycle permanent-income hypothesis in high-frequency
tests is impressive. During the 1990s, however, it became apparent also
that the life-cycle permanent-income hypothesis does not perform so
impressively at long horizons (Carroll and Summers 1991, Carroll

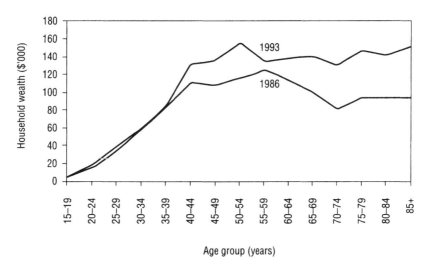

Figure 2.10 Australian household wealth by age group of the oldest person
Note: These age–wealth profiles show average assets per adult, in 1993 dollars,
and in households defined in terms of pooled income units.
Source: Baekgaard (1998), p. 30

1997). The age–earnings profile describes an inverse U shape, with the peak occurring some time before or at retirement. According to the life-cycle permanent-income hypothesis, income should greatly exceed consumption in middle age. In fact, consumption is found to track disposable income rather closely (see Figure 2.12).

In a series of publications (for example, Carroll 1997), Carroll and associates have proposed a *buffer stock* model to resolve the paradox of good model performance over short time horizons and poor performance over long horizons. The model relies on the interaction of three elements. The first is high risk aversion; that is, sharply diminishing marginal utility of consumption. The second is high time preference; that is, strong impatience on the part of consumers. The final ingredient is considerable income uncertainty; in particular, considerable doubt about the dependability of wage incomes over the life cycle

With the help of extensive numerical simulations, Carroll and his associates demonstrate that, over most of the life cycle, buffer stock households will build up some precautionary savings (savings for emergencies), but will not dissave much in youth, nor will they save much until a decade or so before retirement. There is a positive correlation between

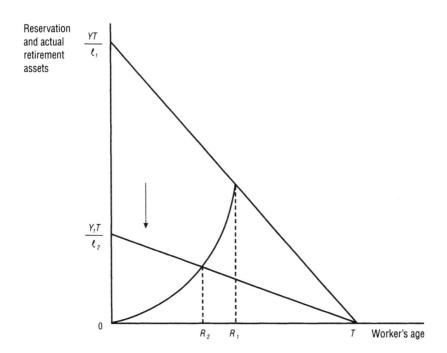

Figure 2.11 Uninsured health setbacks and early retirements

saving and the expected growth of wage income rather than the negative
correlation suggested by simple life-cycle theory. Overall, young households are more timid in using the capital market than the simple life-cycle
story would lead one to expect. Evidence of buffer stock behaviour in the
Australian case is presented by Edey and Britten-Jones (1990).

   Carroll and his associates have treated the date of retirement as
exogenous. In particular, 65 is treated as the 'normal' retirement age,

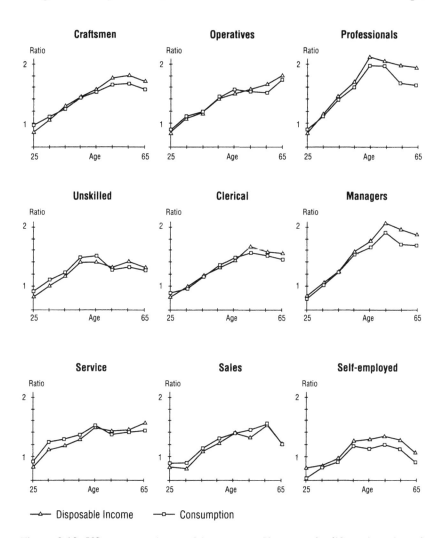

Figure 2.12 US consumption and income profiles over the life cycle, selected
occupations
Source: Carroll (1997), p. 34

as is suggested by Figure 2.12. However, the life-cycle model of retirement is complementary with the buffer stock model of saving in the following ways:

- High risk aversion is also helpful if the life-cycle retirement model is to accommodate the natural explanation of the early retirement phenomenon; namely, younger households responding to higher permanent income by bringing forward their planned date of retirement, even in the absence of DB components among their retirement assets. (Low risk averters, by contrast, respond to higher permanent income by working longer, thereby coming to enjoy much higher consumption over the life cycle.)
- High time preference helps to reconcile life-cycle theory with the fact of early retirement even in the case of some people with modest means and good health. It helps also explain the observed consumption declines in the wake of retirement.
- Uncertainty about the date of retirement reinforces the proposition that there is considerable uncertainty about future wage income.

Further to the point about retirement uncertainty adding to wage uncertainty through the life cycle, retirement itself can be considered a buffer against wage uncertainty, along with the short-term buffering role of saving that is highlighted by the buffer stock model. Notably, an unexpected wage drop can be partly countered by postponing retirement. The life-cycle model of retirement easily accommodates this type of behaviour.

Carroll (1997) is candid about the limitations of the buffer stock model. These can be summarised as follows. First, the buffer stock model does not describe the behaviour of the richest households, wherein consumption does not track wage income. Second, by emphasising impatience it fails to account for the willingness of some young households to pay off an owner-occupied home, and participate in pension plans voluntarily. (The variant of the buffer stock model proposed by Gourinchas and Parker 1999 finds rates of time preference around 5% per annum.) Third, high time preference suggests high real returns to safe securities. Yet, index bonds issued by governments in Australia, Canada, the United Kingdom and the United States have only yielded about $3\frac{1}{2}\%$ per year on average.

Self-control and saving for retirement

There is a richer model of impatience that can account for life-cycle saving even while preserving elements of the buffer stock story.

'Lord make me virtuous, but not yet.' There are pervasive problems with self-control. The classic example is that of a smoker who acknowledges substantial long-term health benefits arising from giving up the habit, and therefore resolves to do so, yet continually procrastinates. Indeed, research by psychologists on animal and human behaviour finds evidence that we discount the near future more heavily than is needed for consistent decision-making.

Pensions research along this line was pioneered by David Laibson and his associates (Laibson, Repetto and Tobacman 1998). In this article the authors cite a 1997 survey that found 76% of respondents believe they should be saving more for retirement. Laibson and others have handled this departure from the standard life-cycle permanent-income hypothesis by postulating a multiple self:

> Self 0 prefers patient tradeoffs at period t, but self t disagrees ... Economists have modelled this situation as an intra-personal game played among the consumers' temporally situated selves. (Laibson et al. 1998, p. 100)

In the case of saving for retirement, households not only understand their self-control problems but go some way towards rectifying them by accepting commitment devices enforced by governments and employers. In the case of 401(k) pension plans in the United States, for example, Laibson et al. (1998) note a number of enforcement mechanisms:

- Members enjoy tax deferrals, and also matching contributions by their employers. In 81% of plans, employer contributions are contingent on employee contributions.
- The standard 401(k) plan requires an automatic deposit system, thereby lessening the temptation to skip contributions.
- Withdrawals can be made freely and without penalty only if the account holder is aged more than 59 years and 6 months. While younger workers can obtain access to their accounts in cases of financial hardship, or separation from the enterprise, this attracts a 10% penalty.

Australia's Superannuation Guarantee and superannuation generally involve even more stringent controls. The employer contribution is mandatory. The Tax Office enforces deposits into accounts by way of tax penalties on the employer's business. The preservation age – the age at which retirement-conditioned assets can normally be accessed – is in the process of being gradually escalated from 55 to 60. While death and disability do trigger access, and financial hardship can provide grounds for access, separation from your employer does not, except in cases of very small accumulations.

Together with discussants of their article, Laibson et al. (1998) draw out a few weaknesses in the case for treating self-control problems as an important part of the puzzle. First, buffer stock savers – high risk averters with high but intertemporally consistent rates of time preference, and facing considerable wage uncertainty – are not easily distinguishable from savers with poor self-control. Thus, in order to demonstrate big social gains from compulsory saving for retirement, it becomes necessary to assume a low coefficient of relative risk aversion. Accordingly, Laibson et al. (1998) highlight the case of a unitary coefficient. Second, in the United States some scope is allowed for using the 401(k) plan assets as loan collateral, and around one-third of account holders avail themselves of it, although the average loan is only $2500. Third, there are indications that retirees may save too much rather than too little (Hurd 1990). While there are various mechanisms to compel retirees to annuitise, these are often motivated by the need to deter the elderly from first concealing family assets; for example, by gifting them to children, and then stepping forward to claim pensions and other forms of state assistance for the impecunious.

Conclusion

The twentieth century was the first one to see older men in the industrial countries choosing to retire *en masse*. During the last decades of the century, the trend to early retirement gathered pace, but may have stabilised by the mid-1980s.

Broadly speaking, early male retirement is consistent with the life-cycle model due to Burbidge, Robb, Fields, Mitchell and others. The life-cycle model relates the planned span of retirement to factors that include accumulated assets relative to wages forgone upon the occasion of retirement, the arduousness of the job, employee impatience and aversion to risk. The twentieth century was the first one during which ordinary people were able to amass substantial retirement assets, including public and private pension entitlements and housing equity.

By contrast, the last third of the century saw increased full-time and part-time participation by older women in the paid workforce. The main explanation is probably the strong rise in women's wages that occurred over the period in question, as the services sector came to dominate the industrial economies. In the case of secondary workers within a household, the substitution effect of a wage rise will tend to dominate the income effect.

While the broad facts fit the basic life-cycle model of work and saving, there are several anomalies at the level of detail. Actual consumption cleaves too closely to household disposable income, at least until about age 40, household consumption drops too much in the immediate aftermath of retirement by the household head, saving by retired households is surprisingly strong, and employees have proved surprisingly willing to surrender control over their life-cycle savings to employers and governments.

CHAPTER 3

Saving for Retirement

Over the past two decades a growing number of countries have introduced multi-pillar retirement income arrangements that rely largely on private mandatory retirement provision. As was outlined in Chapter 1, the minimum requirements for private mandatory retirement saving include a public mandate (rather than public provision), private administration and management, and full funding in individual accounts. So far few countries satisfy these criteria fully. Chile was the first to introduce mandatory private retirement saving in 1981, followed by Switzerland and Australia in the mid-1980s.[1] Throughout the 1990s, many Latin American countries followed the Chilean model, a number of OECD and transition economies have reformed their retirement income arrangements along these lines, while Hong Kong has pioneered private mandatory retirement saving in Asia. Other countries (including the United States) are considering full or partial implementation.

Policy reform in Latin America has followed the Chilean system. As with Chile, the reform process was motivated by the loss of credibility in the public PAYG system although other issues such as population ageing, low coverage of retirement income provision and broader economic goals were also relevant. The reforms commenced in Peru in 1993, followed by Argentina and Colombia in 1994, Uruguay in 1996, Mexico and Bolivia in 1997, El Salvador in 1998 and more recently Costa Rica.

In the OECD, Australia and Switzerland have introduced comprehensive private mandatory retirement saving arrangements, while similar policy development has taken place in the United Kingdom, Denmark, The Netherlands and Sweden. In the United Kingdom, policy reform has been achieved by providing incentives to contract out public pensions into private arrangements, while in Denmark and The Netherlands the private retirement income provision is organised through collective bargaining, rather than a public mandate. Private mandatory arrangements play a lesser role in Sweden where the mandate requires only 2.5% of earnings to be placed in individual accounts.

Elsewhere in the world, Hungary and Kazakhstan introduced private mandatory retirement saving in 1998, Poland in 1999 and Hong Kong in 2000. As well, as discussed in Chapter 1, policy reform along these lines has been advocated for the United States. The broad features of private mandatory retirement saving around the world are summarised in Appendices 1 and 2.

This chapter considers the accumulation (or saving) phase of private mandatory retirement provision. The outcome of this phase is an accumulation amount, which is available to purchase a retirement benefit. As private mandatory retirement provision is based upon defined contributions, the final retirement benefit is a function of the contribution rate, the contribution period and the rate of return on the contributions. However, a range of other factors will determine the final accumulation amount including coverage, the specification of contribution rates and thresholds, labour force participation, the institutional framework, industry practices and governance of the retirement saving entities, government intervention in the form of regulation and taxation, disclosure requirements, and member education. These factors will affect lifetime contributions, and through their impact on asset choice, rates of return and administrative charges, the net returns on these contributions.

A formal analysis of the accumulation phase

Consider the accumulation phase of a private mandatory retirement saving scheme. The aim is to produce an accumulation to convert into a retirement benefit. Expressed in discrete terms, the final accumulation at retirement, A, is:

$$A = \sum_{i=1}^{T} \left\{ C \cdot W \cdot (1 + w)^{i-1} \cdot (1 - \beta_C) \cdot [1 + (\mu - \beta_A)] \right\}^{T-i} \tag{3.1}$$

where: A = accumulation at retirement
C = mandatory contribution rate, %
W = wage to which the contribution rate applies (in period 1)
w = wages growth, % per period
β_C = account administration charge as a percentage of contributions
μ = nominal rate of return of superannuation fund assets, % per period
β_A = investment management charge as a percentage of assets under management
T = number of periods in accumulation phase

It follows that the final accumulation (A) is a function of total net contributions:

$$\sum_{i=1}^{T} \left\{ C \cdot W \cdot (1 + w)^{i-1} \cdot (1 - \beta_C) \right\}^{T-i}$$

and the net rate of return $(\mu - \beta_A)$.

Total net contributions are determined by the contribution rate (C), the wage to which this applies (W), the rate of increase in this wage (w), the period of participation (T) and any outlays made from these contributions, such as account administration charges (β_c), contribution taxes, or insurance premiums.[2] The total net return is determined by the gross rate of return (μ), reduced by investment management charges (β_A) and possibly earnings taxes (not represented here). Contributions and earnings taxes are specifically considered later in this chapter.

Throughout this process, the rate of return, administration and investment charges and taxes, and the duration and continuity of contributions are influenced by other factors, including the institutional framework for retirement saving, the governance structures, and the tax and regulatory environment. These factors are considered below.

Governance

In the context of private mandatory saving for retirement, governance refers to the structure of the entities responsible for the management and investment of the mandatory contributions, and any rules, regulations or practices that may influence the decision-making of these entities. The institutional framework, in conjunction with the regulatory framework, and industry practices largely dictate governance structure. Governance is important because of its possible impact on administrative efficiency, asset allocation and administrative charges, and by implication, the retirement benefit outcomes (Mitchell and Hsin 1997, Useem and Mitchell 2000). Allowable and actual governance strategies differ, both within countries and internationally. The main determinants of governance are industry structure and the regulatory arrangements.

Institutional framework

The process involved in the accumulation phase of private mandatory retirement provision is quite straightforward:

- Individual accounts are created.
- Contributions are placed in the individual accounts.

- The funds in the individual accounts are invested.
- The returns on the assets are credited to the individual accounts.
- Ongoing performance is reported to individuals.
- At a designated retirement or preservation age, the accumulated amount is available for withdrawal, and possible conversion into retirement income.

The institutional framework and therefore the governance structure are important as they have implications for market structure, asset allocation and incentives to deliver high net-of-charges returns to members. In turn, market structure is relevant for economies of scale and scope, marketing requirements and administrative costs and, by implication, net-of-charges investment returns.

Two distinct models of institutional structure are prevalent. These can be classified as 'intermediated retirement saving' and 'direct retirement saving'.

Intermediated retirement saving

Under 'intermediated retirement saving' a private financial intermediary is chosen to manage the retirement savings. In practice, the financial institution has taken the form of a trust or private company. This entity is generally responsible for both the administration of the individual accounts and the investment of the assets (although either or both of these functions may be contracted out to specialist service providers). Generally, the financial intermediaries are established specifically for the management of retirement savings. Examples include pension funds (in many OECD countries), *administrados de fondos de pensiones* (AFPs) or a derivative thereof (in Latin American countries) and superannuation funds (in Australia). Assets may be self-managed or there may be individual or group choice of asset manager(s).

Two main categories of 'intermediated retirement saving' have emerged, which can be broadly classified geographically. Latin America and Eastern Europe have taken a highly regulatory approach with restrictions placed on the institutional framework. Mandatory contributions can only be made to specific 'new' financial institutions, with existing financial institutions not allowed to participate. And, while there is generally member choice of financial intermediary, asset allocation has been restricted to a single portfolio.

The lack of voluntary private retirement saving in many Latin American or Eastern European countries has meant that the necessary institutions, regulatory infrastructure or industry experience have not evolved. For example, when the Chilean AFP arrangements began in 1981 there was no private pension market and the necessary financial entities – the AFPs – had to be established. Initially there were 12 AFPs. By 1995 this had grown to 21, but by 1998 had fallen to 9 as some AFPs merged and others making losses sold out to the profitable AFPs. The AFPs are limited liability companies, tightly regulated, outsource few of their functions and each is allowed to manage only one pension fund. Ownership and control of the AFPs is varied: some are organised on an industry or profession basis, while others are controlled by private Chilean or international financial institutions. This policy design can be traced back to the desire to avoid the political interference and lack of credibility with the previous public PAYG arrangements (Bateman and Valdes-Prieto 1999).

It has been argued that the restrictions in the Latin American and Eastern European regimes are designed to keep the regulation and supervision of the industry simple (Srinivas et al. 2000), although the case is often made that structural regulation inhibits performance (Shah 1998).

In most OECD countries the institutional structure is more varied with private mandatory retirement saving alternatives offered by a variety of providers. The majority of OECD countries have a long history of defined-benefit occupational pensions arranged through single company or industry-wide plans. Many of these have been converted to, or replaced by, defined-contribution plans. As well, personal pensions offered through the retail sector are important (particularly in the United Kingdom and Australia). Reforms in the OECD countries have tended to build upon the existing institutions.

In both Australia and Switzerland, the private mandatory retirement saving was grafted on to pre-existing voluntary occupational arrangements. In Australia, even before the introduction of award superannuation in the mid-1980s, around 40% of the private sector and 65% of the public sector were covered by superannuation and there were many thousands of superannuation funds. Similarly, in Switzerland around 80% of workers were covered by voluntary private retirement income arrangements prior to the introduction of the mandatory arrangements. In both countries, occupational superannuation/pension funds were used as the platform for private mandatory retirement saving; although, the retail sector – through master trusts – is also important in Australia.

Direct retirement saving

Under the 'direct retirement saving' alternative, contributions are made directly to asset managers (such as mutual funds). These need not be entities specifically established for the purpose of retirement saving.

Alternatives include free or constrained choice of asset manager and
the use of a centralised agency (such as a public clearing house) to
collect contributions from members and distribute them to the chosen
mutual funds.[3] A current example includes the new Swedish arrangements, where workers are required to save 2.5% of earnings in
individual retirement saving accounts. A constrained choice of mutual
funds is offered and accounts are administered by the Swedish Premium
Pension Agency. Members can choose up to five domestic or international mutual funds that negotiate an agreement with the Premium
Pension Agency about fees and reporting requirements. In Spring 2000,
the Premium Pension Agency offered a choice of 453 funds provided
by 67 different fund managers (Herbertsson et al. 2000). Variants of this
model have been canvassed for the reform of US Social Security
(Advisory Council on Social Security 1997, Kotlikoff and Sachs 1997,
Feldstein and Samwick 1998, Diamond 1999a).

'Direct retirement saving' allows greater individual control of retirement savings and provides the possibility of greater choice of asset
manager and portfolio type. This gives workers the freedom to decide
for themselves how much risk to accept in order to obtain better
expected returns on their retirement saving (Diamond 1999a). As well,
the asset managers or mutual funds may be able to offer individually
designed portfolios. While this institutional framework may be conducive to high marketing costs, these could be mitigated by offering
constrained choice (as in the case of Sweden) or, as discussed further
below, establish centralised collection.

'Intermediated retirement saving' would facilitate group choice (and
the associated cost savings), and, if appropriately governed, provide
some security for inadequately informed members. Importantly, financial intermediaries such as pension funds facilitate greater risk-pooling
and diversification than could be achieved with individual holdings.
As well, the 'intermediated retirement saving' approach has allowed
some countries (particularly in the OECD) to build their new private
mandatory retirement income provision upon existing voluntary
arrangements. Moreover, this institutional structure facilitates the
provision of complementary benefits and services, such as death and
disability insurance, at low cost. However, 'intermediated retirement
saving' does raise principal–agent issues in relation to incentives to
maximise the retirement accumulation

Both intermediated and direct retirement saving could be associated
with a centralised collection agency (clearing house) established to
co-ordinate and distribute contributions to financial intermediaries or
asset managers. Various forms are possible, ranging from a simple
conduit for contributions (as introduced in Argentina, Mexico and

Poland) to full account administration. Sweden is an example of the latter where the Premium Pension Agency administers the individual accounts, and collects, aggregates and transfers the mandatory contributions to the asset managers. A key design feature of the Premium Pension Agency is that the contributions are aggregated, ensuring that the asset managers administering investments do not know the identity of the investors (Herbertsson et al. 2000). In principle, centralised collection may lead to streamlined administration that could more easily address compliance and the issues of account duplication and 'lost' members. However, while centralised collection may be expected to improve efficiency and generate cost savings, Demarco and Rofman (1999) find that collection costs are higher and coverage no better in Argentina, with centralised collection, than Chile, with decentralised collection.

Implications for governance

Governance takes on particular importance in the case of 'intermediated retirement saving' where the financial intermediary acts as an 'agent' for the contributing member 'principal'. As noted earlier, the financial intermediary may take the form of a trust or a private company and regulations differ internationally as to the composition, duration and duties of the board of trustees (for trusts) and the board of directors (for private companies).[4] As well, decisions of the governing board may need to be sympathetic to statutory investment and institutional restrictions or requirements (such as minimum or maximum asset holdings or performance thresholds).

In Latin America, the financial intermediaries (AFPs or derivatives thereof) are established as private companies governed by boards of directors. In Chile, for example, the relevant financial intermediaries – AFPs – are limited liability corporations either organised on an industry basis, or controlled by private Chilean and international financial groups. While the members of the board have responsibilities as trustees, they have no particular relationship to the AFP members. Under this form of governance, the stakeholders include both AFP members and shareholders, and the governance structure has the dual goals of making profits for shareholders and maximising retirement benefits for members.

In the relevant OECD countries (with the exception of Mexico) the governance arrangements are more varied. This follows from the greater variation in industry structure, industry practices and regulatory requirements. It is common for the governing body to be established as a trust, although the composition, characteristics and duties of boards of trustees differ internationally. For example, the composition of the boards ranges from employer appointees (in the United Kingdom) to equal representation of employees and employers (common in Australia, Hong Kong, Switzerland, Denmark and The Netherlands). Importantly, where the trust is associated with a non-profit entity, the stakeholders are the fund members only.

Under the Australian arrangements, the relevant financial intermediaries are superannuation funds. Most mandatory contributions are placed in industry superannuation funds or a form of retail superannuation fund called a master trust, although other forms are allowed, including public superannuation funds, corporate superannuation funds, self-managed superannuation funds and retirement savings accounts. While industry funds and master trusts coexist and are subject to the same regulatory environment, there are significant differences in the governance structures. Industry funds are non-profit entities established for the purpose of providing a vehicle for retirement saving. They are governed by boards of trustees, which comprise equal employee and employer representation. Master trusts, however, are profit-making entities, which are governed by boards of trustees having no direct relationship with fund members. These and other differences between industry funds and master trusts are considered further in Chapter 7.

In Switzerland, employers generally satisfy their mandatory obligations by making contributions to a foundation (or trust),[5] which may be single or multi-employer based. The foundations must be separate legal entities from the employers, and are managed by a board of trustees comprising equal numbers of employer and employee representatives. Employers whose plans do not satisfy the mandatory requirements are required to join a multi-employer pension foundation.

Fund governance does matter. While research into the governance of privately managed pension funds is sparse, analysis of the governance of public pension funds suggests that governance is an important determinant of performance. In a cross-country study of public pension funds, Iglesias and Palacios (2000) found that pension funds in countries with low governance ratings performed poorly, as compared to pension funds in countries with high governance ratings. They also found that, as compared to private-sector management, public management reduces returns. Evidence suggests that public funds are more likely to comprise political appointees, conduct administration and asset management in-house and be subject to strict investment regulations.

Useem and Mitchell (2000), in an investigation of the performance of US public pension funds, take this analysis a step further. In a two-stage analysis, Useem and Mitchell investigate the impact of governance on asset allocation and then the impact of asset allocation on performance.

Their results strongly suggest that the ways that public pensions are governed have a direct bearing on how they invest their assets, and the investment strategies in turn directly affect the financial performance of their holdings.

It follows that the governance structures of private mandatory retirement saving are likely to have an impact on net investment returns. While it is clear that private governance structures dominate public governance structures, the most appropriate form for the private governance structure is still unclear.

Contributions

In simple terms, aggregate contributions are a function of the contribution rate, the wage to which this applies and the length of the contribution period. However, many other factors come into play including coverage, wage income definitions and thresholds, who bears the legal responsibility for the contribution, and the collection mechanism. These factors are discussed below.

As private mandatory retirement saving is based on defined contributions, the amount and timing of contributions made are crucial. Contributions are only made by, or on behalf of, those covered. No coverage implies no contributions and no retirement accumulation. Those covered are generally workers – who, more often than not, do not include the self-employed – and coverage of these workers may be universal or selective. International practice is summarised in Table 3.1.

In Chile, coverage is comprehensive, with all persons working at least one hour per week covered, while the Australian arrangements restrict coverage to persons aged 18–70 with income in excess of 14% of average earnings. The Swiss arrangements restrict coverage to employees over the age of 24 who are making contributions to the public pension arrangements. With the exception of Hong Kong, none of the private mandatory retirement saving arrangements requires mandatory contributions from the self-employed. Such selective coverage may assist with minimising administrative costs (but at a large design cost).

Coverage may also be determined in relation to coverage of previous (or coexisting) retirement income arrangements. In many Latin American and transition economies, coverage of the private mandatory arrangements is being phased in with workers given the option to join or stay in the previous public PAYG system. For example, when the AFP system was introduced in Chile, existing workers were given the choice of staying in the public PAYG system or contributing to the 'new' private mandatory arrangements. Contribution to the new system was mandatory for all 'new' workers. In Mexico all workers were required to switch to the private

Table 3.1 Contributions – international experience

	Contribution rate	Who pays?	Coverage	Collection mechanism	Access to accumulation
Argentina	7.5% (excluding administrative charges and insurance premiums)	employees	Choice between previous public and new private systems for all dependent workers and the self-employed	Central collection: Employers make payments to tax authorities	Age 65 (males), 60 (females)
Australia	9%	employer	All employees aged 18–70 with earnings in excess of 14% average earnings	Decentralised collection: employers pay to superannuation funds	Age 55 (increasing to 60)
Bolivia	10%	employees	All dependent workers	Decentralised collection: directly to private funds	Contributions cease at age 65. Retire earlier if balance sufficient to finance a pension of at least 70% earnings
Chile	10% (excluding administrative charges and insurance premiums)	employees	All persons working at least 1 hour per week. Existing workers could opt to stay in previous public system	Decentralised collection: Employers deduct from wages and send to AFPs	Contributions cease at 65 (male), 60 (female). Retire earlier if balance is sufficient to finance a monthly pension of at least 50% earnings

Country	Contribution rate	Who contributes	Coverage	Collection	Retirement age
Colombia	10% (excluding administrative charges and insurance premiums)	employees	Option to remain in public system for women aged 35 and above and men aged 40 and above. Can switch between public and private (and back) every 3 years	Decentralised collection: employers deduct from wages and send to AFPs	Contributions cease at 62 (male), 57 (female). Retire earlier if balance sufficient to finance a pension of at least 110% minimum wage
Denmark	5–15%	employees and employers	Workers covered by collective bargaining agreements	Decentralised collection: directly to pension funds	From age 60
Hong Kong	10%	employees and employers	All employees and the self-employed	Decentralised collection: directly to mandatory provident funds	Ages 60–65
Hungary	8%	employees	Mandatory for 'new' workers, optional for current workers	Decentralised collection: employers make payments directly to pension funds	Age 62 years
Mexico	12%	employees and government	All workers (but at retirement can choose between pension calculated under new private or previous public systems)	Central collection	Age 65 years
Peru	8% (excluding administrative charges and insurance premiums)	employees	Choice between new private and previous public systems Irrevocable switch to private system	Decentralised collection	Age 60 (females), 65 (males)

Table 3.1 (cont.)

	Contribution rate	Who pays?	Coverage	Collection mechanism	Access to accumulation
Poland	7.3%	employees and employers	Mandatory for 'new' workers, optional for current workers	Central collection: national social security institution is the central clearing house	Age 60
Sweden	2.5%	employees	Mandatory for all	Centralised pension agency	From age 61
Switzerland	7–18% according to age and gender	at least 50% to be paid by employers	All employees over the age of 24, contributing to the public pension arrangements	Decentralised collection: directly to funds	Age 62 (females), age 65 (males) or earlier for home purchase
United Kingdom	Minimum contributions must satisfy the minimum employer-provided pension	employees and employers	Voluntary, around 70% employees	Centralised and decentralised collection: directly to employer pension funds or via tax agency to personal pensions	Age 60 (women), 65 (men)
Uruguay	7.5% (excluding administrative charges and insurance premiums)	employees	Private system only mandatory for workers under age 40 earning between 5000 and 15 000 pesos per annum	Centralised collection	Age 60 years

Sources: Bateman and Piggott (1998), Queisser (1998), Sundén (1998), Rofman and Demarco (1999), Blake (2000a) mandatory arrangements, but at retirement could opt to take public benefits. In Colombia, workers can switch between the private and public schemes every three years, while elsewhere in Latin America, participation in the private mandatory arrangements is voluntary (but generally irrevocable). It could be argued that voluntary participation in the private mandatory arrangements may ease the transition costs associated with the phasing down of PAYG public schemes. Although, it could equally be argued that such choice merely defers the switch to funded, privately provided retirement incomes, and therefore exacerbates the costs of unfunded public PAYG schemes to future taxpayers.

Another issue to consider is the range of wage income (or self-employment income for the self-employed) over which contributions are mandatory. Ceilings or floors may be set. Further, wage income may be defined variously: taxable, total, after tax or by some alternative definition. Again, these factors may be determined by the requirements of previous arrangements and may be designed to minimise administrative costs.

In defined-contributions plans, the contribution, rather than the retirement benefit, is specified in advance. The contribution can be made by employees, employers or even the government. International experience differs. In Latin America, employee contributions were generally chosen as a means of distancing the new arrangements from the previous inefficient, public PAYG schemes – although in Mexico the government makes a co-contribution. In Australia, employer contributions were considered appropriate in the then industrial relations environment, while in Switzerland both employees and employers are required to contribute. These and other differences are set out in Table 3.1 and are generally due to historical or political factors, rather than economic considerations.

A further issue is the contribution rate and the wage to which this rate should apply. In the absence of other forms of retirement income provision, one would expect a contribution rate be set to target an adequate retirement income benchmark. In developed countries, a replacement rate of two-thirds of pre-retirement income (variously defined) has been endorsed under public PAYG pensions and advocated by the private sector. The actual contribution rate is likely to be related to the rate applying under any previous arrangements, the availability of other forms of retirement income provision and political feasibility at the time of introduction.

A related issue is whether the contribution rate is set gross or net of administrative charges. The international experience differs, again along geographical lines. In Latin America, the practice has been to set a contribution rate and add to this an amount to cover administrative charges and life and disability insurance premiums. Outside Latin America, the practice is to set a contribution rate 'gross' of administrative charges and other outlays. An advantage of the Latin American, 'net' contributions approach is that it provides greater transparency of administrative charges and the amount of the total contribution invested each period. A problem with the 'gross' contribution approach is that the mandatory contribution rate is dissipated by administration charges, life and disability insurance premia and taxes.

In Chile, where the AFP system replaced public PAYG pensions and there was no system of voluntary occupational pensions, the contribution was set at 10% of wages. Notably, insurance and administrative charges of 2–3% of wages are added to this, and there is minimal taxation of retirement savings. Simulations and estimates suggest that, for the average worker, the Chilean AFP system could replace just about all of pre-retirement earnings (Castillo 1993, Baeza Valdes and Burger-Torres 1995).

On the other hand, as Switzerland already had comprehensive public pensions and funded occupational pensions, the Swiss BVG was designed to replace only 20% of pre-retirement earnings for the average worker. Here contribution rates are determined by age and gender ranging from 7% for 25-year-olds to 18% for persons approaching retirement, with the average contribution rate at around 12.5%. However, the BVG contribution rates apply to only part of total earnings – co-ordinated earnings – with the remainder covered by social security taxes. As well, the BVG sets a low minimum rate of return of 4% per annum (nominal).

Finally, in Australia (which had previously lacked a second pillar), the 9% employer contribution rate under the Superannuation Guarantee was reached as a compromise between adequacy and political expediency. There is some concern among commentators and academics that a 9% contribution rate is too low – particularly since administrative charges, insurance premia and taxes (as high as 30%) are all deducted from the 9% contribution. Contribution rates as high as 18% have been canvassed (FitzGerald 1993). Assuming continuous labour force participation and stock market stability, it has been estimated that the 9% Superannuation Guarantee will result in a replacement rate for a single male of around 39% of pre-retirement income, and a total replacement rate (including the first-pillar age pension) of 76% of pre-retirement income (Tinnion and Rothman 1999).

A particular feature of private mandatory retirement saving, which does not apply to public PAYG DB arrangements, is that the contributions must be identified and, with the earnings thereon, placed in individual accounts. This raises the issues of collection and account-keeping. There are two main alternatives: decentralised, where employees and/or employers send the contributions directly to the retirement saving organisation, or centralised, where the employees/employers send the contributions to a centralised (possibly government-run) collection agency. There are advantages and disadvantages with both approaches, and international experience differs (as summarised in Table 3.1). A centralised collection agency operates in Argentina, Mexico, Poland, Sweden, Uruguay, and for personal pensions in the United Kingdom. Elsewhere, the contributions are made directly to the relevant financial intermediary.

Centralised collection may allow economies of scale and scope (due to the large size and the opportunity to incorporate retirement saving contributions with other payments such as taxation). Also, centralised collection may enhance compliance and allow easier tracking of accounts and members – all of which may act to minimise administrative costs and charges. In Sweden, the centralised agency also performs the administration and management of the accounts and passes on the contribution to the member's chosen mutual fund (Fox and Palmer 2000).

Decentralised collection may enhance political insulation (and was chosen in Chile precisely for this reason), and lead to greater competition between financial intermediaries and retirement saving service providers. However, compliance is more difficult and the issues of multiple accounts and lost members may arise – although these issues are also prevalent under centralised collection in Latin America.[6]

A final determinant of aggregate contributions is the length and continuity of the contribution period. Generally, mandatory contributions are required provided a person is employed and has not reached the compulsory retirement or preservation age. Access ages vary internationally, and are summarised in Table 3.1. Mostly, contributions are not made when a person is unemployed or out of the labour force. An interesting feature of some Latin American plans is to permit contributions to cease once an adequate balance has been accumulated. For example, in Bolivia a balance sufficient to finance a pension of at least 70% of earnings is required, while the Colombian system requires a balance sufficient to finance a pension of at least 110% of the minimum wage. In Chile, 'adequacy' is defined as a pension larger than the greatest of 50% of average earnings over the previous 10 years (revalued by adjusting for inflation), and 100% of the current minimum pension. Due to high rates of return, currently 50% of pensions (and annuities) under the AFP system are 'early' pensions, and 50% of those pensioners are under age 55 (Bateman and Valdes-Prieto 1999).

Investment returns

Irrespective of the institutional framework, once a contribution has been made, it is invested. The final retirement benefit will be determined by lifetime contributions and the net rate of return. Crucial to the net rate of return are asset allocation and associated expenses such as administrative charges or taxation.

The importance of the rate of return for retirement savings can readily be appreciated from the following example. Suppose an individual on level earnings of $A40 000 a year for 35 years contributes 10% of salary to a pension fund. If assets are invested at 5% per annum, payable at the end of each year, the accumulation totals $A379 344. At 4%, the accumulation totals $A306 392, while at 3%, it amounts to just $A249 104 – less than two-thirds the 5% total. The lifelong returns to increasing the rate of return through strategic investment policy and efficient asset allocation are evidently very large – the power of compound interest at work.

Regulation

Regulation is an important determinant of asset allocation. Among countries with private mandatory arrangements, the entire spectrum of regulatory possibilities is experienced – ranging from 'highly' regulated to 'unregulated'. Subject to any restrictions, asset allocations will be influenced by the institutional framework. For 'intermediated' retirement saving, the governance of the financial intermediary will be important (as well as the menu of portfolio or asset manager choice offered to fund members). For 'direct' retirement saving, the menu of potential asset managers or mutual funds is relevant.

Investments can be regulated in terms of assets and/or performance. International experience differs and is summarised in Table 3.2 (assets) and Table 3.4 (performance). A notable distinction in investment regulation is found by comparing countries with established principles of trust law with the others. Of those countries that have introduced private mandatory retirement saving, examples of the former include Australia, the United Kingdom and The Netherlands. These countries have little investment regulation: asset allocation is determined subject to the prudent-person standard, whereby pension trustees and managers are obliged to invest in the same way that a prudent person would do on his or her own behalf (OECD 1997). As well, investment practices have been developed through a long history of voluntary retirement saving arrangements. The remaining countries apply varying degrees of regulation to assets, performance, and, as discussed earlier, institutional structure.

Table 3.2 Asset regulations – international comparisons

	Asset regulations
Argentina	Limits: 65% government securities, 40% corporate bonds, 28% mortgage-backed securities, 28% fixed-term deposits, 35% shares (public companies), 14% shares (private companies), 14% mutual funds, 10% direct investment funds, 10% foreign securities, 2% hedging instruments
Australia	No limits
Bolivia	50–90% equities, 10–50% to be invested overseas in foreign securities traded at the New York or London Stock Exchange
Chile	Limits: 50% government securities, 45% corporate bonds, 50% mortgage-backed securities, 50% letters of credit, 50% fixed-term deposits, 37% shares (public companies), 5% mutual funds, 10% real estate funds, 5% venture capital funds, 5% securitised credit funds, 12% foreign securities, 9% hedging instruments
Colombia	Limits: 50% government securities, 20% corporate bonds, 50% bank bonds, 30% mortgage-backed securities, 15% repurchase agreements, 30% shares (public companies), 5% stock index instruments, 10% foreign securities
Denmark	Minimum 60% in domestic or Euro-denominated debt, maximum 40% in property, equities and mutual funds, 20% foreign assets
Hong Kong	Guidelines include: maximum of 10% securities of a single issuer, maximum 70% assets with foreign currency exposure Limits on certain financial assets Not allowed (includes): geared investment vehicles, commodities, direct investment in property, loans, mortgages and debt
Mexico	Limits: 100% government securities, 35% corporate bonds, 10% bank bonds, 0% shares (public companies), 10% preference shares, 10% primary issues (new ventures), 0% foreign securities
The Netherlands	No limits
Peru	Limits: 30% government securities, 35% corporate bonds, 25% bank bonds, 30% fixed-term deposits, 10% short-term margin loans, 20% shares (public companies), 20% shares (worker's shares), 10% mutual funds, 5% foreign securities, 10% hedging instruments

Table 3.2 (cont.)

	Asset regulations
Poland	Limits: 20% bank deposits or securities, 40% listed equities, 15% open-ended investment funds, 5% closed-end funds, 15% publicly traded municipal bonds, 5% untraded bonds, 5% foreign assets, 0% property, derivatives
Sweden	Limits: 5–10% in foreign assets
Switzerland	Limits: 30% domestic equities, 55% domestic property, 30% foreign assets (of which – 30% foreign bonds, 25% foreign equities, 5% property)
United Kingdom	No limits
Uruguay	Limits: 75–85% government securities, 25% corporate bonds, 25% bank bonds, 30% mortgage-backed securities, 30% fixed-term deposits, 25% shares (public companies), 0% mutual funds, 0% foreign corporate bonds/shares

Source: Bateman and Valdes-Prieto (1999), Sin and MacArthur (2000), Herbertsson et al. (2000), Srinivas et al. (2000) Tables A.3 and A.4

Asset regulation

As set out in Table 3.2, typical approaches to asset regulation include limits by asset class, often by placing stringent limits on equities and foreign assets. For example, Peru limits equities to 20% assets and Uruguay to 25% assets, while neither allows investment in foreign assets. Other typical regulations include a high minimum holding of bonds. An example here is Denmark where a minimum of 60% of assets must be invested in domestic or Euro-denominated bonds. Among the countries considered here, none requires a minimum investment in government bonds, but many apply high ceilings on the proportion of government bonds allowed.

The Chilean experience has been that investment guidelines for pension funds have become more liberal over time. Initially, AFPs were not allowed to invest in domestic equities, mutual funds, foreign assets or hedging instruments. The equity restrictions were relaxed in 1985, mutual fund investments were permitted in 1990, foreign investment has been allowed since 1992 and the AFPs have been allowed to use hedging instruments since 1995.

Asset regulation that limits holdings of equities or international assets, or requires investment in government bonds, restricts asset diversification and may dampen the rate of return that could otherwise be

Table 3.3 Portfolio choice – international experience

	Member choice of portfolio or asset manager
Australia	Increasing portfolio choice. Includes choice of investment strategy and of specific fund manager
Argentina	Each AFP is allowed to manage only one portfolio
Bolivia	No choice of fund or portfolio
Chile	Each AFP is allowed to manage only one portfolio
Colombia	Each AFP is allowed to manage only one portfolio
Denmark	No choice of fund (or portfolio)
El Salvador	Each AFP is allowed to manage only one portfolio
Mexico	Each AFP is allowed to manage only one portfolio
Peru	Each AFP is allowed to manage only one portfolio
Poland	Initially each pension fund is allowed only one portfolio. From 2005, pension funds will be allowed to offer two portfolios – one where the assets are allocated as per the restrictions and another restricted to fixed-income securities
Sweden	Choice of up to 5 domestic or international mutual funds that negotiate an agreement with the Premium Pension Agency (PPM) about fees and reporting requirements. In Spring 2000, the PPM offered a choice of 453 funds provided by 67 different fund managers
Switzerland	No choice of fund or portfolio
United Kingdom	Substantial member choice may include: form of retirement income provision, portfolio, and asset manager
Uruguay	Each AFP is allowed to manage only one portfolio

Source: Palacios and Rocha (1998); Queisser (1998), Sundén (1998), Srinivas et al. (2000)

achieved (Srinivas et al. 2000).[7] This has been the experience in Singapore where the Central Provident Fund is required to invest a substantial proportion of assets in government bonds and final accumulations are low in relation to the high mandatory contribution rate (Asher 1999).

Asset regulation is often justified on the grounds that while equities have generated higher long-run returns than other assets, they are associated with greater year-on-year volatility. However, for countries with developed financial markets, any concerns about the volatility of equity markets can be addressed through financial engineering, as proposed by Bateman (1997) for Australia and Feldstein and Ranguelova (2000) in the context of US Social Security reform. These and other issues associated with investing over the life cycle are discussed further in Chapter 4.

As well, strict portfolio restrictions may limit portfolio choice, and therefore the ability of members to integrate their financial portfolio

Table 3.4 Regulation of performance

	Minimum rate of return	Maximum rate of return	Government guarantee[1]
Argentina	relative to average	relative to average	yes
Australia	no	no	no
Bolivia	no	no	no
Chile	relative to average	relative to average	yes
Colombia	relative to markets	no	yes
Denmark	no	no	no
El Salvador	relative to average	relative to average	yes
Hong Kong	no	no	no
Hungary	relative to market[2]	no	yes
Mexico	no	no	yes
Peru	relative to average	no	no
Poland	relative to average	no	no
Sweden	no	no	no
Switzerland	4% nominal	no	yes
United Kingdom	no	no	no
Uruguay	relative to average	yes	yes

1 Excludes safety net pensions.
2 Benchmark under the discretion of the supervisory authority.
Source: Derived from Palacios and Rocha (1998), Sundén (1998), Sin and MacArthur (2000), Srinivas et al. (2000) Table 4

with their human capital portfolio. Few countries operating private mandatory retirement arrangements offer portfolio choice. Current practice is summarised in Table 3.3. It is notable that the Latin American schemes restrict the AFPs to a single portfolio.

Performance regulation

The regulation of performance is summarised in Table 3.4. The international patterns here follow those for asset restrictions and are generally confined to countries without a prior history of private retirement saving arrangements and/or non-common law countries. In practice, the performance requirements are stated in terms of an absolute minimum (Switzerland), a relative minimum (Hungary, Peru, Poland and Uruguay), or a relative band (prevalent in Latin America). For example, Argentina and Chile define their profitability band in relative terms – the minimum of 2 percentage points and 50% of average real return (Chile) or 70% of average nominal return (Argentina) above or below the average return of the industry. The AFP managers have to establish a reserve fund with their own capital (invested in the same way as the AFP), and if this is insufficient to top up the rate of return, the government guarantees the minimum (Srinivas et al. 2000, p. 15).

As with asset regulation, performance regulation has perverse implications for investment returns and therefore the final retirement
accumulation. The absolute minimum rate of return (as applies in
Switzerland) is particularly damaging to retirement saving. Where the
threshold is low and the guarantee applies over the short run, asset
managers will be encouraged to invest in low-return (but low-volatility)
fixed-income investments. The minimum relative rate of return is less
damaging, but is likely to encourage herding – see Queisser 1998 for a
discussion of the Chilean experience.[8] As well, by limiting portfolio
choice, relative rate of return requirements are likely to encourage the
asset managers or financial intermediaries to compete through other
means (such as advertising, gifts, and so on). This had been the case in
Chile (until the late 1990s) and had resulted in marketing costs of
around 10% of the mandatory contribution. Finally, government guarantees (explicit or implicit) facilitate the problem of moral hazard and
may lead asset managers to be less focused on maximising long-term
investment returns.

Taxation and administrative charges

Taxation and administrative charges both lead to lower retirement
accumulations than in their absence. Depending upon system design,
both taxation and administrative charges could reduce net lifetime
contributions and net investment returns. As well, both have behavioural impacts, which may reduce the accumulation period.

Turning first to administrative charges. Administrative charges can be
broadly categorised in terms of account administration charges and
investment management charges. If we assume that the contribution rate
is set gross of administrative charges, account administration charges
reduce the effective contribution amount while investment management
charges reduce the net rate of return. Following the notation introduced
earlier, account administration charges (specified as a percentage of
contributions) of β_c, would lower aggregate contributions by:

$$\sum_{i=1}^{T} C \cdot W \cdot (1 + w)^{i-1} \cdot \beta_c \qquad (3.2)$$

In other words, an account administration charge of 20% (that is,
$\beta_c = 0.20$) would reduce total contributions by 20%. The higher the
contribution charge, the greater the incentive to evade contributions or
find informal employment arrangements. This incentive would be
greater where the administrative charge is identified and paid separately
by members.

Similarly, an investment management charge (specified as a percentage charge on assets under management) of β_A, would lower the net rate of return from μ to $(\mu - \beta_A)$ and reduce the retirement accumulation by:

$$\sum_{i=1}^{T} \beta_A \left\{ \sum_{x=1}^{t} C \cdot W \cdot (1+w)^{x-t} \cdot (1+r)^{x-t} (1-\beta_A)^{x-t} \right\} \qquad (3.3)$$

Administration charges are discussed in greater detail in Chapter 7. It is noted there that aggregate administrative charges are framed by a variety of factors including the institutional framework (which has implications for economies of scale and scope, and marketing requirements); governance (which may affect administrative efficiency and asset choice); contribution policy (particularly coverage and contribution thresholds), which may help minimise the costs associated with small-amount accounts; and member education and disclosure requirements, which may facilitate members' choice of cost-effective investment strategies. Also important is the cost regime chosen. As will be discussed in Chapter 7, investment charges have a greater impact the greater the asset base, therefore providing members with an incentive to retire early, or switch to the informal labour market.

The impact of taxation can be illustrated in a similar manner. Taxation is discussed in greater detail in Chapter 6. At this stage, it is noted that taxes can be imposed on retirement saving at three points – contributions, investment earnings and retirement benefits – all of which will detract from the magnitude of the final retirement accumulation. Also important is the impact of the alternative tax regimes on retirement saving behaviour.

Referring again to the accumulation at retirement defined by equation 3.1, and ignoring the taxation of retirement benefits, we can illustrate the impact of the taxation of retirement savings as follows:

$$A = \sum_{i=1}^{T} \left\{ C \cdot W \cdot (1+w)^{i-1} \cdot (1-\beta_C-\tau_C) \cdot [1+(\mu-\beta_A)\cdot(1-\tau_A)] \right\}^{T-i} \quad (3.4)$$

where: τ_C = rate of tax on contributions
τ_A = rate of tax on investment earnings

As in the case of administrative charges, a tax on contributions would reduce the net contributions (by $\tau_C\%$), while a tax on investment earnings would reduce the net-of-charges rate of return, $\mu - \beta_A$ (by $\tau_A\%$). As well, different taxation regimes have differing behavioural impacts, which may reduce the number of periods in the accumulation phase, T. All of these factors would lead to a lower accumulation at retirement, A.

Other issues

Finally, a range of other factors may impact upon lifetime mandatory contributions and net investment returns.

Where individuals are faced with a choice of financial intermediaries or portfolios, choices will be informed by the extent of their financial literacy and the form and extent of disclosure provided. Therefore, the introduction of private mandatory retirement provision should be associated with accessible disclosure provisions and consumer safeguards. Low financial literacy and/or insufficient disclosure requirements may lead to inappropriate choices. The partial privatisation of pensions in the United Kingdom provides a 'real world' case study of the implications of poor disclosure and inadequate consumer protection.

During the second half of the 1980s and the first half of the 1990s, the United Kingdom undertook a program of pension privatisation. Specifically, the government encouraged workers to 'opt out' of traditional DB plans in order to take out 'personal pensions', of the DC variety, and with maximum portability. Investor protection was intended to come from the Financial Services Act of 1986, which required pension sellers to disclose fully the nature of their product, provide the best advice for the circumstances of the buyer, and allow a cooling-off period (OECD 1997). Between 1988 and 1993 around 500 000 members of occupational pension schemes were persuaded to transfer their pension assets to the new personal plans being sold by insurance companies.

The upshot was that as many as 90% of the 500 000 were advised badly (Blake 1995). There seem to have been two main problems. First, switching to personal pensions often entailed forgoing a pre-existing employer contribution. Second, the actual transfer of vested pension assets triggered losses of up to 25%, to sales commissions and administration charges. A notorious case involved an elderly miner who was persuaded to switch to a personal pension (Blake 1995). In 1994 he retired, aged 60, to a pension of £734 and a lump sum of £2576. Had he remained in the Miners Pension Fund, he would have received a pension of £1791, and a lump sum of £5125.

Conclusion

This chapter has surveyed the accumulation phase of private mandatory retirement saving. Under an accumulation (or defined-contribution) plan, the final retirement benefit is a function of aggregate net contributions and net investment returns.

Aggregate contributions depend upon labour force participation and the contribution rate. For a given contribution rate, aggregate net contributions will be determined by a number of factors including coverage, wage income definitions and thresholds, the tax regime and possibly the collection mechanism. Centralised collection may allow economies of scale and scope and enhance compliance – all of which act to minimise costs and therefore maximise retirement benefits. However, decentralised collection may enhance political insulation and lead to greater competition between financial intermediaries and service providers. Arrangements vary internationally, with an increasing trend towards centralisation.

Net investment returns are a largely a function of institutional structure and governance, asset allocation and regulation. Two types of institutional framework are prevalent across current private mandatory arrangements – 'intermediated' and 'direct' retirement saving. Under the former, contributions to individual accounts are made via a private financial intermediary (such as a pension or superannuation fund), which is responsible for both account administration and investment management. These arrangements facilitate group choice (and the associated cost savings) and the conduit of information to members, but raise principal–agent issues in relation to incentives to maximise the retirement accumulation. Under direct retirement saving, contributions are made directly to asset managers (such as mutual funds). This allows individual control of retirement savings and the potential for substantial choice of asset manager and fund type, but is conducive to high marketing costs.

Irrespective of the institutional framework and mandatory contribution rate, contributions are subsequently invested. Crucial to net investment returns are asset allocation, which is influenced by governance practices and regulatory requirements, administrative charges and taxes. Investment can be regulated in terms of assets and performance. In practice the entire range of possibilities is experienced. For countries with a history of trust law, asset allocation is determined by the prudent-person standard and there is little regulation of assets or returns. The remaining countries apply a variety of restrictions ranging from prescriptions of asset type and weight in portfolio and rate of return requirements to minimal intervention in asset allocation decisions.

Taxes and administrative charges operate to reduce both net contributions and net investment returns. Taxes can be imposed on contributions, investment earnings and retirement benefits, and in all cases will reduce the size of the final retirement benefit. The most common approach is to exempt contributions and investment earnings and tax retirement benefits. However, with the growth of pension fund assets, there is a temptation to tax investment earnings, which may have perverse incentive effects.

Administrative charges are imposed in relation to account administration and/or investment management. Administrative costs (and by implication, charges) are determined by a complex combination of industry structure and practices, governance and regulation. Administrative charges reduce retirement benefits and may discourage participation in the formal labour market (and therefore pension plan coverage).

While international practice varies widely across the accumulation parameters, there is little analysis to guide policy-makers towards the most efficient retirement saving arrangements.

Notes

1 Quasi-mandatory private retirement saving commenced in the mid-1980s with the introduction of award superannuation. The Superannuation Guarantee commenced in 1992.
2 Insurance premia are ignored in this analysis.
3 Centralised collection is also possible with intermediated retirement saving.
4 Public-sector governance is not discussed. Private mandatory retirement saving comprises private management only, by definition.
5 BVG obligations can also be satisfied using a co-operative society or an 'institution of public law'.
6 Centralised and decentralised collection mechanisms are discussed in Demarco and Rofman (1999).
7 Although Davis (1998) suggests that even in countries with prudent-person rules, there is some evidence that pension funds do not achieve market levels of returns.
8 Although it is also suggested that other regulations (such as the limit of one fund per manager) and the structure of capital markets (for example, the supply of liquid investments) are more important than performance regulation in explaining herding and the lack of portfolio diversity – see Srinivas et al. (2000).

CHAPTER 4

Financial Risks Over the Life Cycle

This book is about the worldwide trend away from financing retirement by means of a secure pension from the central government of a nation of which employees have long been resident, or from a large enterprise to which they have given long service, and towards personal pension plans that move with them from job to job or even country to country. This brave new world of retirement finance is one of increased freedom and risk, for high-fliers and ordinary workers alike. The objective of the present chapter is to identify and discuss financial risks over the life cycle, with special reference to managing risks during the accumulation phase of the defined-contribution (DC) pension plans that become predominant once the second pillar is privatised.

Differences in the risk between government-provided retirement benefits and privately managed retirement benefits should not be exaggerated. It is true that, during the second half of the twentieth century, most surprises concerning public pensions amounted to good news for plan participants. In the United States, for example, unexpected enhancements of social security in 1961 saw benefits for males become available at age 62 (see Chapter 2). During the following 50 years, however, surprises are more likely to be unpleasant. In Europe especially, governments have recently been finding ways to write down promised retirement benefits. Even in the United Kingdom, a country that has achieved a comparatively high level of pre-funding of its second pillar, the year 2002 will see a halving of the pensions reverting to spouses of deceased former members of the state-sponsored earnings-related pension scheme. Throughout Europe, preservation ages are on the rise, and CPI indexation of pensions is tending to replace wage-based indexation. In these ways and others, the apparent safety of retirement assets in the form of an entitlement to a government benefit is partly illusory.

Privately managed DC plans can give young households more opportunity to participate in the stock market, thereby enabling a more efficient life-cycle risk-return profile for all but the most risk averse. Moreover, retirement assets in the form of stocks, bonds, property and 'cash' (safe short-term interest-bearing securities) are much more liquid than accrued entitlements to government-provided retirement benefits. Provided employees have investment choice, they can choose to rebalance their portfolio whenever their pre-existing asset allocation has become unpromising. This is not so easy in the case of accrued entitlements to defined retirement benefits.

Regardless of the types of pension schemes to which a household belongs, the cash flows entailed by its life-cycle saving can be summarised by Figure 4.1. This diagram transfers the concept of free cash flows from its usual context of business to one of households. In the case of a business firm, free cash flows at each point in time are defined roughly as income from operations less the business investment needed routinely to maintain and expand operations. Sole proprietorships have a finite life-span, entailing a terminal cash flow, whereas public companies can be infinitely lived, with potentially no terminal cash flow. Similarly, in the case of households, one may or may not take a dynastic perspective. If the dynastic perspective is preferred, inheritances from and bequests to relatives must be left out of account.

Figure 4.1 begins with children and adolescents, a cash flow-negative time of life. Next come several cash flow-positive decades in the labour force. Finally come the cash flow-negative retirement decades. This chapter, however, is less concerned with the expected magnitude of these cash flows than their riskiness.

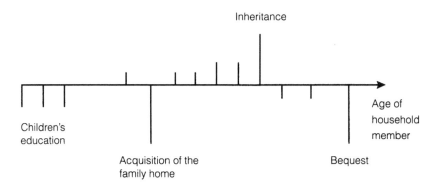

Figure 4.1 Free cash flows through the life cycle

A taxonomy of household investments

This section lists the assets in which households invest over their life cycles (with special reference to the pre-retirement phase) and discusses the risk characteristics of each of the assets mentioned. Entitlements to government benefits and their associated riskiness are largely left out of account.

Human capital

For most of us the most valuable asset we will ever own is our *human capital*, hence the importance of employment-related pension plans. A simple back-of-the-envelope calculation makes the point. Consider a hypothetical household with wage income of $23 764 per annum, and at the outset of 30 years in the labour force.[1] Assume conservatively that it can expect total wage rises of 1% per annum, by way of annual real salary progression plus an economy-wide productivity dividend. Assume wages are paid one year in arrears, and let the discount rate for future wages be 5% real per annum; this is equal to the index bond rate plus a rough 'risk premium' of $1\frac{1}{2}$ percentage points. We thereby arrive at the following estimate of the present value of household earnings:

$$= \frac{23764}{1.05} \times 1.01 + \dots + \frac{23764}{(1.05)^{30}} \times (1.01)^{30}$$

$$= 22858 + \dots + 7411$$

$$= \$405\ 498$$

Apart from being rough, such estimates give no indication of the split between earnings derived from skills, and earnings derived from exertion. A famous study of a cross-section of countries by Mankiw, Romer and Weil (1992) put the split at 50–50 in the case of the industrial nations.

Of particular interest from a finance standpoint are the risk characteristics of wages. Aggregate wage data are particularly unsuitable for analysing labour income risk, because they mask such things as spells of unemployment undergone by particular households. In the United States, however, annual life-cycle wage data from the Panel Study of Income Dynamics have long been available, and have been analysed in a pensions context by Campbell et al. (1999) and Gourinchas and Parker (1999). In the former study, labour income is defined inclusive of unemployment compensation, workers' compensation and related transfers. Only households with a working-age male head are considered. Wage surprises are generated by deviations from fitted deterministic functions of age and education that represent underlying age–earnings profiles. Once calculated, wage innovations are then decomposed into permanent and temporary components; this procedure serves to distinguish between innovations in wages arising from, say, promotion on the one hand, and a stint of unemployment, on the other. Results on the volatility of household labour incomes are not presented in a way that enables ready comparison with standard formats for representing the volatility of financial asset returns (see below). On the other hand, results on correlations between wage innovations and stock returns are readily interpretable. In the case of households headed by men without a high school education, the correlation of wage innovations with returns to a broad-based index of stocks, lagged one year, is 0.32. In the case of households headed by men with a college education, the correlation rises to 0.52. In these ways, households in the United States are found to have considerable latent exposures to the stock market.

The study by Gourinchas and Parker contains readily interpretable results on the volatility of household labour incomes, but abstracts from the question of stock market correlations. In the case of households headed by high school graduates, the volatility (standard deviation) of permanent shocks to labour income is found to be 17% per annum, which is comparable to aggregate stock market volatility in the United States. Davis and Willen (2000) confirm the importance of idiosyncratic shocks to wages.

That young wage-earners have a considerable indirect exposure to the stock market is disputed by Davis and Willen, on the basis of panel data constructed from various issues of the Current Population Survey in the United States, from 1968 to 1994. They find little evidence for the proposition that income innovations at the occupation level are correlated with aggregate stock returns.

That human capital is risky recalls the existence of life insurance and income insurance markets where a household can buy cover against the economic loss occasioned by death and disability. The financial economics of life insurance are analysed by Purcal (1996), who finds that young households especially need substantial death cover, consistent with the inexorable decline in household human capital with advancing age. Markets for this type of contingent claim are, however, especially prone to problems of adverse selection and moral hazard (a point emphasised by Shiller 1993). Hence the small market for income insurance, and the correspondingly large reliance on group-based arrangements such as employer-sponsored death and disability insurance, and government-provided income streams for people burdened with disabilities.[2]

Housing

Paying off your own home is a traditional cornerstone of financial planning for retirement. Likewise, renting residential property is a popular type of unincorporated business activity (see below). Indeed, in the case of Australia at the end of the twentieth century, total dwelling assets amounted to 54% of all traded assets, with owner-occupied housing wealth constituting 49% of traded assets (see Appendix 1). In the United States, by contrast, owner-occupied real estate amounted to 33% of traded assets, while total real estate assets including rented dwellings, stood at 48%. (In the case of Europe, the importance of public housing makes for difficulties in such comparisons.)

Shiller (1993) recalls the experience of New Haven, his place of residence. During the mid-1980s, house prices rose at up to 40% per annum, followed by tumbling house prices in the early 1990s. A famous example of volatile real estate prices comes from Japan, which in 1987 experienced an appreciation of land value that was greater than total Japanese gross domestic product for that year. Shiller points out that housing wealth is not very liquid, with transactions costs of the order of 6–8% of capital values. He points out further that there have not been deep markets for the kinds of financial instruments that could insure against economic risks to housing wealth, even though insurance against real damage to a house and its contents has long been available.

A mitigating factor in the financial risks associated with home-ownership is that households only need to change their place of residence infrequently. In the meantime, the household can sit tight and hope to enjoy a steady flow of services, without major disruptions to cash flow (apart from those arising from any borrowings associated with the original purchase). Campbell and Viceira (1999) point out that this benefit is analogous to the avoidance of reinvestment risk when one purchases a long-term bond rather than a short-term interest-bearing security.

In the case of real-estate investments apart from the family home, a subtle economic risk came to light in the Australia of 1985, and Thailand and South Korea in 1997. In all three countries there arose a fashion for domestic real estate financed by foreign currency loans. A major problem with this strategy was that the effective interest rate on such loans tends to have a negative correlation with returns to domestic real estate, because the value of services from real estate, as a non-traded good, tends to move in sympathy with exports. Yet this risk was unrecognised by some investors and their advisers. In the Australian case, for example, the historical correlation between increases in Australian house prices and declines in the Swiss-franc value of Australian dollars turned out to be −0.25 (Kingston 1995).

Corporate equities

With or without a movement to privatised pensions, corporate equities are playing an increasingly important role in the portfolios of ordinary households around the world.

At the end of the twentieth century, shares and other equity amounted to 7% of the traded wealth of Australian households (Commonwealth Treasury of Australia 1999). In the United States in 1990, the total value of listed stocks amounted to about half the total value of residential real estate (Shiller 1993).

Returns to particular listed stocks are subject to *market risk*; that is, the sensitivity of individual returns to returns on the stock market as a whole, as measured by the coefficient beta. A high expected return comes at the price of a high beta. There are deep markets in financial instruments that insure against either the risks associated with particular listed stocks or the market as a whole.

Interest-bearing securities

Apart from the family home, the traditional safe haven for investing households has been interest-bearing securities. Young households tend to have a negative position, collateralised against the family home. Old households tend to have a positive position. *Interest rate risk* – financial distress experienced as a consequence of unexpected changes in interest rates – therefore tends to change sign as the household ages. At the end of the twentieth century the average Australian household was a net debtor to the tune of 3.7% of household net worth (Australian Bureau of Statistics 1999).

Within the category of interest-bearing securities, a traditional distinction in investments terminology is between fixed interest, that is interest-bearing securities which mature in more than one year, and 'cash' or 'liquids', that is interest-bearing securities which mature in less than one year. Their difference in riskiness depends partly on the investor's horizon. Specifically, the market value of fixed-interest securities will fluctuate, yet they are less subject to *reinvestment risk*; that is, the possibility interest rates have fallen by the time reinvestment in the cash flows from interest-bearing securities is required.

Davis and Willen (2000) find that in the United States the returns on long-term bonds have been positively correlated with innovations in the wages paid in some industries.

Inflation risk – the possibility that unexpected acceleration of the rate of general price increase acts to erode the real rate of return on fixed-interest investments – is a traditional enemy of the self-funded retiree. During the twentieth century in Australia, for example, the average rate of inflation was surprisingly high, at 4% per annum, as a consequence of war-related inflations during the 1910s, 1940s, 1950s and 1970s. For this reason the average real return to fixed-interest securities came in at a meagre 2% per annum.

At the end of the twentieth century most Anglo-Saxon economies were running fiscal surpluses, with the consequence that managed funds were increasingly being driven into corporate (rather than government) securities. In this way, *credit risk,* that is unexpected delays in the repayment of interest or principal, together with insufficient collateral to compel legally the repayment of debts due, was becoming an increasingly important consideration. However, as with liquid securities generally, there are increasingly deep markets for financial instruments that insure against such things as interest rate risk and credit risk. Moreover, inflation-indexed securities were becoming more widely available. As noted by Campbell and Viceira (1999), an inflation-indexed perpetuity would come close to being the ultimate safe asset for households with long investment horizons.

Equity in unincorporated businesses

Business owners naturally expect their asset to play a major role in financing their retirement. As a consequence, issues for ordinary employees, notably diversification, and delegation of portfolio decisions to specialist managers, have less relevance. The interplay between the distinctive risks faced by entrepreneurs in the United States and their portfolio choices is studied by Heaton and Lucas (2000). As might be expected, entrepreneurs have significantly less exposure to listed stocks, other things being equal. In other words, business owners recognise their latent exposure to the stock market. In Australia the distinctive needs of business owners are accommodated by a special retirement saving vehicle called the self-managed fund.

Managed funds

Outside the small business sector, households tend to delegate retirement portfolio decisions to specialist managers. One reason for delegation is that there are substantial economies of scale in achieving portfolio diversification if investments are collective – even if allocated to individual accounts – rather than on a household-by-household basis.

A second reason is that, in the case of pension funds, there tend to be multiple stakeholders, as mentioned in Chapter 2. Figure 4.2 portrays the typical administrative structure in common law jurisdictions.

In Figure 4.2 the arrows indicate lines of authority. The custodian is the legal owner of the fund's assets (without being the beneficial owner). Trustees are sometimes advised by asset consultants on the best choice of investment managers.

Yet another reason for collective investments arises in the case of insurance companies. They rely on the principle of risk-pooling in order to manage down risks on the liability side of their balance sheets. (Risk-pooling is of course different from diversification, which cannot counter market risk.)

Asset classes

Managers of the assets of insurance and pension funds traditionally begin with a fourfold taxonomy of 'asset classes'. These are listed below by decreasing order of expected return and volatility:

- equities
- commercial property
- fixed interest
- 'cash' (or 'liquids').

Each of the four asset classes has an 'offshore' or 'international' counterpart. For example, an Australian fund manager might give some weight to North American, European or Asian equities, in order to get a broader spread across different industries.

Historical returns and risks

This section reports historical returns and risks to the main asset classes, from the perspective of an Australian investor. We begin in Table 4.1 with returns.

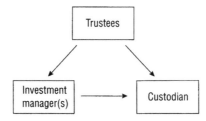

Figure 4.2 Managed fund structure

Table 4.1 Mean returns, % per annum

	Aust. Equities	US Equities	Aust. Property	Aust. Bonds	US Bonds	Aust. Cash
Nominal	14.4	17.8	12.1	13.2	7.7	10.0
Real	10.5	14.0	8.3	9.4	3.9	6.2

Note: The data are quarterly and span 1987 to 2000.
Sources: ASX, Bloomberg, Datastream, JP Morgan, Intech and the ABS Cat.
no. 6401.1

Table 4.1 is fairly typical of findings for the last decades of the twentieth century. Note, however, that for the purpose of estimating the equity premium for the twenty-first century, analysts including Bateman (1997) and Campbell et al. (1999) view an historical equity premium of 14.4 − 10.0 = 4.4 percentage points as being slightly high, reflecting abnormally high price–earnings ratios and low dividend yields during the last decades of the century. They have worked instead with a forward-looking equity premium of 4 percentage points. Time will tell.

Historical volatilities are shown in Table 4.2.

A robust feature of estimated volatilities of diversified Australian equity investments is that they routinely exceed their United States counterparts by the order of 9 or 10 percentage points. In this context it makes little difference whether one uses US dollars or Australian dollars for measuring US returns. This may reflect the comparatively narrow base of Australian industry.

A natural reaction to the finding of highly volatile returns to Australian equities is to study correlations with risky assets overseas. Substantial international diversification would seem to make sense. Table 4.3 shows historical correlations between domestic and overseas real returns to the risky asset classes.

Clearly, international diversification offers scope for risk reduction.

Table 4.2 Volatilities (standard deviations), % per annum

	Aust. Equities	US Equities	Aust. Property	Aust. Bonds	US Bonds	Aust. Cash
Nominal	22.2	13.2	9.8	10.6	8.5	5.1
Real	22.3	13.5	10.0	10.9	8.1	2.9

Sources: ASX, Bloomberg, Datastream, JP Morgan, Intech and the ABS

Table 4.3 Correlations between real returns to risky assets

	Aust. Equities	US Equities	Aust. Property	Aust. Bonds	US Bonds	Aust. Cash
Aust. Equities	1					
US Equities	0.57	1				
Aust. Property	0.47	0.73	1			
Aust. Bonds	0.30	0.07	0.61	1		
US Bonds	0.29	0.65	0.16	0.20	1	
Aust. Cash	−0.11	−0.26	0.18	0.50	−0.03	1

Sources: ASX, Bloomberg, Datastream, JP Morgan, Intech and the ABS

Asset allocation

Asset allocation refers to decisions about portfolio composition, primarily decisions about weights given to the broad asset classes, but possibly also to the selection of particular securities. Apart from self-managed funds (see above), the average asset allocation by the Australian superannuation industry in mid-2000 is portrayed by Figure 4.3.

Home bias

When comparing Figure 4.3 with Tables 4.1 to 4.3, the actual average exposure to overseas assets, at 18.2% of the total, seems meagre relative to the apparent potential for diversifying risk without substantially sacrificing returns. This impression is consistent with the theory of *home bias* whereby there is a tension between the low extent of international

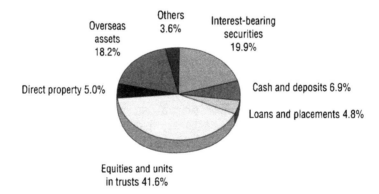

Figure 4.3 Asset allocation
Source: APRA Superannuation Trends, June 2000

diversification actually practised and the apparent benefits from so doing. The term is due to Cooper and Kaplanis (1994) who examine the tax and regulatory costs of investing offshore, along with the possible loss of a natural hedge against home-inflation risk. They find, however, that the bias against investing offshore is too strong to be explained by those factors. Brennan and Cao (1997) examine information differentials as a possible barrier to international portfolio investment flows. They find that foreign investors are indeed more likely to be trend followers ('momentum investors') than their domestic counterparts. However, Brennan and Cao do not venture an opinion on whether actual information differentials are sufficient to explain the observed home bias.

A literal reading of basic portfolio theory suggests that a fund's exposure to risky domestic investments should be proportional to the weight of risky domestic investments in the world market portfolio of risky investments. This prescription would place Australian fund managers 98% in offshore assets – a far cry from the 15–20% weightings that characterised the 1990s. A sophisticated treatment of the Australian case, including the currency-hedging aspect of the problem, is given by Black and Litterman (1992). They find that, compared to Group of Seven countries, Australia's 15–20% weighting has actually been on the high side. By the same token, Australian investors benefit much more from international diversification than investors in a number of comparable nations, and would therefore be advised to lift their offshore exposures, on the Black–Litterman argument.

Active versus passive management

Active fund management is an investment strategy characterised by willingness to take large bets on particular asset classes, or on particular stocks, bonds, properties or currencies, even if doing so entails significant transactions costs. Passive management, by contrast, seeks to maintain broad diversification of the fund, while avoiding transactions costs through a 'buy and hold' strategy (except for rebalancing of the portfolio).

The right mix of these approaches for particular investors is to some extent best left to the 'discovery' function of markets. It will never be fully ascertainable from academic research. By the same token, we note that finance research has tended to be sceptical about the value added by active management. First, there is necessarily a zero-sum aspect to it; as more and more investors seek to act on (what they believe is) superior information, their endeavours must become progressively less rewarding, on average. Second, to the extent that the average market timer is

Table 4.4 A possible investment strategy

Asset class	Neutral benchmark (%)	Asset ranges (%)
Domestic shares	40	30–50
Foreign shares	40	30–50
Direct property	6	0–15
Listed property	6	0–15
Domestic fixed interest	12	0–35
Foreign fixed interest	11	0–35
Domestic cash	5	Balance

Source: Randall et al. (1996, p. 90)

neither better nor worse informed than the average market participant, he or she will actually subtract value, as a consequence of transactions costs, and through the efficiency cost of an uneven exposure over time to investment risk, analogous to the efficiency cost of a house-and-contents insurance policy that is in force intermittently rather than continuously.

An Australian innovation in the development of regulations is that trustees are required to formulate and give effect to a written *investment strategy* that establishes target bands for portfolio weights in the main asset classes. In other words, trustees are not permitted simply to 'make it up as they go along'. This regulation has the potential to discourage ambitious market-timing endeavours, a fund management style criticised by Hathaway (1992) among others. Details of one 'possible strategy,' due to Randall et al. (1996), are presented in Table 4.4.

Note in Table 4.4 that this candidate strategy involves intermediate exposures to offshore investments at best, consistent with the phenomenon of home bias, but contrary to Australia's meagre 2% share of the world market portfolio.

Common law jurisdictions typically do not require guaranteed minimum rates of return on individual accounts in pension funds. This is in contrast to civil law jurisdictions including Switzerland and Chile (see Chapter 3). A consequence of such guarantees is of course a need on the part of fund managers to adopt conservative asset allocations.

Investment risk, age and wealth

Investment risk and age

The leading theoretical proposition on the relationship between investment risk and age is that rational households will progressively reduce their proportionate exposure to risky assets as they move closer to retirement – an investment policy described as *age-phasing* (P.A. Samuelson 1989), or as *lifestyle* fund management (see, for example, Blake 2000c).

The rationale for age-phasing is reviewed by Bodie, Merton and Samuelson (1992), Kingston, Bateman and Piggott (1992), and Bodie and Crane (1997). There are two main arguments. The first applies to the extent that the wage plus transfer income of a household is substantial, dependable and uncorrelated with investment income. This set of circumstances is analogous to holding a safe term annuity; that is, a long position in interest-bearing securities (as distinct from equities). To the extent that a household desires a stable exposure to safe assets, broadly interpreted, it needs to build up interest-bearing securities as available working years run out.

The second argument is that a young household holds embedded options that enable it partially to self-insure against bad luck with risky investments. Here is a list of labour supply possibilities that amount to self-insurance (Kingston et al. 1992):

- seek overtime
- seek part-time work after hours
- reduce full-time home production within the household
- work more intensively during ordinary time; for example, by switching to more arduous yet better-paid work
- study part-time towards qualifications for better-paid work
- plan to postpone retirement.

Bodie and Crane (1997) report evidence on age-phasing behaviour from a 1996 survey of members of the Teachers Insurance and Annuity Association–College Retirement Equities Fund in the United States.[3] Each net-worth quartile showed unambiguous phasing down of exposure to equities relative to fixed-income securities. In the second lowest quartile, for example, respondents aged 25 to 44 allocated 67% of their equity-plus-fixed-income investments to equities, compared to 39% in the case of respondents aged 65 plus.

At the end of the twentieth century, comparable data for Australia were not available. However, Baekgaard (1998) put together data from the 1993–94 household expenditure survey that shed light on this question. These are the basis of Table 4.5, which shows assets per adult resident in Australia held by households in the year 1993 by asset type and also by the age cohort of the oldest household member.

Table 4.4 shows that total wealth per adult in 1993 averaged $91 900, excluding human capital. At $45 400 per adult, net owner-occupied housing wealth came in at 49% of the total, compared with superannuation assets at $17 500, or 19% of the total.

Table 4.5 Household assets by type and by the age of the oldest member (average assets per adult, Australia 1993)

				$000				Per cent	
	(1)	(2)	(3)	(4)	(5)	(6)	(7)	(8)	(9)
Age group of oldest member	Housing gross	Housing loans	Housing net	Interest-bearing assets	Super-annuation assets	Other assets	Total wealth	Interest-bearing assets share [(4)÷(7)]	Other: assets share [(6)÷(7)]
15–20	0.7	0.3	0.4	1.2	0.7	0.4	2.8	43	14
21–24	4.2	2.4	1.8	4.0	4.2	4.7	14.7	27	31
25–29	20.8	10.4	10.4	3.6	10.7	8.9	33.6	11	26
30–34	39.6	15.9	23.6	4.9	16.4	13.8	58.7	8	24
35–39	53.5	14.9	38.6	6.9	23.5	16.4	85.3	8	19
40–44	77.0	14.9	62.1	9.5	29.6	31.1	132.2	7	24
45–49	79.7	12.8	66.8	11.4	35.1	22	135.4	8	16
50–54	76.9	7.2	69.7	16.6	39.9	29.4	155.6	11	19
55–59	73.5	4.4	69.1	14.8	23.9	26.9	134.7	11	20
60–64	80.4	2.2	78.2	23.6	15.9	21.3	139.1	17	15
65–69	80.1	0.4	79.7	36.1	8.0	17.7	141.4	25	12
70–74	82.3	0.5	81.8	28.9	7.8	12.9	131.4	22	10
75+	88.3	0.2	88.1	42.8	8.0	7.6	146.5	29	5
Averages:	53.2	7.8	45.4	13.2	17.5	15.9	91.9	14.4	17.3

Source: Adapted from Baekgaard (1998, p. 27)
Note: 'Other assets' consist of dividend-yielding assets plus net rental property plus net business assets.

Two columns are of particular interest from the standpoint of age-phasing. One is column (8) which shows interest-bearing assets relative to total wealth. According to the age-phasing proposition, interest-bearing assets are at the safe end of the spectrum, and should therefore register an increasing weight in household portfolios as households age. Indeed, beginning especially with the 60–64 cohort, that is more or less what the data show. For example, the 75+ cohort holds 29% of its wealth in interest-bearing assets, relative to the weighting across all age cohorts of 14.4%.

The other relevant column is (9), which shows dividend-yielding assets plus net rental property plus net business assets, collectively shown as a percentage of total wealth. This composite asset is at the risky end of the spectrum. The trend can be seen to be more or less downwards through the age cohorts, consistent with age-phasing. On the other hand, the 15–20 age cohort holds only 14% of its wealth in this risky composite. Campbell et al. (1999) suggest one explanation: gaining exposure to risky assets tends to involve fixed costs, and wealth per head has to build up to a certain level before it is worthwhile incurring such costs. Another obvious explanation is that many within the 15–20 age group will have delegated asset allocation decisions to parents.

Investment risk and wealth

The leading theoretical proposition on the relationship between investment risk and wealth arises from the structure of household preferences. If households have some fixed minimum subsistence requirement, or even if they have a subsistence requirement that varies with past consumption or with the consumption standard of their neighbours, there is a case for increasing proportionate exposure to risky assets as total household wealth rises. Conversely, as household wealth falls, a household should progressively concentrate its wealth in safe assets, in order to protect the dependable income needed to cover 'subsistence' consumption. The theoretical foundations of this argument were laid by Merton (1971). A second argument for this type of behaviour is based on fixed costs of investing in risky assets.

Bodie and Crane report evidence for this type of behaviour in their 1997 study. Almost every age cohort showed increased exposure to equities relative to equity-plus-fixed income investments. In the 45–54 age group, respondents in the lowest net-worth quartile allocated 48% to equities, compared to 64% to equities in the case of the highest net-worth quartile. Unfortunately, directly comparable Australian data are not available.

Table 4.6 Viceira's results on age-phasing

Expected time until retirement (years)				
	30	20	10	0
Coefficient of relative risk aversion	Percentage – portfolio of stocks			
2	256	175	133	90
5	63	52	44	36
10	22	20	19	18

Source: Viceira (2001, p. 448)

'Default' asset allocation

'Default' asset allocation refers to the question of how the trustees of a defined-contribution plan should manage a portfolio on behalf of a quiescent plan member with known age but unknown risk tolerance, or total net worth, or labour supply flexibility. Research by Viceira (2001, especially Table 1) probably constitutes the best scientific advice to date on this important practical issue for trustees and managers.

Viceira considers a stylised world of two financial assets: stocks and cash. All investors are assumed to have a constant coefficient of relative risk aversion, which obviates the need for fund managers to know the net worth of individual fund members (see, for example, Campbell 2000 on this implication of constant relative risk aversion). The equity premium on stocks is assumed to be about four percentage points per year. Drawing on recent research based on the Panel Study of Income Dynamics in the United States (see above), the growth of the investor's labour income is assumed to have a 25% correlation with stock returns. Permanent shocks to the investor's labour income growth are assumed to have a volatility of 10% per year. Labour supply flexibility is assumed absent. A subset of Viceira's simulation results is reproduced in Table 4.6.

Table 4.6 shows that in the case of a coefficient of relative risk aversion (see Chapter 2) equal to two, young investors should have highly levered portfolios. Even on the cusp of retirement, 90% of the portfolio is allocated to stocks. On the other hand, a coefficient of relative risk aversion equal to 10 leads to lifelong conservative portfolios. By contrast, the boxed intermediate case looks reasonable. Notably, exposure to stocks at the point of retirement is 36%, which is fairly typical of actual portfolio proportions in the 'allocated pensions' and 'allocated annuities' that dominated the market for purchased retirement income streams in Australia at the turn of the century (see Chapter 5). Working back in this way, the boxed allocations amount to promising candidates for 'default' asset allocations.

Managing investment risk

The worldwide movement away from defined-benefit (DB) pension plans that act to replace wage income will require ordinary workers to participate more in the financial markets. Yet developments in those markets have made it easier for businesses and households alike to manage investment risk. Notably, *derivative instruments* – financial securities with payoffs that can be specified as functions of two or more underlying securities – have become readily available in prepackaged form.

Among derivative instruments, the out-of-the-money put option may be the quintessential instrument of financial risk management (Stulz 1996). The out-of-the-money feature acts to reduce premium costs, as with a deductible in standard insurance policies. At the same time, having *some* downside protection in place guards against the disproportionate cost of extreme financial stress. Appendix 3 contains a review of option basics.

Puts and pensions

Put options are important in retirement finance because they are used in some guise or other for *portfolio-insurance* strategies, whereby life-cycle savings are managed so as to display a *convex payoff profile*, that is, upside potential combined with downside protection. The term portfolio insurance gained a bad name as a result of disappointments with a particular product in the United States following the 1987 stock market crash. Yet versions of portfolio insurance have proved ubiquitous. Figure 4.4 is inspired by Blake (2000c). It portrays the payoff profile of a portfolio consisting of risky underlying assets with value A, together with a protective basket put with strike price L, chosen to equal the value of the underlying assets at the beginning of the reporting period.

As shown by Figure 4.4, if the underlying assets finish the relevant period with value greater than L, the pension plan participant enjoys all the upside. If the underlying assets finish the relevant period with value less than L, the protective put finishes in the money, with the result that pension assets hold their initial value L.

In the United Kingdom, so-called *targeted-money-purchase* pension plans are characterised by this sort of payoff structure, as Blake (2000c) observes. Let *TMP* stand for the value of a payout from a targeted-money-purchase plan. Then the payout is given by:

$$TMP = max\ (A,\ L)$$

In Australia, however, targeted-money-purchase has been uncommon, and is not generally recognised as a generic type of scheme. Rather, the traditional classification of pension plans is a twofold one, into defined benefits and defined contributions.

Defined-benefit schemes

The traditional pension plan for managers in large businesses and for public-sector workers has been a DB one, whereby retirement benefits are predetermined by reference to factors such as final salary and years of service. To the extent that the plan is funded, benefits are paid from a pool formed from employer and employee contributions over the years, plus the investment earnings on past contributions. In general, however, the assets underlying defined pension benefits are better viewed as collateral than as actual components of the retirement wealth of fund members.

The employer/sponsor undertakes to stand ready to make up the difference in the event funds available fall short of payouts due. Thus the employer/sponsor bears the investment risk. On the other hand, to the extent that investment earnings on the underlying assets are building up a surplus well in excess of the present value of benefit obligations,

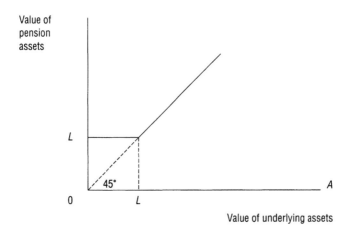

Figure 4.4 Portfolio insurance: underlying assets with put option protection

the employer/sponsor is entitled to take a contributions holiday, and/or return surplus capital to the enterprise's stakeholders.

Blake (2000c) is among a number of financial economists to have analysed the options embedded in DB plans. He observes that what is effectively happening is an exchange of options: the employee/member holds a put on the employer/sponsor, while the employer/sponsor holds a call option on the employee/member. Figure 4.5 makes the point in more detail. The member of a DB fund ends up with pre-specified payout *DB* regardless of the underlying value *A* of the fund's investments. (For simplicity, we abstract from the real-world complication of unusual fund surpluses that lead to an *ad hoc* enhancement of members' benefits.) The member can therefore be viewed as being long in a put and short in a call, each with strike price *L*.

According to Figure 4.5, the retiring fund member receives a defined benefit *DB*, regardless of how the fund has performed. If fund assets *A* fall short of the present value of benefit obligations *DB*, then the employer/sponsor makes up the difference, and this is analogous to the granting of a put option to the employee. If fund assets exceed the present value of benefit obligations the employer/sponsor is entitled to the surplus, and this is analogous to the granting of a call option to the employer.

The expertise needed to keep DB funds on track is provided by the actuarial profession. The actuary certifies funding and solvency, upon having been satisfied that the sponsor's contributions (on top of member ones), plus investment earnings, are sufficient to meet contingent liabilities to members as and when they fall due. Factors considered by actuaries include:

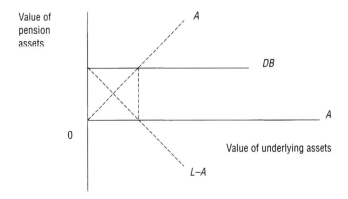

Figure 4.5 Defined-benefit scheme

- expected rate of inflation of members' wages
- prospective resignations, retrenchments and deaths leading to early payouts
- expected investment returns.

Specifics of the regulatory requirements typical of common-law jurisdictions can be found in Randall, Higgins and Goddard (1996). In the United States, back-up protection for members is provided by the Pension Benefit Guarantee Corporation (PBGC), which levies sponsors of DB plans in exchange for underwriting benefits. For an analysis of the put options embedded in this regulatory arrangement, see Hsieh, Chen and Ferris (1994).

Defined-contribution (accumulation) schemes

'Defined-contribution' or 'accumulation' schemes are the simplest. Employees and/or employers pay in prespecified contributions. Each member has a specifically allocated account. The member's retirement benefit is the total of accumulated contributions on his or her behalf, plus their investment earnings during fund membership. In this way, members bear all the investment risk. Figure 4.6 portrays the case of accumulation funds. 'What you see is what you get'; the member of an accumulation scheme simply ends up with contributions made on his or her behalf, plus the investment earnings on contributions over the years.

One complication to the simple story portrayed by Figure 4.6 in practice is that some employer-financed benefits may be subject to a

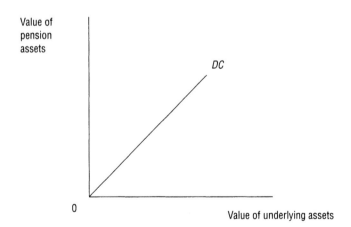

Figure 4.6 Defined-contribution (accumulation) scheme

vesting scale whereby they are not fully credited to the account of the employee unless and until conditions such as sufficient length of service with the employer have been met. (Vesting provisions are especially prevalent in the case of employer contributions to DB funds.) There are additional complications arising from 'heterodox' investor behaviour, as is discussed next.

Myopic loss aversion

Myopic loss aversion refers to the phenomenon of strong distaste for investment losses along with frequent reviews of the value of one's portfolio, even in the case of life-cycle saving by young households with dependable wage income. The term is due to United States researchers into investment behaviour; in the United Kingdom the term 'short termism' has similar connotations. Thaler et al. (1997) report the results of controlled experiments involving 80 paid undergraduate experimental subjects from the University of California, Berkeley. Subjects provided with frequent feedback about the progress of the experimental portfolios managed by them generally chose more conservative investments than subjects not so informed.

Members and trustees of Australian accumulation funds seem to have been susceptible to this type of behaviour. Take the case of a year of high investment returns. Trustees need to decide how much should be credited to members' accounts and how much should be taken to reserve. In years of negative returns, trustees need to choose between a negative crediting rate (a course of action that is actually prohibited by many trust deeds), or drawing down reserves, in order to bring the bad year's crediting rate more into line with those of good years. In practice, the earning rate actually credited has often been a moving average of the most recent three years of returns to the underlying assets of the fund.

In the case of DB funds, reserving can easily be handled fairly, as well as being integral to the management of that type of fund. In the case of DC funds, by contrast, heavy reserving is a policy riddled with potential for unfairness. For example, a fund with high reserves might merge with a fund with low reserves, thereby subsidising one group of contributors at the expense of another group. Reserves also might be strongly accumulated during a member's years in the fund, only to be credited to members' accounts shortly after he or she has retired and drawn down his or her balance with the fund.

High and uniform crediting rates during a run of good years in the financial markets may lull fund members into a false sense of security concerning the riskiness of their investments. Hathaway (1992) finds that, given a fairly aggressive asset allocation, and on the basis of a long span of historical data, implicit or explicit promises not to credit a negative rate could be violated as often as one year out of every 10.

Hathaway points out that some trustees of accumulation funds are in effect attempting to mimic the smooth, predictable crediting rates delivered by defined-benefits funds – which have of course the luxury of a sponsor willing to bear investment risk. In terms of options terminology, such trustees are in effect following a *collar* strategy, whereby the fund's members have upside potential capped by the sale of calls, and downside risk protected by the purchase of puts (see Figure 4.7).

This analogy with options suggests that, in place of smoothed crediting rates, trustees might consider the outright sale of calls and purchase of puts. This would eliminate the risk of broken promises (subject of course to counterparty and clearing house performance in the market for traded options). The first systematic investigation of the likely life-cycle performance of accumulation funds managed by option-based strategies, including option-based collars, is due to Bateman (1997), who treated the Australian case. Bodie and Crane (1999) treat the United States case, without considering the case of collars. Feldstein and Ranguelova (2000) focus on collars.

Bateman finds that, compared either to put options alone, or balanced investment strategies without options, the performance of collars is at best mediocre. The reason is that surges in the value of risky assets, intermittent as they are, prove to be valuable over the life cycle. Put another way, careful analysis of the underlying asset allocation required

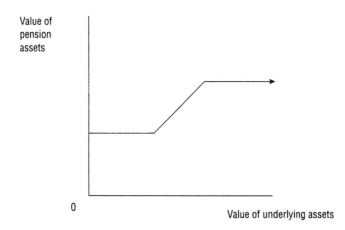

Figure 4.7 Collar strategy for defined-contribution (accumulation) schemes

to guarantee a collar reveals it to be surprisingly conservative. A good analogy comes from owner-occupied housing. Most home-owners are keenly aware of the historical record of periodic surges in house prices, and their potential importance for long-run household wealth, not least for security in retirement. Moreover, most households can time their retirements, in particular, wait unless and until there has been a surge in household net worth, in this way 'surfing' out of the labour force (Kingston 2000 examines the theory of flexible retirements by workers exposed to investment risk).

Conclusion

At the end of the twentieth century, no country with a privatised second pillar could be said to have surmounted all the associated risk management problems. In civil law jurisdictions, for example, heavy regulation of investments or their returns tended effectively to rule out major investments in domestic corporate equities, even on behalf of young households. Nowhere had there been international diversification to the extent advisable in the light of finance research. As the first common law nation to have introduced a wholly privatised second pillar, Australia had made instructive progress, yet problems remained.

In the year 2000 the average asset allocation of Australian managed funds involved a 42% weight on domestic equities, consistent with the substantial weight on equities that has long characterised pension funds and insurance company portfolios in common law jurisdictions (with or without a mandated second pillar). Total overseas assets, by contrast, were weighted at just 18%, and this represented the voluntary choices of fund managers. Even 18% was a high figure by international standards, consistent with the pattern of home bias seen in pension funds around the world.

Australians have tended to age-phase their wealth outside the formal retirement income system. Yet this had not caught on as a general principle for pension fund managers, even though some pension plans have enabled and encouraged members to switch into conservatively managed funds as retirement draws near. United States data suggest in addition that the weight given to risky assets tends to increase with household wealth; directly comparable Australian data are not available.

In contrast to members of DB funds, members of DC funds (which predominate in privatised second pillars) have to bear investment risk on their own account. However, trustees of Australian DC funds have often sought to make the pattern of benefit accrual resemble the smooth upward trend that characterises benefit accrual in bank savings deposits, or in DB pension funds (except at vesting dates, or around 'normal' retirement ages). This is consistent with myopic loss aversion on the part of fund members, a behavioural trait familiar to pensions researchers in the United Kingdom and the United States.

A common response by Australian trustees has been to make each member's annual crediting rate a moving average of investment earnings during the preceding few years. Pooled investment fluctuation reserves are thereby built up in good years, with the objective of bolstering crediting rates during years of low investment earnings. Such a strategy could go awry in the aftermath of a stock market crash, especially in the emerging environment of member investor choice, which may also see sophisticated, footloose investors promptly leaving funds with depleted reserves and joining those funds that are flush with reserves (and without a fee structure discouraging opportunistic behaviour). Bateman (1997) points out that an alternative to investment fluctuation reserves is provided by risk management strategies using put options. In the context of the United States, Bodie and Crane (1999) and Feldstein and Ranguelova (2000) make related points concerning possibilities for options-based management of investment risk over the life cycle.

Age-phasing of portfolios could also be implemented by put options. Specifically, young contributors could have partial insurance against investment risk, by way of inexpensive out-of-the-money puts, while their elderly counterparts could have at-the-money put protection (Bateman 1997).

Notes

1 The figure of $23 764 can be viewed as an estimate of the annual earnings of the median 'young' Australian household, in 1995–96, and excluding households that depend primarily on government pensions and allowances; see *Year Book Australia 1998*, p. 227.

2 In mid-2000, 600 000 Australians out of a total resident population of 19 million were receiving disability benefits, eligibility for which was conditioned on at least 20% medical impairment. Accordingly, at the end of the twentieth century disability pensions were shaping up as a major new pathway to early retirement, following a trail blazed by several European nations (see Chapter 2).

3 TIAA–CREF is a non-profit organisation that provides self-directed life-cycle savings products to workers in 6000 secondary and tertiary educational and research institutions in the United States. Members tend to be college educated. A total of 1503 survey respondents provided at least partial information; 916 respondents filled out the forms completely, including questions on their net worth.

CHAPTER 5

Retirement Income Streams

This chapter explores mandatory retirement income streams in a privatised retirement policy environment. Within such policy designs, the decumulation or payout phase of saving through the life cycle has received surprisingly little attention. In countries adopting a privatised mandatory retirement policy, the associated payout profiles have thus far been conditioned more by the pre-reform retirement policy status quo than by dispassionate consideration of sensible policy design. Yet this is where many of the financial risks associated with the elderly, which cannot be adequately insured against in an unregulated private market, are confronted. These risks, discussed in Chapter 1, underlie the economic case for central intervention in retirement provision – to recapitulate, they include replacement, longevity, investment and inflation risk.

Adverse selection in the voluntary annuities market, prudential considerations, and the implications of interactions between annuity payouts and first-pillar-type social welfare, all suggest that privately administered retirement provision will require a policy position on the nature of retirement benefits. Under mandated, privately administered, DC plans, regulations and employer obligations associated with the accumulation phase typically expire at retirement, and payout regulations must be separately stipulated. Throughout this chapter, we assume this arrangement will prevail.

Why do we need retirement income streams?

Hannah (1986) reported that in the late nineteenth century in Great Britain, the traditional life-cycle consumption smoothing model described the behaviour of the business and professional classes quite well. However, hunger and other needs pressing on low-income workers through their working lives led them to discount the value of their future consumption to the point that little retirement provision resulted. Similar observations have been made about the United States. Samuelson (1987), for example, asserted that in the century prior to 1937 the United States was the richest country on earth, yet the bulk of its retirees relied on charity in retirement.

These circumstances motivated the development of organised retirement plans. The best known of these are, of course, the publicly provided plans that are now well established in most OECD countries. Known collectively as social security, they typically pay out a pension to the retiree, with the payment depending on years of service and earning levels and patterns.

These are examples of defined-benefit (DB) plans. By contrast, defined-contribution (DC) plans only define the contribution, usually as a fraction of wages. This idea is carried over into mandatory saving plans, which require workers or employers to contribute some proportion of wages into a pension fund. Under this type of plan, there is no risk-spreading between different parties in the plan – everyone has their own account. This characterises the typical mandatory retirement policy paradigm.

First-pillar designs

Most countries in a position to contemplate mandatory second-pillar development will have some form of first-pillar support in place. First-pillar design will affect the structure of second-pillar benefits. More often than not, first-pillar support is financed from general revenue, involves modest payouts and is at least partially means-tested. It usually comprises some form of social assistance or 'social welfare', and often has a minimum pension guarantee, subject to a qualifying contribution period. This is the generic first-pillar design that will be assumed here.

Means-testing is sometimes criticised on the grounds that very high effective marginal tax rates (EMTRs) are implied. It is easy to generate EMTRs of close to 100% by combining the impact of income withdrawal and income taxation. However, it is important to recognise that in the absence of means-testing, general revenue funding requirements would be higher, and that these will increase marginal tax rates (which may already be very significant) on the working-age population.

Neither is it clear that the income withdrawal should be gradual. While low-rate tapers reduce the EMTR faced by retirees, the lower the taper, the more retirees confronting the EMTR. In an insightful paper, Blinder and Rosen (1985) argue that 'notches' may be a better solution to policy dilemmas of this type than low-rate tapers. However, like many other issues raised in considering retirement income provision and mandatory annuity design, this has not been much researched.

The form of first-pillar support will have an impact on aggregate replacement rates. But in addition, the first pillar will interact with second-pillar payouts. Whether a retiree will be entitled to first-pillar payments, and to what degree, will be determined by the means-test specifications of the first pillar and the second-pillar payout pattern.

Annuity design

At retirement, some arrangement must be made as to how to invest the accumulation to finance the retiree's retirement. Regulations sometimes exist that direct the retiree to organise this in specific ways, but there is a clear cut independence between the accumulation and liquidation phases.[1]

If we assume that individuals desire at least some form of equivalent consumption smoothing, then instruments that provide a relatively even flow of income through time would appear to be suitable. Annuities comprise an important class of such instruments. This chapter focuses on annuity products and annuity markets in the context of mandatory retirement schemes.

Annuity design is important because insurance against retirement risks, whether provided by governments or privately, is expensive. Successful policy design must be sensitive to these costs, and responsive to the subtle trade-offs between insurance and expected income that they imply. Indeed, retirees can be seen as increasing their exposure to what Bodie (1990b) terms 'replacement rate risk' – that is, the risk that in retirement you have not adequately replaced working-life income – the more comprehensive is their coverage against other kinds of retirement income risks. The greater the insurance, the lower will be the promised income stream. In this section, we first examine the fundamental mechanics of an annuity, for simplicity confining attention to single individual instruments, and then discuss alternative annuity designs.

An annuity, literally, is a stream of annual payments. However, the term usually refers to a stream of payments specified against a set of contingencies such as death. An annuity specified against this contingency is called a life annuity. It insures against outliving one's resources or leaving an unintended bequest by converting assets into a continuous stream of income contingent on survival. Life annuities allow the pooling of longevity risk and can – at least in principle – offer a higher periodic payment than an equivalently valued non-annuitised asset with no longevity insurance. Those annuitants who die early implicitly share their estate with those annuitants who survive.

For any financial security, its value must equal the expected present value of the stream of payments it promises. It is convenient to begin by abstracting from uncertainty entirely, and setting out this equivalence for an annuity promising a stream of equal payments of $y per year for T years. This is referred to as a term-certain annuity. The relationship is specified as:

$$K = \sum_{t=1}^{T} \frac{y}{(1+R)^t} \tag{5.1}$$

where R is the risk-free rate of interest (that is, the rate on nominal default-free bonds) and K is the annuity value. K can be thought of as the accumulated sum that the retiree has to invest to fund their retirement.

To solve for the value of y, given some value K, we have:

$$y = \frac{K}{\left(\sum_{t=1}^{T} \frac{1}{(1+R)^t} \right)} \tag{5.2}$$

Equation 5.2 can be readily extended to deal with varying payments. For example, if the stream of payments were to be escalated by a constant proportion each year, it would be modified to:

$$y = K / \left(\sum_{t=1}^{T} \frac{(1+s)^{(t-1)}}{(1+R)^t} \right) \tag{5.3}$$

where s is the escalation factor, and y denotes the year 1 payment. The exponent on the $(1+s)$ term is lagged by one period for convenience, to allow the first-year payment to be written as a set value.

The analysis thus far has developed the skeleton of an annuity structure. While income streams for set periods are generated by these annuities, we have not yet introduced uncertainty, and insurance features of these instruments have therefore not been specified.

It is possible to design and market private annuities that provide full insurance against longevity, investment and inflation risk. Full coverage will inevitably mean that exposure to replacement risk is increased: for a given accumulation, the overall expected income stream will be lower, the more comprehensive the insurance offered by the annuity. There are potential trade-offs between various retirement risks in choosing an annuity. This fact has not been lost on annuity-issuers. In what follows, we explore the properties of some annuity products that have been developed to capture preference across patterns of risk exposure. We

Table 5.1 A simple example of life annuity payments

Year	Interest $	Principal $	Probability of survival	Total $
1	15 000	98 438	1.00	113 438
2	10 313	103 125	0.5	113 438

Note: Assumes $K = \$150\ 000$, $R = 10\%$, $_1p_x = 1$, $_2p_x = 0.5$ and $_3p_x = 0$.

begin with simple life products, and then extend the discussion to more complex products.

Longevity insurance and life annuities

Longevity risk might be described as the risk that you will outlive your financial resources. An individual may insure against this risk by purchasing a life annuity. In entering into such a contract, the individual is taking advantage of the risk-pooling that life annuities exploit.

An issuer provides actuarially fair *single-life annuities* if the premium charged for each contracted t-year-ahead dollar of payment is calculated by the formula $_tp_x / (1 + R)^t$, where $_tp_x$ is the annuitant's probability of survival t periods from age x. The general formula for the actuarially fair annuity payment is given by:

$$y = K / \sum_{t=1}^{\omega} {_tp_x} \frac{(1 + s)^{(t-1)}}{(1 + R)^t} \tag{5.4}$$

where ω is set at the maximum potential life-span, measured from the annuitant's age, given by x, at $t = 1$.

Table 5.1 reports a simple example, with $s = 0$. Year 2 payouts have been adjusted to reflect mortality; the sum of reported principal repayments exceeds $\$150\ 000$ by $\$51\ 563$, equal to the principal remaining after the year 1 payout, because they are paid only one out of two times.

Risk-pooling, then, would appear to work well – the corresponding annual payout for a term-certain annuity is $\$86\ 429$. But this result depends on the assumption of an actuarially fair quote, one which accurately reflects the real risks insured against. In the section on annuity pricing and market failure we explore reasons why annuity insurance may not be able to offer products that are actuarially fair on a population basis, in a voluntary market.

Life annuities are frequently sold with survivorship provisions. Following the death of the primary annuity holder, a nominated survivor continues to receive an annuity payout, sometimes at a reduced rate, until his or her death.

Investment risk, variable annuities and phased withdrawals

Investment risk involves the risk of unevenness in consumption resulting from income flows that fluctuate because of volatility in the returns earned by underlying investments. An annuity promising a series of payments that does not vary with the performance of financial markets provides full insurance against investment risk.

Full investment insurance comes at a price. The simplest context in which to demonstrate this is to abstract for a moment from annuity products and other kinds of uncertainty, and consider two alternative investment strategies. Individuals who know they are going to live for exactly 20 years could assure themselves of a steady income by purchasing a long-term (20-year) government (that is, default-free) bond. This might be thought of as safe, although, as we shall see shortly, a steady nominal income does not guarantee a steady flow of real consumption because of inflation risk.

Alternatively, the retiree might purchase a diversified portfolio of shares. On the US stock market, for example, over the last 75 years shares have offered an average annual rate of return of 12.31%, but have demonstrated considerable volatility over that time, ranging from –43% to about 54% on an annual basis. Another way of expressing this volatility is to calculate the standard deviation of returns – about 20%. The cost of eliminating this volatility has been between six and seven percentage points of annual return – the so-called equity premium.

It would be open to the investor to combine these portfolios in some proportion. For example, he or she could place 50% of his or her funds in bonds of the appropriate maturity and 50% in stocks. This would provide the investor with a guaranteed minimum annual income flow, along with a higher expected income than it would be possible to generate from bonds alone.

If this trade-off between risk and return is present for direct investments, it must translate into the terms of offer available on annuities. Conventional annuities such as those already discussed insure against investment risk, and their payouts reflect 'safe' rates of return. By contrast, an annuity design that transfers risk from issuer to annuitant would provide the potential to offer higher average income flows.

Variable life annuities have been designed to provide insurance against longevity risk, while at the same time delivering higher expected returns by transferring investment risk to the annuitant. The annuity is written on the basis of an assumed investment return (the AIR). Payouts,

Table 5.2 A simple example of a variable annuity payment stream

Year	Interest $	Principal $	Probability of survival	Total $
1	21 000	96 226	1.00	117 226
2	4 302	107 547	0.5	111 849

however, are adjusted by the relationship between the performance of the underlying portfolio – which may be specified by the annuitant – given by R^m, and the AIR. The formula is:

$$y_t = y_{t-1}\left(\frac{1 + R^m}{1 + \text{AIR}}\right) \tag{5.5}$$

where y_0 (not actually paid) is determined according to Equation 5.4, with $s = 0$.

To illustrate, modify the life annuity example given above in Table 5.1. Assume an AIR of 9%, and assume further that the actual rates of return turn out to be 14% and 4%. The outcome is reported in Table 5.2.

The stream of payments is fairly even in this case. However, a sequence of bad years for stock returns would see the annual payments from a variable annuity decline rapidly. For example, if the returns were –20% and –10%, the stream of payouts would be $82 264 and $67 925.

This kind of outcome is by no means unheard of on the stock market. The annuitant is likely to want to insure him or herself against this kind of risk. It is possible to select quite sophisticated portfolios to underwrite a variable annuity. Of particular interest are portfolio designs that exploit options and other derivatives to limit downside risk. Retirees may wish to accept some degree of investment risk, but not wish to risk losing all their capital. Portfolio insurance strategies, involving the use of options, offer this possibility. Current research (Doyle and Piggott 1999) is aimed at developing this idea, along lines analogous to those that Bateman (1997) applied to pension accumulations.

Before concluding the discussion of investment risk another annuity-type product should be introduced. This is the so-called *phased withdrawal*. The phased withdrawal appears at first sight to be more like a pure investment instrument than a retirement income stream product. Its essence is that a sum of money is invested at retirement, in a portfolio over whose composition the retiree has considerable control. Both income and capital can be drawn down to meet the retiree's needs.

The drawdowns, however, are limited to a range, with both upper and lower bounds. In Australia, the bounds are determined using uniform statutory valuation factors to age 80. The maximum drawdown factor is specified on the basis that the individual will live to age 80, while the minimum is calculated on the basis that he or she will survive until the actuarial probability of survival from the date of purchase approximates zero. These 'valuation factors' apply to the account accumulation each year. The account accumulation at time t is given by

$$K_t = K_{t-1}(1 + R^m) - y_t \qquad\qquad (5.6)$$

and the payout at time t of a phased withdrawal may be written as:

$$\frac{K_{t-1}}{F_{t-1}^1} \le y_t \le \frac{K_{t-1}}{F_{t-1}^2} \qquad\qquad (5.7)$$

where F_t^1 is the minimum drawdown factor, and F_t^2 is the maximum.

The current Australian drawdown factors are such that on an initial $150 000 investment, with a 12% nominal rate of return, the first-year payout range for a male aged 65 at the time of purchase is $10 701 to $19 086. If the minimum is consistently drawn down, then the account balance will continue to increase for about 15 years, until it reaches an expected maximum of about $230 500, and thereafter diminishes. If the maximum drawdown is taken, the account declines monotonically until exhausted at age 80. In Australia, phased withdrawals, known as 'allocated annuities', are the fastest growing segment of an admittedly small retirement income product market.

It is in principle possible to combine phased withdrawals with *deferred life annuities* starting at age 80. This arrangement has considerable intuitive appeal, combining capital drawdown flexibility with partial longevity insurance. Assuming retirement at 65, for the first 15 years, the annuitant has considerable flexibility in arranging drawdown patterns. The deferred annuity then cuts in, offering a rest-of-life annuity with an initial payout indexed to inflation, thereafter escalated at a predetermined rate. The annuitant bears the investment risk, but derives some long-term inflation protection from the correlation between movements in the price of physical capital and the price level generally, and enjoys insurance against investment risk under the deferred life annuity. In the event of death before age 80, a bequest results.

The deferred life annuity is not expensive – a 65-year-old male needs to commit only about 10% of his accumulation to the deferred annuity. This result occurs because of the combination of the probability of death before payouts begin, and the compounding of investment returns in the 15 years prior to the first payout, and lower life expectancy at age 80. Formally, the expression for a deferred annuity life payout is:

$$y = K / \left\{ \left[\frac{_d p_x (1 + s)^d}{(1 + R)^d} \right] \sum_{t=1}^{\omega - x} {}_t p_x \frac{(1 + s)^{t-1}}{(1 + R)^t} \right\} \tag{5.8}$$

where d is the number of years that the annuity payouts are deferred from the date of purchase. The term in square brackets represents the increase in the capital sum with which the annuity was initially purchased over the period of deferral, including the implicit sharing of the accumulations of those who die before payouts begin with those who survive the deferral period.

Inflation risk and inflation insurance

Inflation risk refers to the possibility that the purchasing power of an annuity stream will be eroded over time because of price level increases. Even a modest inflation rate of 4% will halve purchasing power in 18 years. Combined with 1% wage productivity growth, purchasing power relative to community standards will halve in 14 years. For a retiree with a life expectancy of 15 or more years, as a male retiring at 65 would have in Australia, erosion of purchasing power through inflation is thus a significant risk. For women, the risk is even greater.

A natural response is to offer annuities with escalation equal to expected inflation. Equation 5.4 provides the mechanics for this with a set equal to expected inflation, or, in the case of a community standard instrument, expected nominal wage growth. However, this does not offer insurance against unanticipated inflation, which perhaps more than anticipated inflation 'creep' is the larger danger to annuitant welfare, precisely because of its unpredictability. It has been possible to purchase annuities indexed to the Consumer Price Index (CPI) in Australia and the United Kingdom for some time. These products have recently become available in the United States.

How much will insurance against the risk of inflation cost? Consider an annuity that guarantees indexation to inflation – an inflation-indexed life annuity. Equation 5.4 can be amended to accommodate this. To cover the risk of unanticipated inflation, the issuer could secure the option to purchase CPI-indexed bonds, assuming such bonds are on offer. The option value A_t effectively prices the inflation risk:

$$K = \frac{K}{\sum_{t=1}^{\omega} {}_t p_x \left[\frac{1}{(1 + R)^t} + A_t \right]} \tag{5.9}$$

One way in which the cost of inflation insurance might be reduced is to offer an annuity providing inflation insurance above some threshold of cumulative inflation. Formica and Kingston (1991), in the spirit of Bodie (1990c), proposed and provided the analytics for such a product, which can be thought of as providing partial inflation insurance, or inflation insurance with a deductible. These annuities are considered further in following sections.

Trading off the risks

It is possible to envisage a trade-off between the various retirement risks identified here in choosing an annuity. Consider first how well these alternative annuity types cover payout-related risks. The insurance coverage that each provides is rated as low, medium or high. Generally speaking, a term-certain annuity offers little longevity insurance and is rated 'low' on this category. However, a term annuity whose term is set equal to life expectancy, which is offered in Australia, could be seen as offering medium longevity coverage. In contrast, annuities with some longevity insurance features score better on this category. Those with life features score high, while the phased withdrawal–deferred annuity combination, which offers some longevity insurance but admits the possibility of resource exhaustion prior to the expiry of the deferral period, rates a medium.

Turning to investment risk, nominal annuities offer high coverage, as does a full CPI-indexed instrument. By contrast, annuities that leave the purchaser with most or all of the investment risk – variable annuities and phased withdrawals – score poorly here.

Inflation risk is not well covered by products offering a nominally fixed periodic payment. It is fully covered by a CPI-indexed annuity. Instruments in which the annual payout is related to the investment return of a portfolio representing claims on physical assets would appear to offer some inflation protection in the long term, although there is evidence that in the short term, inflation and investment returns would be negatively calculated.

In one sense, full coverage against these payout risks is desirable. However, as we emphasised earlier, it is expensive. This quickly exposes retirees to replacement rate risk. A CPI-indexed annuity is therefore rated as providing only medium coverage against replacement rate risk

As Table 5.3 reveals, no annuity design dominates in all risk categories. Overall, the pattern of insurance coverage suggests that *partial* exposure to some of these risks may be acceptable, in return for a higher expected income or consumption flow.

Table 5.3 Insurance coverage offered by alternative annuity designs

Annuity Type	Longevity	Investment	Inflation	Replacement
Term-certain annuity	Low	High	Low	Low
Nominal life annuity	High	High	Low	Medium
Variable life annuity	High	Low	Low	High
Partial inflation insurance life annuity	High	High	Medium	Medium
Phased withdrawal with deferred annuity	Medium	Low	Low	Medium
Inflation-indexed life annuity	High	High	High	Medium

Annuity price variation

Annuity prices may vary through time. This effect, sometimes referred to as annuity rate risk, poses an immediate problem for a policy requiring private annuity purchase on retirement. The date of purchase can significantly affect rest-of-life income. Annuity rate risk has apparently motivated recent policy changes in the United Kingdom, in which individuals who have opted out of the state-run pension scheme into personal pension plans may postpone annuity purchase for some time after retirement, financing their consumption in the interim by a form of phased withdrawal.

Annuity price variation is likely to occur when inflationary expectations are being revised. An instrument that offers full insurance against inflation risk is likely to exhibit a less volatile annuity rate than one that passes on inflation risk to the annuitant. To illustrate, Figure 5.1 depicts variation in Australian annuity quotations for CPI-indexed and 3.25% escalated life annuities, for 65-year-old males, from 1986 to 1993, a period over which inflationary expectations in developed countries were revised downward.[2]

The relatively smooth annuity rate on indexed annuities is striking. This is a fairly short run, of course. But the annuity formulas given above imply that the difference between nominal and real interest rate volatility will largely determine relative annuity rate volatility on the two annuity types. We measured Australian interest rate volatilities over 10-year spans using long bond rates and long spans of inflation, covering the period 1950–1995, and found real interest rate volatility to be much lower than nominal interest rate volatility. The standard deviation of real rates was 0.46 and of nominal rates 0.83.

Annuities for males aged 65

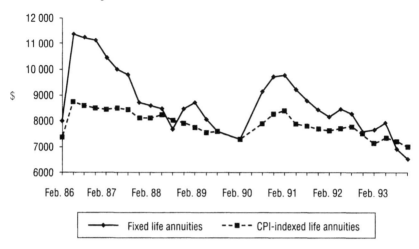

Figure 5.1 Annuity rate variability in Australia, 1986–1993 (first-year payout for $A100 000 purchase)

Infrastructure for secure privately provided retirement income streams

Much economic policy analysis is predicated on the view that in practice markets work well in the fundamental social task of allocating resources. In moving from government pension provision to private annuity mandation, it is necessary to ask what regulations might be needed to facilitate resource allocation.

For a price system to operate effectively in allocating resources efficiently in a sophisticated society, three prerequisites can be identified. Property rights must be allocated and enforceable, information about possible transactions must be available on a fairly general basis, and contracts must be enforceable over time. These requirements lie behind the legal, administrative and regulatory environment that must develop to support a comprehensive annuity market.

Viewed from this perspective it is easy to see why the regulation of annuity-issuers is so pervasive, and why it assumes so much importance. Property rights to pensions are frequently blurred by public regulations and complicated vesting conventions. Relevant information is not common between annuity buyers and sellers, and very long time periods sometimes elapse between annuity purchase and the final payment promised by the annuity-issuer, thus raising the real possibility of default, either explicitly or implicitly through changes in the interpretation of contingency obligations.

Life insurance and annuity-issuer regulation

Robust legal and reliable financial infrastructures are features of most developed economies. It is hard to see how long-term saving and investment could otherwise be facilitated through market channels (Mitchell 1998b provides an accessible discussion of these issues, emphasising the evolving nature of legal and financial infrastructure). The annuity issue raises a number of specific regulatory concerns, addressed in the quite sophisticated mechanisms developed economies use to govern annuity-issuers. This group of agents typically overlaps heavily with life insurance companies. Typically, life insurance regulations cover professional competence, reporting and disclosure requirements, reputation and capital adequacy (or solvency). Often, the public sector will already be supplying annuity and life insurance services. Effective privatisation of, or the introduction of private competition in, annuity provision should be implemented in ways that allow regulatory authorities to draw upon information already available from these public-sector activities.

The sequence of privatisation and deregulation therefore needs to be carefully considered. Annuity providers are typically licensed and are limited in number. Privatisation may be best undertaken by initially implementing tight regulations, with gradual deregulation to follow as the market matures. For example, registered annuity-issuers may each be allocated a basket of contracts, with price and conditions set by the regulator. Subsequently, migration between issuers at regulated transfer fees may be permitted, followed by some price deregulation. A parallel may be found in the Chilean approach to regulating investments in pension funds. Equity investments were not permitted until 1985, were limited to 30% of the fund's assets over 1985–95 and since 1995 are limited to 37%. International investment is now allowed.

Annuities and the structure of government debt

A rather different policy issue pertaining to the annuity market relates to the structure of government debt. The safety of annuities could be increased (lowering default risk) and the price of a given annuity stream decreased (reducing replacement risk) by changes in the structure of government debt issue. This is especially true of annuity streams with some degree of inflation insurance. Annuities could be made more attractive if sellers had access to securities that are indexed and of long duration.

A seller of an indexed annuity to a buyer aged 55 with reversion to a younger spouse is committed to indexed payouts over 40 years or more. Because of the long durations involved, and the impossibility of predicting inflation over such a period, default risk in this context is real. It could arise if, for example, an annuity seller supported his or her obligations with assets that failed to perform as expected, or if his or her reserves proved inadequate. With adequate indexed and long-term government bonds, however, it is possible to replicate any upcoming schedule of annuity payments. Feasibility of this type of safe and judgement-free annuity management strategy requires adequate availability of indexed and long-duration government securities. If long-maturity indexed government securities are unavailable, annuity sellers will build up reserves, to protect themselves, and the cost of this will be passed on to the purchaser.

It is hard to see how debt management objectives would be impeded if indexed and long-duration bonds in public debt were undertaken. This is an excellent example of how policy towards retirement income provision could be improved without adding significantly to demands on consolidated revenue. One of the implicit costs is reduced options for inflating away the real burden of nominal debt. By the same token, indexed bonds, as opposed to nominal bonds, might well encourage beneficial monetary discipline in countries where, from time to time, governments are tempted to overuse inflation to decrease the real value of government debt.

If annuity purchase is mandatory for retirees, further policy and implementation issues arise. These include the specification of minimum criteria for annuity insurance features, and annuity offer regulations directed at annuity-issuers. Mandated annuity purchase is a natural complement to mandated retirement accumulations, and a natural response to annuity market failure – an issue to which we return below.

International practice

Whether compulsory DC plans are administered in the public sector or the private sector they bring with them the policy challenge of associated payout design. That this is controversial is evident from Table 5.4. It reports a wide range of payout designs and provisions, and largely bears out the view that payout patterns reflect what has gone before.

The first three countries considered in Table 5.4 are those with the most mature private mandatory systems. Table 5.4 then summarises payout regulation in five Latin American nations that have recently introduced private mandatory retirement provision, and concludes with two economies with provident funds. Countries with pre-existing PAYG social

Table 5.4 Retirement benefits in countries with mandatory accumulation retirement policies

	Australia	Chile	Switzerland
Preservation age	Current preservation age is 55 years for both men and women. To be increased to age 60 by 2025	Men: 65; women: 60. Early retirement is permitted for high accumulations	Preservation age is set at 65 years for men, and at 62 for women. Early access to accumulated benefit for home purchase
Benefit type	Employees may access the accrued benefits either as a lump sum or as an income stream. Mostly taken as a lump sum. Phased withdrawals are the most popular form of income stream	Choice of phased withdrawals and life annuity. Lump-sum withdrawals are permitted for high accumulations. Phased withdrawal compulsory if annuity is greater than the minimum pension unaffordable. So far, most retirees have taken life annuities	Benefits paid as monthly pensions. Lump sums may be available if small accumulations or for home purchase. No income stream choice
Reversion	Not compulsory	Reversion is required	Reversion is required
Replacement rate	40-year employment history, retiring at 65 years, 76% replacement for single male. This includes both annuity and public pension income	Average replacement rates have reached 78% and have been higher for those opting for early retirement (82%)	Aims to increase total retirement replacement rate of average earnings from around 40% (under the public pillar) to 60% after 40 years of contributions
Integration with public safety net	Poor integration. Preservation age not co-ordinated with public pension eligibility age. Dissipated lump sum not counted under means tests	Well integrated with safety net. Minimum guaranteed pension to those with 20 years employment	Well integrated with public pensions. Minimum pension guaranteed
Taxation	Lump sums are taxed at 15% above an indexed threshold. *Annuities and Superannuation pensions are taxed as ordinary income for all types of superannuation schemes, subject to 15% tax rebate*	All of the pensions are subject to income tax – but the tax-free threshold is high	Benefits subject to income tax

	Argentina	Peru	Mexico
Preservation age	Men: 65; women: 60	Preservation age is 65. Early retirement possible for high accumulations	Preservation age is 65 years for men and women. Early retirement possible for high accumulations
Benefit type	Choice of phased withdrawals and life annuity. 'Fragmented withdrawals' are available for those whose accumulated funds are not large enough to allow for withdrawals equivalent to half the basic pension. Lump-sum withdrawals are permitted for high accumulations	Choice of phased withdrawals and life annuity. Also third option combining temporary phased withdrawals with a deferred annuity	Workers with 1250 weeks of contributions can opt to purchase a life annuity or to receive phased withdrawals from the fund, and government minimum pension guarantee applies. Workers with fewer than 1250 weeks of contributions are not entitled to minimum pension, but are allowed to withdraw balance of account as a lump sum if they prefer not to purchase annuity or take planned withdrawals
Reversion	The dependants of a worker who dies before retirement are entitled to receive a survivorship pension, which is equivalent to a percentage of the worker's average income received in the five years prior to death	Reversion is required	Reversion is required
Replacement rate	Basic universal pension set at about 27.5% of average salary. PAYG benefits calculated as percentage of average last 10 years earnings for each year of contributions. Funded scheme benefits depend on the level of accumulations	Benefits depend upon value of accumulation. Early retirement is possible if the balance accumulated can finance a pension equivalent to 50% of average salary during last 10 years	Minimum pension is equal to the minimum wage (about 40% of average earnings), for those who satisfy contribution requirement. Funded scheme benefits depend upon value of accumulation

Table 5.4 (cont.)

	Argentina	Peru	Mexico
Integration with public safety net	Well integrated with universal basic pension	No public pillar or minimum pension guarantee	Minimum pension guaranteed to those aged 65 and with 1250 weeks of contributions
Taxation	Benefits subject to income tax	Pension contributions are paid out of after-tax income and pension benefits are also taxed	Withdrawals are not taxed up to a limit of nine times the minimum wage, and there is a higher limit for tax exemption when employees withdraw all their funds at once

	Colombia	Uruguay
Preservation age	Preservation age is 62 for men and 57 for women. Early retirement is possible for high accumulations	Men: 60; women: 55, rising to 60 by 2003
Benefit type	Choice of phased withdrawals, purchase of life annuity, or a combination of both. If accumulated balance is sufficient to finance pension of 110% of minimum wage, excess capital may be used for purposes other than retirement	Life annuity only
Reversion	Reversion is required	Reversion is required
Replacement rate	Minimum pension represents a replacement rate of around 60% of average earnings. Funded scheme benefits depend upon accumulation amount	Minimum guaranteed pension pays at least 50% of average salary of the last 10 years, rising if retirement is postponed. Funded scheme benefits depend upon level of accumulation
Integration with public safety net	Government guarantees minimum pension (equal to the minimum wage, or about 60% of average earnings) provided reached official retirement age and contributed for at least 1150 weeks	Minimum guaranteed pension to those with 35 years of contributions at retirement age, or those aged 70 with 15 years of contributions

Taxation	Pension benefits are tax exempt up to the limit of 20 minimum wages. However, if funds accumulated in individual account are used for non-retirement purposes, taxes are due	Benefits subject to income tax
	Singapore	**Malaysia**
Preservation age	Preservation age is 60 for both men and women. Lump sum may be available at age 55	Full retirement benefits available at age 55, and partial benefits at age 50. Early withdrawals permitted for home purchase
Benefit type	Retirement account funds must be used to purchase a life annuity. Members may withdraw a lump sum at age 55 provided they retain a specified minimum sum in their retirement account	Benefits can only be taken as lump sums. However, the member can withdraw the annual dividend only or leave the funds in the account after age 55 and can continue to contribute
Reversion	If a member dies, the full amount of the accumulation is available to beneficiaries	If a member dies, the full amount of the accumulation is available to beneficiaries
Replacement rate	No explicit target replacement rate but the scheme is intended to provide members with an income of 20–40% of pre-retirement earnings, sufficient funds to meet medical expenses during retirement, and a home commensurate with their income level	The average amount of the full withdrawal is about the same as one year of an annual salary for a typical employee
Integration with public safety net	98% of Singaporeans over 21 are covered by Central Provident Fund (CPF). Strict means-tested safety net assistance provided to destitute aged and those not covered, or inadequately covered by the CPF	No public age pension. Means-tested benefits available to those aged 60 and over who are homeless or destitute and do not have families to support them
Taxation	Lump-sum withdrawals at age 55 years are tax-free. Normally, pensions paid from age 60 years are also tax-free; however, any pension amount paid from contributions in excess of those required on a mandatory basis is taxed as income	Benefits are untaxed

Source: Bateman (1997), Bateman and Piggott (1997), Davis (1995), Hepp (1990), Feldstein (1998), Barrientos (1998), Queisser (1998), Stanton and Whiteford (1998) security usually preserve some part of life annuity as the standard payout, although variants, such as the phased withdrawal, are sometimes introduced.

Some developing economies, often those with links to British colonialism, such as Singapore and Malaysia, have established what are generically known as 'provident funds' to help finance retirement. These are essentially mandatory DC plans administered by the national government, sometimes through a separately established board of management, which maintain individual accounts for employees and which usually pay a lump sum, comprising the worker's net contributions and investment earnings, at retirement.

To make discussion about payout design more concrete, it may be useful to briefly describe the benefit types available in Australia, Switzerland and Chile, the three countries with the most mature privately administered mandatory accumulation schemes.

Australia

Until the advent of private mandatory retirement provision coverage in 1992 (known as the Superannuation Guarantee), Australia was almost unique among developed countries in having no second pillar. Mandatory contributions, payable by employers, are being phased in, and will rise to 9% of employees' earnings by 2002. Before this, voluntary private-sector occupational superannuation had quite low coverage, and benefits were mostly drawn as a lump sum.

The practice of taking lump sums has continued under the Superannuation Guarantee. About 85% of the value of superannuation benefits are paid in this form. About 10% are taken as an income stream and the remainder are taken as a death, temporary or permanent disability benefit. Although income streams are not compulsory, they are encouraged through a variety of tax incentives and first-pillar means-test provisions.

Retirement income streams that attract preferential tax and/or means-test provisions can be broadly classified into *immediate annuities* (comprising both term and life annuities), *superannuation pensions* (from DB schemes) and phased withdrawals.

Recently, amendments to first-pillar means-testing arrangements have served to encourage what might be termed *life-expectancy* products.[3] These must guarantee an escalated or CPI-indexed income stream for the life expectancy of the retiree at the time of purchase. There can be no commutation or residual capital value. Retirement accumulations used for these purchases are not counted in the assets test, one of two means tests applied to the first-pillar age pension. (The Australian arrangements are discussed in Appendix 1).

Switzerland

Switzerland has traditionally had a standard OECD-type three-pillar retirement support policy. In 1985, another component was added to the second pillar, the BVG, which is a privately administered compulsory occupational scheme. This supplements the employment-related social security pension, which is financed by social security tax payments from employers and employees. The two schemes combined aim to provide a total retirement pension of 60% of covered earnings after 40 years of contributions for the average worker. There is a means-tested social assistance pension for those on very low social-security pensions.

Contributions for the BVG are required from both employers and employees, with the employer to contribute at least 50%. The contributions vary according to gender and age, and range from 7% of earnings for the young to 18% of earnings for those approaching retirement. There are additional contributions of 2–4% for survivors and disability insurance, 1% to allow for the indexation of benefits, 0.02% for the security fund and 0.2% for administration.

Benefits from both social security and the BVG are generally paid as monthly pensions. Alternative benefit designs are not available. For small BVG accumulations, lump-sum benefits are possible, and early withdrawal of benefits for housing purchase is available under certain circumstances.

Viewed as a DC plan, the BVG incorporates minimum requirements: a minimum contribution rate, a minimum rate of return and a minimum annuity conversion factor. (Annuity factors must be gender uniform.) The security fund guarantees minimum retirement credits and by covering DC as well as DB plans the Swiss guarantee arrangements are unique in the OECD. Reversion is required. While the BVG is essentially DC based, many of the benefits actually paid exceed the minimum requirements and are formulated on a DB basis.

Chile

Chile's current second-pillar retirement income policy was established in 1981, with the old social security system gradually being phased out. It is of the DC type, publicly mandated but privately administered. The government guarantees a minimum pension to workers whose accumulations fall short of set limits. The value of the minimum pension is adjusted by inflation every time the accumulated change in the CPI reaches 15%. First-pillar support comprises a targeted social assistance scheme. A subsistence pension is payable through that scheme to those not eligible for the minimum pension.

Retirees may make phased withdrawals from their individual account, regulated to guarantee income for their expected life-span, or buy an annuity to provide lifetime benefits, or choose a combination. Phased withdrawals require reversion, but life annuities do not. Some lump-sum withdrawals are permitted. However, this is only allowed if it still leaves enough in the account to fund a benefit that is a 70% replacement rate and equals 120% or more of the guaranteed minimum pension. Only 25% of the eligible retirees in Chile have taken lump sums. Of the current pension beneficiaries of the new system, some 60% have taken up a lifetime annuity.

Under the phased withdrawal, the accumulated funds are drawn according to an actuarially determined schedule. Any balance remaining after the beneficiary dies is inherited by heirs. Complete longevity risk is provided only insofar as the government will pay the minimum pension if funds are exhausted.

Annuity pricing and market failure

In previous sections, we have cast our discussion in terms of annuities that are actuarially fair from an economy-wide perspective. Even on this basis, retirement insurance purchase is expensive. However, in practice, retirement income streams offering insurance are even more costly for a variety of reasons to which we now turn.

Voluntary annuity markets are thin everywhere. The reasons are not clear. Possible explanations are a bequest motive, the desire to hold precautionary balances to cope with uninsurable events, and over-annuitisation through publicly provided social security. What does seem clear is that life annuity prices are high, relative to population life expectancy and alternative investment returns. In an early widely cited paper that computes estimated loadings, Friedman and Warshawsky (1990) reported that a typical male aged 65 in the United States in the 1980s would have enjoyed a premium of 4.21% per annum, had he purchased a government bond rather than a life annuity. High annuity prices are frequently attributed to adverse selection.

The extent and nature of adverse selection are among the most intractable issues in annuity analysis. The primary efficient market requirement that is violated is commonality of information. If individuals know more about their own survival prospects than the insurer, those with longer life expectancy will be more likely to buy an annuity, and will be more likely to buy annuities of higher value.[4] Such behaviour will lead to rising annuity prices, thus leading more 'good risks' – in this context, people with low life expectancy – to drop out of the market. Adverse selection has set in.

If insurance companies and annuitants had common information and each individual were able to purchase an annuity based on his or her own survival probabilities, this kind of market failure would not arise. In practice, however, insurance companies do not have enough information about survival prospects to individually tailor annuities in this way. Either information held by annuity purchasers can be successfully withheld from the annuity-issuer, or regulation may preclude insurers from statistically discriminating between groups; for example, by compelling the use of unisex mortality tables.

The efficiency costs of adverse selection

While the presence of adverse selection in annuities markets is generally acknowledged, its importance is difficult to determine. There is little well-documented evidence about the welfare costs of this market failure. Among the difficulties confronting researchers are the existence of government-provided retirement income schemes, the link between income and mortality, and the possibility that implicit family contracts may mitigate the costs of formal market failure.

It is possible to characterise annuity market failure by thinking of a utility-maximising consumer, averse to consumption variability, or risk, making choices over two retirement periods. He or she survives the first with certainty, but survives the second period with probability less than unity. Kingston and Piggott (1999) present a rigorous two-period geometric treatment of the welfare costs of annuity market failure along these lines, and provide some illustrative estimates of the associated efficiency cost. In the absence of an annuity market, individuals will typically opt for some consumption variability, trading off the risk of outliving their resources against the prospect of leaving an unintended bequest from which they gain no utility. It is exactly this risk that a well-functioning annuities market allows individuals to pool.

Using a simple logarithmic power utility function, implying a risk-aversion parameter set at unity, welfare costs of about 5% of retirement wealth are calculated. Efficiency costs decrease with increasing risk aversion. This results from the uneven consumption stream that individuals are forced to adopt to maximise their welfare in the absence of an annuities market, and suggests that the efficiency costs of annuity market failure are worth taking seriously.[5]

In a well-known paper, Kotlikoff and Spivak (1981) reported much larger welfare gains for single individuals gaining access to a perfect annuities market. However, in most cases, their calculations do not correct for the unintended bequests of those who die before their resources are exhausted. The major focus of their paper is the role of the family in an incomplete annuities market; we return to it below.

Why the annuities market is different

The prevalence of information asymmetry in insurance markets generally, and consequential adverse selection and moral hazard problems, means that insurers are experienced at designing contracts with characteristics that minimise these difficulties. These frequently involve deductibles and co-payments. In addition, truthful disclosure is often checked prior to meeting a claim. All these practices are observed, for example, in the health insurance market. Health insurance premia are frequently differentiated on the basis of whether the insured smokes, and lower premia are offered to 'good risks'.

By contrast, the annuities market does not exhibit these characteristics. For example, annuity-issuers do not offer lower premia to heavy smokers. Instead, we typically observe thin markets with significant premium loadings that are at least in part attributable to adverse selection.[6]

The distinctive features of the annuity market are discussed by Walliser (1997a). First, whereas with most other insurance contracts, multiple coverage is easily monitored, the annuity seller cannot control, or even observe, the amount of annuity purchased, making the use of market strategies such as those discussed above difficult. Even if an annuity contract explicitly restricted further purchases of annuities, this might not suffice since monitoring would be very difficult. This is because the receipt of annuity payments from different insurance companies would not be observable. Issuers typically quote on a dollar's worth of annuity, and leave the quantity purchased up to the annuitant, a practice consistent with this monitoring problem.

As Walliser additionally points out, in contrast to other insurance markets, the contingent event (the annuitant's death) ends the involvement of the insurance company rather than creating it. This fact precludes withholding payments and investigating compliance with the insurance contract, as occurs in life insurance or car insurance markets.

An obvious response to this market circumstance is to offer group annuities, in which participation of some population, such as employees of a firm, is mandatory. This limits adverse selection, and allows better terms to be offered. Separate annuitant mortality tables are available for group and individual annuities. The study by Finkelstein and Poterba (1999), discussed below, is relevant here.

In an environment of individual accounts, however, it is not clear that precommitment of this kind is possible. One possible approach to social security privatisation in the United States is to begin by randomly assigning annuitants to insurance companies, at least as a first step (Diamond 1999a). This would presumably be accompanied by some form of price regulation.[7]

Evidence on adverse selection

Market evidence on adverse selection begins with the calculation of load factors on market premia, relative to actuarially fair annuity offers. A number of studies, of which the first was the already cited work of Friedman and Warsharsky, attempt to assess their size.

In Australia, Doyle and Piggott (1998) compared payouts from equivalently valued term-certain life expectancy and full-life products. Quotes from a major Australian financial service provider suggested that in August 1998, allowing for commission costs of 6%, a 15-year term-certain annuity was priced using a nominal interest rate of 5%. Using standard Australian mortality tables, corresponding quotes for a life annuity for a male aged 65 imply a nominal rate of 2.5%. The difference in the implied rates of return must largely reflect adverse selection. Apart from the monitoring of death, administrative costs do not appear to be greatly different in the two cases.

In making comparisons of premium loadings on these annuities, it is important to note that with a positive discount rate, the present value of a fixed single-life annuity paying $1 a year will be lower than the present value of a $1 fixed term-certain annuity where the term is set at life expectancy. The result is at first counter-intuitive – a life annuity provides insurance, which is expensive. It occurs because of the compounding effect of discounting. The present value of an annuity-issuer's expected payout to the holder of a life annuity will involve mortality probability-weighted income streams that are of both shorter and longer duration than life expectancy. With a discount rate set at zero, these would in aggregate exactly offset each other. However, with a positive discount rate, the present value of payout streams on an annuity for a long-lived individual involves terms that are heavily discounted. To put it another way, the annual payout of an actuarially fair-life annuity bought with a given accumulation will be greater than the annual payout of a term-certain annuity with a term equal to life-expectancy bought with the same accumulation. This result, which is standard in the actuarial profession, means that loadings cannot be computed by direct comparison with the payouts offered on life-expectancy term-certain products.

The Australian quotes referred to above, for a $A100 000 purchase price, were (about) $A9500 a year for the life annuity, and $A11 400 a year for the term-certain annuity. The actuarially fair-life annuity payout, assuming that the commission payments and rates of returns for the two contracts are identical, is more than $A11 900. Adverse selection has reduced the annual payout on the life annuity by about $A2400, or 20% of the actuarially fair value.

Using a much more sophisticated methodology, Mitchell et al. (1997) reported load factors on actuarially fair quotes (the difference between the premium and the expected pension benefit) of 18% in the United States for 1995, although some of this is due to overhead costs. They attributed about half of the load factor to adverse selection. They also reported a significant increase in the effect of adverse selection with age and a significantly smaller effect of adverse selection on annuity prices for women.

Finally, Finkelstein and Poterba (1999) studied the United Kingdom annuities market, focusing on both group and individual contracts. They found that selection effects are more pronounced in the voluntary (individual) than in the compulsory (group) market, but that even compulsory annuitants are not a random sample of the UK population. While the expected present value of the annuity payout stream from a typical voluntary annuity is 13% higher for a typical 65-year-old male voluntary annuitant than for a typical 65-year-old male in the United Kingdom, in the compulsory annuity market, the cost of adverse selection is between one-third and one-half of this. Annuitants also select across types of annuity products with different payout profiles, even within the compulsory market.

For most retirees, these load factors are an effective deterrent to voluntary life annuity purchase. Estimates of this magnitude suggest that adverse selection is pervasive in individual annuity markets. They may give an exaggerated picture of the efficiency costs of annuity market failure, however, because informal substitutes may be effective in meeting the longevity insurance requirements of many elderly people. Kotlikoff and Spivak (1981) argued that implicit or explicit family bargains play a significant role in providing annuities on an informal basis. This clearly occurs, at least implicitly, in many countries lacking formal retirement income provision.

Explaining low annuity demand

Of the alternative explanations for low annuity demand, economic analysis has focused mainly on the bequest motive. While a desire to leave bequests would no doubt discourage voluntary annuity purchase, observation suggests that even those who might be supposed not to have a strong bequest motive (for example, the elderly with no children) do not purchase annuities. Hurd (1990) considered the interaction between private annuities and bequests in some detail, and tentatively concluded that the bequest motive is not necessary to explain the lack of demand for individual annuities. Further, many people who have the possibility of securing an individual life annuity in developed countries own their own homes, and their bequest motives may be satisfied through the transfer of this asset.

This assessment would appear to lead back to adverse selection as a major reason for the lack of demand for individual annuities. Hurd, however, also reported that in at least two experimental programs, elderly people in subsidised housing programs were offered the choice between a lump sum and an actuarially fair annuity. Almost all took the lump sum, even though many had no children. One plausible explanation for this is the desire to hold precautionary balances to cope with uninsurable events, what we term contingency outlay risk. A second possible explanation is that the annuity promised a flat payment path, and it may be that very elderly individuals prefer lower consumption in return for higher consumption possibilities earlier in their retirement. Finally, the participants in these programs had relatively low incomes, and may have been 'overannuitised' through social security.

Adverse selection and the impact of social security has recently been investigated in detail by Walliser (1997b, 2000), using a simulation model calibrated to US data. This model reproduces three stylised facts about the US annuities market: a 7–10% loading on annuity prices, a link between age and the strength of adverse selection, and the gender difference in adverse selection. His model simulations suggest that eliminating social security reduces the annuity price loading by about two percentage points, and that annuity mandation is in aggregate welfare enhancing. This last result is consistent with the much simpler Kingston–Piggott example reported above.

Regulating mandatory annuities

Given that individual tailoring of annuity contracts is infeasible, there is a strong case for mandating life annuities. Adverse selection is limited when everyone must buy an annuity, provided appropriate restrictions are placed on annuity offers. Compulsion may reduce commission costs, and in addition, mandatory annuities address the possibility of preference inconsistency continuing in retirement.

An alternative approach to limiting adverse selection has been put forward by Brugiavini (1993). She suggested incremental-deferred annuity purchase throughout the accumulation phase to exploit the observed feature of annuity markets that adverse selection increases with age. A similar idea has been suggested by Boskin et al. (1988). Incremental deferred annuity purchase would also serve to spread annuity rate risk, since the terms of annuity purchase would vary with each increment purchased (Bateman and Piggott 1999a). Especially in the context of developing countries, however, deferred annuity purchase covering an overall span of many decades may test the enforceability of long-term contracts.

Minimum annuity design criteria deemed to satisfy the mandating requirement must be developed, and should address the risks outlined earlier, including replacement rate risk. It is impossible to lay down a single set of criteria that must be met for all applications. Rather, the aim here has been to set out an approach that takes the most important features of mandatory annuities into account.

That said, however, a major regulatory issue confronting annuity mandation remains. Regulation should be sensitive to the size of the accumulation to be invested. A common problem in mandating annuities is that administration costs render the annuitisation of small accumulations infeasible. Often, in practice, if an accumulation lies below some small amount, it may be withdrawn as a lump sum. If an all-or-nothing regulation is introduced, so that annuity purchase of the whole accumulation is required beyond that sum, then there may be incentives to keep accumulations small. If there is a minimum pension guarantee, then the lump sum can be absorbed into the minimum pension, and this overcomes the difficulty.

Consumer preference, public outlays and mandatory annuity design

The idea of annuity mandation immediately raises the issue of what features of annuities might be specified. We have already seen that a variety of annuities exist, offering differing degrees of insurance against longevity and the financial risks especially associated with retirement. One approach to this question is to consider consumer preference towards different annuity types, and to weigh these preferences against the first-pillar government outlays, which might be expected under alternative annuity designs (Doyle and Piggott 1998, 1999).

A natural first point of comparison across annuity types is the value of the initial payouts offered. Table 5.5 reports year 1 payouts for a range of annuities types. It specifies a number of examples of the broad annuity designs we have discussed, and compares first-year payouts for a range of actuarially fair annuity designs, using Australian data specifications. In the case of the variable annuity and the phased withdrawals, expected values are used. First-year payouts vary from $A16 409 to $A24 432, a very broad range.

Table 5.5 Alternative annuity products, and first-year payouts

Annuity type	Nature of annuity payout	Year 1 payout $A
Nominal life annuity	Provides a constant nominal income stream until death	22 031
Variable life annuity	Provides an income stream until death, with payments contingent on the market performance of some specified underlying portfolio. The AIR is set to generate an expected 3% escalation	24 432
'Life-expectancy' term-certain annuity	Provides a prespecified income stream, escalated at 3% per annum, over life expectancy at the time of purchase	16 409
Phased withdrawal and deferred life annuity	Income can be drawn down at the retiree's discretion within a range specified by regulation; typically, maximum drawdown limits are set to exhaust resources by life expectancy from time of purchase. Deferred standard life annuity payments then commence; the deferred annuity is valued at 9% of the product purchase price	19 333
Partial inflation-indexed life annuity	Provides a lifetime income stream escalated at 3% with an inflation 'deductible' providing a real protection factor of 85% – payments are indexed to inflation above this cumulative price level increase	17 843
CPI-indexed life annuity	Provides a lifetime income stream indexed to the CPI	17 002

Note: Assumes annuity purchase price: $A166 970 (35-year accumulation at 9% of average wages; historical investment returns); annuity return assumptions; real safe return: 4%; real risky return: 8%; expected inflation: 4%; standard deviation on risky portfolio: 20%; standard deviation on inflation: 2%. Life expectancies: average 65-year-old Australian male. Deferred annuity: 9% of purchase price, invested at risky rate for deferred period of 15 years. Average wages at retirement: $A40 154.

Direct comparison of income streams generated by different annuity products offers only a limited guide to their social merit. Of greater importance are individual preferences towards alternative income (or consumption) profiles. In assessing the effectiveness of alternative policies, economists often base their recommendations on metrics associated with individual welfare, or utility. All that is required of a utility score is that it ranks alternatives in the order of preference of the individual.

This approach is readily adapted to the present policy design problem. Doyle and Piggott (1998), for example, explored the implications of alternative mandatory annuity designs in a privatised social security environment, for both consumers' preference and first-pillar public outlays. They assume a retirement policy framework in which mandatory DC accumulations are paid out at retirement, and regulations over retirement income streams must be separately stipulated. The insurance coverage and payout profiles for a 65-year-old male are used to gain insight into their implications for social welfare benefits, and the potential ranking of alternative products by the retiree.

Income flows associated with different annuity types are calculated. Stochastic techniques are used to simulate investment and inflationary processes. Income-tested public-sector first-pillar payments are then added in. The resulting real income in each period is assumed to finance consumption in that period alone – there is no borrowing or lending in retirement, and no other source of income. This gives an estimate of consumption for each period, and provides the basis for the utility score calculation.

Illustrative results are reported in Table 5.6, for annuities with specifications given in Table 5.5. A pension guarantee set at 20% of average earnings is assumed. The present values of public pension outlays and, where applicable, expected bequests are also reported.

The first important message from Table 5.6 is that a CPI-indexed annuity scores reasonably well, across a range of risk aversion, for those on average incomes and above. Longevity risk spreading is important here, as is the complete coverage against inflation and investment risk. It is worth reiterating that these results assume population-based actuarially fair annuity pricing (see Finkelstein and Poterba 1999 for evidence of high loadings on annuities of this type). Associated first-pillar payouts are very low. For those who are very risk averse, this is the preferred product, except for the very poor.

The variable annuity offers a higher rate of return, but with exposure to investment and inflation risk. For those who are less risk averse, this is a preferred product. Expected public pension payouts are, however, higher. This is why the poor prefer it – they can take more advantage of the safety net than higher income individuals. For the very risk averse, however, the variable annuity does not do so well.

At the other end of the ranking scale, the term annuity, a life-expectancy product, scores very poorly. This is probably because there is no consistency of exposure to volatility over time. For the first 15 years, a safe, smooth return is offered; this appeals to the very risk averse, while those less averse to risk miss out on the higher expected returns generated by products associated with riskier portfolios. After

Table 5.6 Utility rankings of mandatory annuities by annuity type and present values of pension and bequests, by income level ($A)

	Annuity type	Utility ranking by risk aversion (γ)			Present value of	
		0.5	1.5	2.5	Public pension ($A)	Bequests ($A)
50% of average earnings	Nominal	3	3	3	9 253	
	Variable	1	1	1	10 845	
	Term	6	6	6	17 562	17 086
	Phased withdrawal	2	2	2	13 781	17 916
	Partial inflation-indexed	4	4	4	2 616	
	CPI-indexed	5	5	5	815	

	Annuity type	Utility ranking by risk aversion (γ)			Present value of	
		0.5	1.5	2.5	Public pension ($A)	Bequests ($A)
100% of average earnings	Nominal	5	4	4	488	
	Variable	1	1	3	2 924	
	Term	6	6	6	14 436	34 173
	Phased withdrawal	3	5	5	2 134	35 831
	Partial inflation-indexed	4	3	2	0	
	CPI-indexed	2	2	1	0	

	Annuity type	Utility ranking by risk aversion (γ)			Present value of	
		0.5	1.5	2.5	Public pension ($A)	Bequests ($A)
200% of average earnings	Nominal	5	4	3	3	
	Variable	1	1	4	653	
	Term	6	6	6	14 436	68 346
	Phased withdrawal	4	5	5	290	71 662
	Partial inflation-indexed	3	3	2	0	
	CPI-indexed	3	2	1	0	

Note: For utility evaluations a standard iso-elastic utility function is used:

$$\left[EU = \frac{1}{1-\gamma} \sum_{t=1}^{\omega} {}_tp_x \frac{C_t^{1-\gamma}}{(1+\rho)^t} \right] \text{ where } {}_tp_x \text{ is the probability of surviving from age}$$

65 to age 65+t, C_t is the value of the payout (and consumption) at time t, γ is the **risk-aversion** parameter and ρ is the discount rate set at 0.035.

Source: Bateman, Doyle and Piggott (1999)

that time, there is a considerable movement in consumption flows that the risk averse dislike. No matter how preference towards risk is specified, this product has unattractive features. Furthermore, the public pension payout associated with term annuity purchase is very high. This product may of course score better if a bequest argument were incorporated into the preference function.

One of the more innovative products to be developed (but not marketed) in Australia, and available in the United Kingdom and Peru, combines a phased withdrawal with a deferred annuity. Notwithstanding the fact that this product does not exploit longevity risk-spreading for a duration equal to the life expectancy of the purchaser it has considerable appeal. It is difficult, however, to capture its appeal in the preference framework used here. It generates a significant value of expected bequests, and also leaves considerable discretion over capital drawdown for the duration of life expectancy. Neither of these features is captured in our preference function, yet both are valued by individuals. Expected public pension outlays are about the same as for a variable annuity.

Time-discounting may go some way to explaining why annuities offering partial inflation insurance score so poorly. An annuity offering inflation insurance with a deductible generates a payout profile whose real value reduces early in retirement and is thereafter insured against. Yet the opposite pattern will score better in a preference function with time-discounting. There is also some anecdotal evidence that individuals prefer to front-load their retirement payouts, presumably on the basis that they will be less active in their later retirement (see Hurd 1990).

Partial inflation-insured annuities tend to score better with individuals who are highly risk averse. In practice, load factors on CPI-indexed annuities are higher than on standard life annuities. While the conventional explanation for this is couched in terms of inflation risk and the costs of building a matching asset base, it may be that adverse selection plays a further role here – only those with very long life expectancies are concerned about purchasing power a long time into the future.

To summarise, results indicate that while a CPI-indexed actuarially fair life annuity is likely to score well from both individual and social perspectives, products that offer only partial insurance against the major retirement risks – longevity risk, investment risk and inflation risk – may dominate. In particular, both the variable annuity and the phased withdrawal coupled with a deferred annuity scored well. There do seem to be advantages in allowing some flexibility in mandatory annuity design.

Conclusion

Many elderly people want insurance coverage against financial and longevity risk, but find that it is expensive, and sometimes impossible, to purchase in an unregulated market. This chapter has considered the retirement insurance issue in countries that use a private mandate paradigm for retirement saving. Modest social welfare safety net support, with some degree of means-testing, is assumed. On this scenario, remaining retirement risk can best be addressed through some form of income flow through retirement.

We argue that for a reliable annuities market to be established in any economy, basic financial infrastructure, including a robust banking sector, must be present. Contracts spanning many years, even decades, must be credible. In addition, annuity-issuers must meet standard regulatory criteria relating to solvency, competence and disclosure.

We confirm the widely held view that annuity prices are not actuarially fair, partly because of adverse selection in the voluntary annuities market. Results are reported that suggest markups of 10% on actuarially fair prices are common, and that the load factor can be much higher. Implied rates of return on an actuarially fair basis can be as low as 1%. The inefficiency of the market is thought to be one reason for the lack of demand for individual annuities, although other possibilities exist.

The surest way to minimise adverse selection in the annuities market is to mandate annuity purchase. This is a natural complement to private mandate accumulation. As well as addressing the adverse selection problem, it may ameliorate other difficulties, including individual misjudgement and high marketing and administration costs.

Mandating annuitisation of retirement accumulations requires the specification of a set of minimum criteria that annuity-type instruments must meet. We show that full insurance coverage against investment and inflation risk may be very expensive, even when annuities are priced fairly. Partial coverage is an attractive alternative.

Inflation insurance for annuitants is best underwritten by indexed securities. It would be sensible to encourage governments to include long-duration indexed bonds as part of their debt issue, both to allow immunisation of inflation-insured annuities and to encourage governments to control inflation.

In addition, phased withdrawals, possibly coupled with a deferred life annuity, offer the possibility of increased liquidity to cover unexpected expenses, especially uninsurable events, while retaining some degree of longevity insurance. This will be especially important when unexpected health outlays might arise, and health insurance policy will therefore be relevant here.

There appears to be no reason why the idea of varying mandatory requirements with accumulation value should not be extended to the mandating of alternative income stream products. For example, it may be possible to require investment in a phased withdrawal for smaller accumulations, and in more comprehensive life instruments (a deferred life annuity add-on, or a variable life annuity) for higher accumulations.[8] Accumulations and their disposal would have to monitored, which may prove difficult where employees maintain multiple accumulation accounts. However, no analysis has been undertaken to examine the impacts of these possibilities.

We conclude that there is no one preferred mandatory annuity design. Minimum criteria should ensure that adequate, if partial, insurance is provided, consistent with the size of the accumulation. Integration with the first pillar should be designed to ensure that affluent retirees are not able to inappropriately exploit first-pillar support. Annuity rate risk is determined by volatility in the relevant interest rate. Where the annuity rate depends on the nominal interest rate, coverage against annuity rate risk is low; where payout is tied more closely to the real interest return, coverage against annuity rate risk is high.

Notes

1 Australia's Superannuation Guarantee, for example, guarantees only that a stipulated proportion of an employee's wage will be paid into a 'superannuation' or plan account. The government guarantees nothing about benefits, even in the event of loss of fund assets, although political independence may be tested in such an eventuality. Chapter 4 provides a formal analysis of the relationship between DC and DB plans, using option concepts.

2 Australian inflation currently runs at about 3%. The Australian government has been issuing CPI-indexed bonds since the mid-1980s. There are also privately issued indexed bonds, arising from private-sector infrastructure projects.

3 Statistical life expectancy of an Australian male retiring at 65 in 1998 was 15.49 years.

4 Adverse selection can of course only arise if individuals possess private information about their own life expectancy, information that they can successfully hide from any prospective insurer. Two studies (Hamermesh 1985, and Hurd and McGarry 1995, cited in Walliser 1997a) suggest that individuals are able to assess their own survival prospects based on factors generally unobservable to insurers. This finding supports the idea that there

is sufficient private information about longevity to cause adverse selection in annuities markets.

5 The compensating variation, or CV, is defined as the amount of money that must be taken from an individual after a change in order to make him or her exactly as well off as he or she was before the change. The equivalent variation, or EV, is the amount of money that must be given to an individual to make him or her as well off as he or she would have been after a proposed change, supposing that the change does not eventuate.

6 We ignore moral hazard, which in this context would occur if annuity purchase precipitated behaviour designed to prolong life. The question of moral hazard in the annuities market, associated especially with social security policy, has been investigated by Kuhn and Davies (1987) and Philipson and Becker (1998).

7 In Australia this procedure was adopted for motor vehicle third-party insurance, which is compulsory and had traditionally been provided by government insurers. Privatisation was initiated by initial random allocation with price control, followed by phased price deregulation and consumer choice of provider.

8 Blake (1999c) discussed some alternative arrangements, in what he called a 'four tier' structure, comprising an inflation-indexed annuity, a nominal annuity, a variable annuity and lump sums.

CHAPTER 6

Taxation of Retirement Saving

The taxation of retirement saving and payouts is one of the most subtle design issues in public finance. This is partly due to the current state of public finance theory, partly to the nature of retirement saving, and partly to the nature of political institutions and practice in most developed economies. In this chapter, we begin by reviewing the economic approach to taxation analysis in general. We emphasise the income versus expenditure tax debate because it turns out that an early design decision in pension taxation focuses on the choice of tax base. We then schematise and assess pension taxation[1] practice across a range of countries.

We conclude that the system most often found in developed countries is probably the best, but warn that this design, while common in most OECD countries, is less often associated with private mandatory retirement policies. Perhaps this is because the political temptation to tax the large capital accumulations in mandatory-funded systems is considerable. It may also be because some policy-makers believe that if a contribution is mandatory, the incentive issues central to the economic analysis of tax design are no longer relevant.

We argue that it is important for successful implementation of a mandatory policy that best practice is followed. First, while compulsion does indeed blunt behavioural response to taxation, mandatory retirement saving is usually integrated with a more extended voluntary system. It is usually possible to save more than the compulsory minimum within the framework of employment-related retirement provision. Any voluntary saving will take place at the margin, where incentives impact. Second, one of the advantages of mandatory private retirement saving is that it provides political insulation. This is seriously compromised if such saving is separately taxed – experience in Australia amply demonstrates this (see Appendix 1 for details).

In other words, two of the most important policy questions in pension taxation are: how preferential should the taxation of pension saving be? And at what point – contributions, earnings, benefits – should pension saving be taxed?

Some standard criteria in normative tax analysis

It is perhaps a truism to say that taxation alters economic behaviour. Behavioural changes occur because not all activities are taxed or taxed at the same rate. Taxation diverts economic activity from taxed to untaxed areas or from areas with higher taxes to areas of lower tax. No-tax areas include leisure, production within the household sector and 'cash economy' activity. In each case, behavioural change can take several forms. For example, more leisure might mean putting in less effort on the job, working short hours, beginning work later in the life cycle or retiring earlier.

It is conventional to approach the economic analysis of taxation with reference to three criteria: efficiency, equity and administrative simplicity. Of particular importance in the present context are the first two, which are used extensively in the popular debate on tax reform, but are often not well understood.

Efficiency

Efficiency, in this context, does not refer to the organisation of a single firm or industry. Rather, it is an economy-wide concept: resources are used efficiently in the economy as a whole if they cannot be reallocated to make someone better off without making someone else worse off.

The theory of price tells us that such an allocation of resources will occur in a competitive economy, provided certain conditions hold. These are never completely satisfied in practice. However, experience tells us that economies that rely on the price mechanism to perform most of the allocation task do a lot better over time than economies relying on alternative mechanisms, such as centralised control. This suggests that efficiency considerations may be of critical importance in the tax reform debate.

When economists talk of taxes being distortionary, they mean that the price mechanism is being interfered with in a way that is likely to adversely affect its capacity to allocate resources efficiently. There are, of course, occasions when taxes are used to help efficient resource allocation; for example, when the price mechanism fails because it is technically infeasible to implement (pricing use of a crowded city intersection) or when property rights cannot be satisfactorily defined (pollution). In these cases, taxes can be used to proxy the price system, given market failure, and can raise revenue as well.

But mostly, though necessary to raise revenue for transfer and other purposes, taxes distort prices. And what matters most is price distortion *at the margin*. For example, the tax paid on the last dollar earned will be more important in choosing whether to supply more or less labour than the tax paid on average. This sets the stage for the first element in any tax reform debate – which tax arrangements generate the least damaging price distortions, measured in terms of the costs of the resulting inefficient allocation of resources.[2]

In the context of income and expenditure taxation, three major price distortions emerge. The first is between marketed goods and leisure. One way or another, all market goods are taxed, either because inputs are taxed or because consumption is taxed. By contrast, leisure is untaxable (along with household production and cash economy activity). This fact almost certainly means that more leisure is consumed than would be the case in an economy without taxation.

The second is between consumption bundles at different points in time. An income tax bears more heavily on saving than an expenditure tax, and this effectively makes future consumption more expensive than current consumption. By contrast, an expenditure tax does not distort prices across time. In times of inflation the distortionary effect of an income tax may be even greater, as nominal returns can be taxed. In this case the post-tax real rate of return will fall even further below the pre-tax real rate of return, whereas under an expenditure tax the pre-tax and post-tax rates of return will be equal whatever the level of inflation.

Third, income taxes typically operate like an expenditure tax where owner-occupier housing is concerned, because the return on capital invested in owner-occupied housing (the imputed rent) is not taxed. This leads to an inter-asset price distortion, between housing and other productive investments, unless there are means of circumventing full income taxation when saving and investing.

Each of these effects is represented in the debate about the taxation of retirement saving, and will be expanded upon below.

Equity effects

The second major group of economic effects to be analysed relates to equity. The most common interpretation of equity in tax analysis relies on the notion of capacity to pay – the spread of the tax burden over poor and rich. If a tax bears disproportionately on the rich, it is said to be 'progressive'. If it bears disproportionately on the poor, it is said to be 'regressive'. This interpretation will be used here.

The index of economic welfare is important in incidence analysis. If 'income' is chosen as the index of welfare – with those with low current income called poor and those with high current income called rich – a given tax change may be regressive. If 'consumption' is chosen (those with high current consumption are rich, those with low current consumption poor), then the same tax change may be progressive.

More mechanically, choice of the consumer unit – individual, household, family, and so on – and time period – a year, a lifetime, and so on – make a significant difference to the measured distributional impact of a tax change. Time period choices matter in the present context because redistribution through government policy over the life cycle is more important than redistribution between consumers in the same age cohort. Most people benefit from government policy early in life (free schooling, student loans), pay taxes through their working life and receive government transfers after retirement (social security, subsidised health care).

These choices – over consumer unit, time period and welfare index – are important, not only because they determine the interpretations that can be drawn from a given set of data on a distribution of, for example, wealth, but because they generate quite different perceptions of the equity impact of a given tax reform. If perceptions drive policy, as is frequently said, then much caution must be exercised in interpreting distributional impacts of tax changes. This caveat is especially relevant in the context of retirement-saving taxation, where the consuming unit and time period choices are inevitably difficult, and the income–expenditure distinction is blurred.

These ideas are well illustrated by the debate between income and expenditure taxation. It is worth taking a step back from considering pension taxes specifically to examine this issue.

Income or expenditure taxation

The distinction between income and expenditure taxation may be usefully seen as centred on the taxation of saving. An expenditure tax levies outlays on consumption. An income tax does this, but in addition taxes income that is saved.

The idea that direct taxation should be based on expenditure or consumption, rather than income, has a long history and has many distinguished supporters. J.S. Mill, Alfred Marshall, Irving Fisher and Lord Kaldor have been among the advocates of expenditure taxation.

From time to time, the idea enjoys a renaissance, most recently in the 1970s, when the US Treasury and a major report in the United Kingdom both supported such a reform (see the US Treasury's 'Blueprints for Tax Reform', and the UK Meade Report (Meade 1978)).

A major theoretical efficiency argument in favour of an expenditure tax is that it avoids the distortion associated with the taxation of saving under an income tax. An expenditure tax levies present and future consumption at the same rate. It is therefore sometimes said to be 'neutral' between present and future consumption. However, an expenditure tax is not itself a lump-sum tax, and neutrality between two components of choice, while other price distortions are sustained, does not necessarily improve efficiency. An expenditure tax affects in particular the labour leisure choice. Since it is not the number of distortions that is relevant in welfare analysis, but the impact on allocation, this argument is not conclusive.

A rather different kind of efficiency argument focuses on the level of savings, rather than the distorting impact of the tax imposition. This may be important because there are other grounds for supposing that the level of saving in many economies is suboptimal.[3] However, the impact of taxation on saving and capital accumulation has been the subject of a longstanding debate (see, for example, Schmidt-Hebbel and Serven 1997). On one hand, it is argued that savers respond to the disincentives of high taxes, which in turn reduces capital and output growth, with potentially serious long-term consequences for living standards and economic development.

Alternatively, it is argued that aggregate saving and investment are determined by factors such as the riskiness of returns to saving and the sophistication of the financial system, with taxes having little effect on saving and investment decisions. In this view, savers can avoid paying taxes through careful tax planning, and the introduction of tax concessions is more likely to lead to savers enjoying windfall tax breaks by shuffling assets between different forms, than to an increase in aggregate saving.

It appears likely that both these arguments carry weight, differentiated by consumer type. For most consumers in developed economies, the major long-term capital accumulation channels remain housing purchase and employment-related pension saving, and the saving of this group is likely to be affected by saving tax treatment. For a minority of rich households, the alternative view outlined above may well be more correct. Although this group is small numerically, it may be responsible for a large fraction of aggregate private saving.

This debate is exemplified in the recent US literature on the impacts of tax-deferred saving schemes. Poterba, Venti and Wise (1996) contended that the bulk of contributions to tax-privileged IRA and 401(k) plans are net additions to private saving. On the other hand, Engen, Gale and Scholz (1996) argued that saving incentives have a strong effect on the allocation of saving or wealth, but little or no effect on the level of saving. In a further paper, Hubbard and Skinner (1996) concluded that further research on consumption and saving behaviour in general, and on variations in saving behaviour among similar individuals in particular, is needed before consensus on whether saving incentives increase the level of saving can be reached.

With these basic ideas in mind, we now turn to the comparison of alternative retirement saving tax regimes.

Alternative pension tax designs

It is frequently observed that it is possible to tax retirement saving at three points: on contributions, on fund earnings and on benefits. The situation is more complex than this, however, even at the level of taxonomy. Contributions and benefits can be taxed either in the hands of the contributor, which allows individual differentiation, or in the hands of the fund, which does not.[4]

At the moment, most countries tax either contributions or benefits (or sometimes both) in the hands of the individual. More often than not, the tax is levied on benefits only. Table 6.1 reports current practice for a number of countries. We report the taxation of contributions, investment fund earnings and benefits, and identify any specific pension taxes. If contributions or benefits (but not both) are taxed, and fund earnings are tax exempt, then this corresponds to an expenditure tax treatment of pension accumulations. A contributions plus earnings (or benefits and earnings) tax structure corresponds to income taxation. Most countries reported take the former approach.

Formal relationship between alternative pension tax designs

In policy debate one proposition is frequently encountered: that for a given revenue target it doesn't matter how pension saving is taxed. This belief is seriously mistaken, but to fix ideas, it is useful to begin by specifying the conditions under which the proposition would hold. We consider the case of proportional taxation, so that our analysis applies to both fund- and individual-based arrangements. No general equivalence can be demonstrated for progressive taxation, since the effective average and marginal tax rates will vary through the life cycle.

On these assumptions, it is trivial to show that contributions and benefit taxes are equivalent, if levied at the same rate. Consider a pension fund scheme spanning two years. A contribution, c, is made at

Table 6.1 Taxation of private pensions in selected countries

Country	Contributions	Investment fund earnings	Benefits[1] Income streams	Lump sums [2]
OECD				
Australia	Employer contributions tax deductible. 15% tax in hands of fund	Taxed[3]	Taxed (with 15% rebate)	Taxed at 15% above threshold
Austria	Tax deductible	Exempt	Taxed	Taxed at 50% of marginal income tax rate
Belgium	Tax deductible	Taxed[4]	Taxed (with tax credit)	Taxed at 16.5%
Canada	Tax deductible	Exempt	Taxed	Taxed
Denmark	Tax deductible	Taxed[5]	Taxed	Taxed at 40%
Finland	Tax deductible	Exempt	Taxed	Taxed at age-dependent rates
France	Tax deductible	Exempt	Taxed (some deductions)	No lump sums
Germany[6]	Employer contributions tax deductible	Exempt	Taxed	Taxed
Iceland	Employer contributions tax deductible	Exempt	Taxed	Taxed
Ireland	Tax deductible	Exempt	Taxed	Taxed with some exemptions
Italy	Tax deductible	Taxed[7]	Taxed	Taxed at 12.5%
Japan	Employer contributions tax deductible	Taxed[8]	Taxed	Taxed
Mexico	Tax deductible	Exempt	Taxed – subject to high tax-free threshold	Taxed above high threshold
The Netherlands	Tax deductible	Exempt	Taxed	Taxed
New Zealand	No tax deductions	Taxed	Exempt	Exempt
Norway	Tax deductible	Exempt	Taxed	Taxed
Portugal	Employer contributions tax deductible. Limited tax deductions for employee contributions	Exempt	Taxed (subject to specific rules)	Taxed (income tax rate on 20% of benefit)

Spain	Tax deductible	Exempt	Taxed	Taxed (lump sum included in global income and taxed at average personal income tax rate)
Sweden	Tax deductible	Taxed	Taxed[9]	Taxed
Switzerland	Tax deductible	Exempt	Taxed	Taxed
United Kingdom	Tax deductible	Exempt	Taxed	Taxed with some exemptions
United States	Tax deductible	Exempt	Taxed	Taxed (but eligible for concessions)
Other Latin America				
Argentina	Tax deductible	Exempt	Taxed	Lump sums tax
Chile	Tax deductible	Exempt	Taxed	Lump sums tax
Colombia	Tax deductible	Exempt	Taxed?	Taxed with some exemptions?
Peru	Taxable	Exempt	Taxed?	Taxed?
Uruguay	Tax deductible	Exempt	Taxed	No lump sums
Other Asia				
Korea	Tax deductible	Exempt	Exempt	Exempt
Singapore	Exempt	Exempt	Exempt	Exempt
Other Europe				
Czech Republic	Tax credit	Exempt	Exempt	Exempt
Hungary	Exempt	Exempt	Taxed	Taxed?

1 Unless otherwise stated, *taxed* refers to the personal income tax.
2 Only Australia allows unlimited lump sums.
3 Nominal earnings taxed at 15%, real capital gains taxed at 15%.
4 There is a tax of 0.17% levied on the assets of non-profit associations plus differential taxation of earnings of alternative assets.
5 Investment income in excess of 3.5% real is taxed.
6 This refers to the more common book reserve approach to financing pensions. Where pensions are financed through direct insurance, both company and employee contributions are taxed, there are no earnings to be taxed and benefits are taxed leniently (or not at all if paid as a lump sum).
7 Taxed at 50% company tax rate plus local taxes.
8 Pension fund asset returns in Tax Qualified Pension Plans taxed at 1.173% per annum.
9 Benefits are taxed as earned income where initial contributions were tax deductible, but are tax exempt if initial contributions were not deductible. Countries with mandatory private schemes are shaded.

Sources: Dixon (1982), Johnson (1992), Dilnot (1992), OECD (1994), Davis (1995), Bateman (1998), Queisser (1998) and Whitehouse (1999) the beginning of year 1, and earns a rate of return r, which is credited at the end of each year. At the end of year 2, the retirement benefit is paid. Assuming a rate τ_C on contributions, value of the benefit payout, P_C, is given by:

$$P_C = (1 - \tau_C)c(1 + r)^2 \qquad (6.1)$$

and the present value of tax revenue collections, PVT_c is:

$$PVT_c = c\tau_c \qquad (6.2)$$

The analogous expressions for a benefit tax are:

$$P_b = c(1 + r)(1 - \tau_b) \qquad (6.3)$$

and

$$PVT_b = c(1 + r)^2\tau_b/(1 + r)^2 \qquad (6.4)$$
$$= c\tau_b$$

Equivalence of P_c and P_b, and of PVT_c and PVT_b, is therefore guaranteed for $\tau_c = \tau_b$.

The equivalence of a tax on earnings is, however, a little more complicated. Assuming a tax rate τ_E on fund earnings, the value of the benefit payout, P_E, is given by:

$$P_E = [1 + r(1 - \tau_E)][c + cr(1 - \tau_E)] \qquad (6.5)$$

The present value of tax revenue collections, PVT_E is:

$$PVT_E = \frac{cr\tau_E}{(1 + r)} + \frac{c[1 + r(1 - \tau_E)r\tau_E}{(1 + r)^2} \qquad (6.6)$$

The relationship between τ_E and τ_c required to satisfy tax yield equalisation is obtained by combining (6.2) and (6.6).

$$\tau_c = \frac{r\tau_E(1 + r) + r\tau_E(1 + r[1 - \tau_E])r\tau_E}{(1 + r)^2} \qquad (6.7)$$

Substitution into (6.1), and rearrangement gives the result that subject to (6.7), $P_c = P_E$. That is, under our assumptions, the value of the retirement payout is the same, for equal tax yield, whether revenue is raised by a tax on contributions or a tax on earnings. It is straightforward to generalise this result to a many-period setting. Kingston and Piggott (1993) proved a Ricardian equivalence theorem along these lines, formulated in continuous time.

Table 6.2 Examples of different pensions tax regimes

		EET	TEE	TTE	ETT
Tax on contributions/benefits		30%	30%	15.565%	15.565%
Tax on earnings		0%	0%	15.565%	15.565%
Decade 1	Fund accumulation	50 312	35 218	40 969	48 521
	Tax	0	12 000	7 552	1 571
Decade 2	Fund accumulation	81 952	57 367	61 949	73 369
	Tax	0	12 000	11 420	6 151
Decade 3	Fund accumulation	133 492	93 444	93 674	110 943
	Tax	0	12 000	17 268	13 078
Decade 4	Fund accumulation	72 484	152 211	141 646	105 406
	Tax	144 960	12 000	26 111	85 903
Total	Fund	338 239	338 239	338 239	338 239
	Tax	144 960	48 000	62 352	106 703
	Present value of tax	21 620	21 620	21 621	21 621

Note: The analysis assumes that the individual earns $40 000 per annum for 40 years, 10% of earnings are paid as pension contributions, and the rate of return is 5%.

A numerical example of these design options, giving decade-by-decade values of tax collections and accumulations, is reported in Table 6.2. In this table we use the frequently encountered shorthand that indicates which of the three possible points of taxation attract tax and which are exempt. A contributions tax is represented by TEE (contributions taxed, earnings exempt, benefits exempt), and so on. The first two columns represent variants of an expenditure tax regime, while columns 3 and 4 report income tax variants. The table shows that benefits and contributions taxes at the same rate provide the same benefit payout and present value of taxes, while under an income tax different tax rates are required to provide equivalent benefits and tax values.

The EET principle can be seen as a tax deferral, since the benefits are taxed on receipt. As Table 6.2 shows, however, at any point in time through the accumulation period, the EET paradigm does result in a net reduction in the tax take of the government compared with TEE. It is this that leads to the erroneous conclusion that, even in the context of expenditure taxation, pension schemes provide a mechanism for tax avoidance that should be restricted.

An important implication of the above analysis is that while equal tax rates on contributions and benefits have equivalent impacts on tax revenues and benefits, the tax rate required for equivalent earnings taxation varies with the time span of contributions. Conversion of a fund earnings tax regime into an equivalent contributions or benefits tax regime, in circumstances where individual contribution periods differ, is thus not feasible. Combined with the difficulty of taxing accruing fund earnings differentially by individual, this makes earnings taxes very awkward to reconcile with broader tax design objectives.

This equivalence analysis assumes that there is no behavioural response to pension taxation. In practice, individuals are likely to respond to the pension tax regime they confront, as are fund investment managers, who are likely to be sensitive to pension fund tax rules when choosing asset allocations. We now turn to this issue.

Efficiency issues in pension taxation

The unifying thrust of the economic theory of tax design lies in the question it poses: how to minimise, or reduce, the economic cost of resource misallocations through the whole economy that will occur as taxes distort prices and the choices of agents are adversely affected. At an abstract level, it is possible to envisage a set of taxes levied at rates that minimise these costs for a given revenue target, and where appropriate, for given equity criteria. This is the optimal tax approach alluded to earlier.

The luxury of *de novo* tax design, however, is not available to policy-makers, who must wrestle with options that modify existing structures. Improvements (that is, changes which reduce distortionary cost), taking into account constraints imposed by unchangeable features of the tax system and equity concerns, are all that can be hoped for.

In this section we take this latter position as a starting point. We are therefore able to finesse issues of *de novo* tax design. We take as given that, at least in countries with well-entrenched income-based tax systems, the income tax base is here to stay, and that equally, major institutional features of the income tax, particularly the tax preference to owner-occupier housing, are permanent as well.

This allows us to consider what major resource allocation effects might result from alternative pension tax designs, given the existing tax structure, and what these imply for pension tax design. Perhaps the clearest resource allocation effect is the impact on aggregate saving, and the implied flow of domestic funds available for investment. Two further important effects are the allocation of assets in the economy generally and the retirement decision. All three are likely to be directly affected by pension taxation.

Aggregate saving and investment

In the context of pension taxation, the taxation of saving has special relevance because there are other grounds to suppose that the level of saving is suboptimal. These include the existence of a publicly funded age pension and undersaving by some groups in the community (for analysis of this latter phenomenon, see Bernheim 1994 and Laibson 1996). The compounding effects of capital income taxation are therefore likely to be especially costly.

It is sometimes argued that many developed economies with income taxes at the centre of their fiscal systems are already part way to a consumption tax reform, and that the impact of the income tax on aggregate saving and investment is therefore overstated. Owner-occupier housing, which constitutes a major component of privately held wealth, at least in developed economies, is typically taxed under what is effectively an expenditure tax regime. This is because the return on capital invested in owner-occupied housing (the imputed rent and, typically, the real capital gain) is not taxed. Pension accumulations are often given similar tax preference.

While capital income taxation applies elsewhere, these two channels of tax-preferred saving – housing and pension – are seen as a partial move towards expenditure taxation, albeit through specific saving deductions from an income tax base. They are easily the most important long-term saving channels for most individuals who undertake any significant saving on their own behalf. Granting tax preference to saving through these channels is therefore likely to generate a welfare improvement relative to comprehensive income taxation.

The significance of inter-asset distortions

If, however, pension saving is not given expenditure tax treatment, as is the case with owner-occupied housing, price distortions are introduced that adversely affect asset choice. There is evidence to suggest that applying differential tax regimes to various forms of saving leads to greater efficiency costs than taxing all forms of saving the same.

Owens and Whitehouse (1996) compared the tax treatment of different saving vehicles in a number of countries. In Canada, France, the United Kingdom and the United States pensions have the most generous tax treatment, being tax subsidised in the United Kingdom and given expenditure tax treatment in the other three countries. In Germany, pensions are behind housing, which receives a large tax subsidy, while in Japan pensions have the least generous tax treatment in comparison with housing, equities and bank deposits, and are taxed at a higher rate than the comprehensive income tax.

An important paper by Hamilton and Whalley (1985) suggested that a hybrid system, offering expenditure tax treatment to housing (but to no other form of saving), is dominated from an efficiency standpoint by both a pure expenditure tax regime and a comprehensive income tax regime.

Using a dynamic general equilibrium model of the Canadian economy, fully taxing imputed housing income at the marginal rate applying to other capital income increases aggregate economic welfare by 0.3 %. For a switch to pure consumption taxation, the estimated gain is 0.8 %. That is to say, the efficiency costs of the inter-asset distortion introduced by a hybrid system can dominate the efficiency gains from the reduced price distortion on intertemporal choice.

A second contribution, by Jonathon Hamilton (1987), used Merton's (1969) continuous time model of the lifetime portfolio choice and consumption decision to analyse the taxation of capital income. Two assets were modelled – one risky and one safe. Three types of capital taxes were considered: a tax levied on wealth each period; a tax on interest income, that is the returns to safe assets; and a tax on dividend income – the returns to risky assets. Hamilton then calculated the efficiency costs for these different kinds of capital taxes, relative to a consumption tax. He also modelled a general wealth tax.

While the compensating variation (a measure of efficiency cost) for a general wealth tax is about 1% of initial wealth, the compensating variation of an interest income tax is 3.2%, and is dramatically higher for a dividend tax. In the latter two cases, all revenue is raised from the return to one type of asset. The static distortion from asset misallocation thus dominates the dynamic distortion from the misallocation between current and future consumption. Interestingly, although the two analyses use entirely different approaches, the Jonathon Hamilton result is consistent with the Hamilton–Whalley finding that inter-asset distortion resulting from a hybrid income expenditure tax system dominates the costs of the distortions of a comprehensive income tax.

As we indicated above, housing has been a longstanding manifestation of inter-asset distortion in many developed economies. Australia provides a good example. In 1997, Australian dwelling assets amounted to 54% of private marketable wealth. Australian owner-occupied housing is untaxed, and does not severely curtail eligibility for age pension payments. About 70% of households with retired heads depend predominantly on the age pension for their income, even though most retirees own their homes outright.

A second type of inter-asset distortion arises when pension funds face earnings taxation. This is because, in all economies, various financial assets are affected by differential capital income tax treatment. Again the Australian experience provides an example of this, where pension funds may hold assets that may not give the best financial return but that provide tax credits.

Since the introduction of dividend imputation in 1987, most dividends from Australian companies provide offsetting credits for recipient entities subject to the Australian income tax, while dividends from foreign countries do not. In this way, there has arisen an inter-asset distortion whereby managers of Australian pension funds seek credits to offset against the 15% taxes on contributions and investment earnings. With the statutory corporate income tax at 36%, funds enjoy a 21% tax credit. This typically enables fund managers to reduce the 15% tax to somewhere between 3 and 10%, depending on the fund's asset allocation decision. Wood (1997) argues that Australian fund managers are likely to respond by overweighting Australian equities.

Current tax policy thus reinforces the pre-existing tendency in Australia and elsewhere towards so-called 'home bias' in asset allocations. The proportion of offshore investments in Australian superannuation funds has fluctuated between 15 and 20% in recent years, which is high compared to several other OECD countries. In Australia, however, the domestic market is itself less diversified than in the United States. For example, major industries such as pharmaceuticals and electronics are almost non-existent. Black and Litterman (1992) find that the benefits of international portfolio diversification are larger in Australia than in major OECD countries, which report lower international diversification. It follows that Australia's target level of international diversification might be higher than those of economies with greater domestic diversification.

The retirement decision

There has been a trend over the last three decades towards earlier retirement, although this has brought about costs in terms of high budgetary outlays for government and lower productive capacity for the economy as a whole. There are reasons for thinking that an income tax treatment of pensions may further encourage early retirement.

Between the early 1970s and the early 1990s, the labour force participation of men aged 60 to 64 in OECD countries dropped from three-quarters to one-half. This is discussed in detail in Chapter 2. Possible causes can be debated. What is now beyond doubt is the fact of flexibility on the work/retire margin. In the context of pension tax design, this represents the labour leisure choice.

The interaction between taxation and retirement has been neglected in the literature. Public finance specialists have tended to see the retirement decision as a special case of the labour leisure choice; labour economists have not viewed taxation as an important determinant of the retirement decision.

Table 6.3 Fund accumulation by decade under contributions and earnings taxes

	10% tax on pension contributions			8.696% tax on pension fund earnings		
	Contributions	Earnings	Tax	Contributions	Earnings	Tax
Decade 1	36 000	9 280	4 000	40 000	9 302	886
Decade 2	36 000	37 757	4 000	40 000	37 044	3 528
Decade 3	36 000	84 142	4 000	40 000	80 395	7 657
Decade 4	36 000	159 699	4 000	40 000	148 139	14 110
Total	144 000	290 878	16 000	160 000	274 880	26 181

Note: The analysis assumes that the individual earns $40 000 per annum for 40 years, 10% of earnings are paid as pension contributions, and the rate of return is 5%. Administrative charges are ignored.

While in an important sense retirement is simply one dimension of the lifetime labour leisure choice, there are many important institutional features associated with retirement that do not bear so directly on labour supply decisions taken earlier in the life cycle. Important among these are the availability of social security and pensions, and the tendency for the retirement decision to be irreversible.

Current policy in many developed countries encourages premature retirement. In Australia, this occurs through the age pension and lump-sum entitlement to superannuation accumulations from a relatively early age. Applying the Mitchell–Fields rule (see Chapter 2, page 36) indicates that progressive income tax compounds this effect, since a prospective retiree can look forward to moving from heavily taxed wage income to somewhat lower but lightly taxed retirement income.

Taxing the investment earnings of pension fund accumulations will, under the Mitchell–Fields rule, further encourage early retirement. Because increments to pension accumulations late in the life cycle are weighted relatively heavily towards investment earnings rather than contributions, the taxation of earnings relative to an equal present value tax on contributions will lead to an earlier retirement decision.

Table 6.3 illustrates how this may occur by comparing contributions and earnings tax impacts on a given accumulation over four decades, for an equal tax yield measured in present values. Under the earnings tax, final decade tax collections are more than three times those under the contributions tax. It follows that working an extra year is worth less to an individual in an earnings tax regime than an equivalent person in a contributions tax regime.

Along with the historical evidence on the flexibility of the work–retire margin, appeals to the high efficiency costs of compounding distortions suggest that earnings taxes encourage retirement behaviour that will become increasingly costly in mandatory retirement saving policy environments. Of course, many countries with PAYG social security systems face similar problems, although the reason is badly designed benefit formulas, rather than badly designed tax and transfer policies.

Other issues in pension taxation

Equity

Equity and redistribution are best viewed as the outcome of a combination of policies. It is in our view futile to expect the taxation of retirement saving to target equity as an independent objective.[5] At the same time, however, a pension tax regime, which is consistent with broader tax-related equity objectives, is likely to serve those goals effectively, and therefore to be more resistant to political attack on equity grounds.

There are two equity issues that arise specifically in the context of retirement saving. The first relates to the taxation of pension fund earnings. This is likely to impact relatively unfavourably on those whose typical working lives involve early full-time labour force participation, followed by broken participation patterns later in life: a pattern associated with female employment. Such a contributions pattern will lead to heavy reliance on the investment earnings component of the final pension accumulation, and its taxation is therefore likely to adversely affect this group, relative to a tax on benefits or contributions. Table 6.3 illustrates this proposition.

The second relates to owner-occupied housing purchases. Suppose, as is usually the case, owner-occupier housing is granted expenditure tax status. If a mandatory retirement savings plan is introduced, it is likely that wages will be lower as a result. To the extent that owner occupation is standard in such an economy, some relatively poor employees will be forced to downgrade their owner-occupier housing purchase, or even be forced out of the housing market altogether. If mandatory retirement saving is taxed under an income tax regime, then these individuals are being forced out of a lightly taxed asset into a heavily taxed one. This inequitable outcome is avoided if expenditure tax treatment is accorded mandatory retirement saving. It is one particular manifestation of the more general idea that if the income taxation of owner-occupier housing is infeasible, then efficient asset allocation and equity will both be well served by more general income taxation concessions.

A further point to bear in mind concerning equity in the context of the debate between income and expenditure taxation is that a switch between the two is likely to have significantly different effects on different age cohorts. For example, a switch from income to expenditure taxation is likely to penalise all those households who have accumulated their assets under an income tax, and now must spend the proceeds under an expenditure tax regime. On the other hand, a young household will reap the benefits of the additional taxation of the old resulting from this reform, and will therefore enjoy somewhat lighter taxation through its life cycle. This effect should not be over-blown – indexed transfers will ensure that the poorer households within the older cohorts are largely protected from this negative impact. Nevertheless, intergenerational issues are frequently overlooked in the context of tax reform and should at least be noted. They have particular relevance to the introduction of mandatory retirement saving schemes, because the equity implications of the transition from PAYG to full funding are intergenerational.

Tax expenditures

It is argued by some commentators that the preferential tax status for pension saving relative to other financial saving, in particular the concessional tax rates applying to employer contributions and to fund earnings, results in a significant revenue cost. This point has its origins in the tax-expenditure methodology developed by Surrey (1973); it has been emphasised in the context of Australian occupational superannuation by Knox (1991; 1993), although he carefully qualified his results. Essentially, the employee is seen as enjoying tax saving from the superannuation tax concessions. In the Australian case, the 1997–98 revenue cost was estimated to be $9.1 billion, or around 1.6% of GDP and is generated largely by the tax deductibility of employer contributions and the concessional tax rate applied to superannuation fund income. The implication here is that taxing superannuation in line with other financial saving would lead to increased revenues.

However, there are a number of objections to this proposition. First, a simple single-year analysis of this type fails to capture the effects of the time dimension; a long-term perspective on superannuation fund contributions shows that the present value of the cost of the superannuation tax concession is much reduced once lower future age pension payouts are factored in (Brown 1993; Bateman and Piggott 1992). Another objection is that they are based upon an assumption of no behavioural impact; however, the removal of tax concessions would change the relative attractiveness of superannuation savings, with the likely result of consumers increasing current consumption, or transferring savings into other concessionally treated forms, such as housing.[6] Third, calculations are typically made on a single-year basis, with contribution and earning tax concessions added together; but once the contributions tax revenues are recouped, earnings tax revenues would be lower.

These calculations, then, although consistent with the tax-expenditure concept, give a misleading picture of both revenue cost and equity impact. The negative equity result is based on two assumptions that are unrealistic for most people: that equivalent saving would be undertaken in the absence of the tax concessions; and that this saving would attract full income taxation, as it would in a conventional savings bank account.

Neither is it clear that the comprehensive income tax should be accepted uncritically as a natural benchmark. An appealing alternative is the expenditure tax. On this basis, it has been calculated that, for the Australian case, over-taxation through superannuation taxes stood at $775 million in 1995–96 (Clare and Connor 1999a). Official tax-expenditure estimates reported under-taxation of $8.3 billion. Similar exercises for the UK case (Dilnot and Johnson 1993a, b) report dramatic reductions in estimated revenue cost from pension tax preference.

Taxation and political insulation

A major advantage of mandatory private retirement savings schemes is the long-term political insulation that they offer their beneficiaries. However, governments are still able to compromise this independence by changes to pension taxation. We pointed out in the introduction to this chapter that while either contributions or, more often, benefits taxation, using income tax rate schedules, are standard in countries with PAYG second-pillar systems, this is less common in economies with private mandated retirement saving regimes. Seen from the perspective of political insulation, alignment of pension taxation with the personal income tax rate schedule, combined with a saving deduction, is equally important for these regimes. Once established, they help protect beneficiaries from sudden and arbitrary tax change.

The development of taxation policy towards private retirement saving in Australia provides a dramatic illustration of how pension tax changes can compromise the political independence of private mandatory saving regimes, if they are not integrated with broader tax design. The development of the Australian second pillar was accompanied by various tax changes (see Appendix 1). But rather than leave pension taxation as part of the income tax, the reforms applied taxes to superannuation funds themselves. These changes thus signalled separation of the taxation of superannuation from personal income taxation. The consequent lack of integration between the two tax systems has led to numerous legislative and regulatory changes, which have undermined the credibility of the superannuation tax system, and has produced an instability in the taxation of retirement benefits, which is likely to persist until integration is re-established.

Of the many changes to the taxation of superannuation that have been introduced since the announcement of the second pillar, one example serves to illustrate the consequences of a lack of tax integration. This is the so-called 'superannuation surcharge'. It sought to reverse the momentum of the previous decade, towards taxing superannuation funds rather than individuals, by linking fund tax liability to the financial circumstances of the individual fund member, with the intent of addressing perceived inequities in superannuation taxation.

The surcharge has highlighted the tension between the concept of fund taxation and the equitable tax treatment of fund members. By making a legal entity – a superannuation fund – liable for tax payments computed on the basis of the taxable income of other legal agents – fund members – the surcharge has created unacceptable administrative complexities. It has also further undermined public confidence in Australia's retirement provision policies, and generated severe price distortions that have already led to undesirable behavioural responses by superannuation fund members and employers. These might be expected to have serious economic efficiency implications as the new tax becomes entrenched in our public finance system.

Ultimately, of course, all taxes are paid by individuals. If equity is a serious concern, then taxes that directly assess individuals offer a ready means of individual differentiation. If pension taxes could be converted back from a fund basis to an individual basis, equitable tax treatment could be achieved in a much more consistent and administratively straightforward manner.

Pension tax design assessment

So, which pension tax design is best? We are inclined to the view that an expenditure-based tax is to be preferred. Specifically, benefits taxation is best. This judgement is partly based on the formal analysis presented above, suggesting that earnings taxes are likely to be awkward, and to lead to greater efficiency costs compared with expenditure taxes. It is reinforced by various non-formal considerations that have been raised in this chapter. Because the debate is somewhat complex, it may be worth recapitulating the main points against taxing pensions fund earnings, before considering the choice between contributions and benefits taxation.

The taxation of pension fund earnings

Even if capital income as a whole is taxed, the earnings from pension funds should not be. This is because:

- enforced preservation funnels the individual disincentive effects of such taxation into a relatively narrow timeframe late in the life cycle, where it is especially likely to induce socially inefficient retirement and saving decisions
- it adversely affects asset allocation, penalising interest-paying securities and tending to discourage international diversification
- the taxation of pension fund earnings is likely to impact relatively unfavourably on women whose typical working lives involve early full-time labour force participation, followed by broken participation patterns later in life.

This issue of pension earnings taxation is likely to become more important in many industrialised countries over the next couple of decades. With population ageing, retirement saving will increase and tax-preferred pension fund saving will be an attractive retirement saving channel. This transformation will be magnified because for many households discretionary financial saving only becomes possible towards the end of working life. Prior to that, saving (of a more or less rationed type) takes the form of human capital formation, owner-occupier housing purchase and children's education. In addition, equivalent income tends to rise sharply relatively late in the working life of many households, with the departure of children from the family home, or their entry into the workforce.

To the extent that pension fund assets rise, the introduction of a tax on earnings will be increasingly tempting for policy-makers confronted with a non-pension capital income tax base that is, generally speaking, shrinking. International financial deregulation has provided many new opportunities for capital income tax avoidance, and lower inflation, if sustained, will mean that the capital income inflation tax take will erode. Countries that have already introduced taxes on pension fund earnings include Japan, Australia, New Zealand and Brazil.

Furthermore, countries with generous unfunded national pension schemes are viewing future commitments implied by the ageing of the population with alarm, and have begun to manoeuvre to reduce their future liabilities. Debate on the best means of converting unfunded pensions to a funded base is already active, and if such conversions

occur to any significant extent this will add further to the funded
pension capital base. There has been a very substantial increase in
pension fund assets over the last decade in a number of countries, and
already there have been suggestions that pension fund earnings may
provide an appropriate tax base on which to levy revenue to fund such
conversions. In our view, this idea is to be resisted, in spite of its
expediency.

Contributions or benefits taxation

The formal model presented earlier suggests that contributions and
benefits taxation are equivalent, for the same present value of tax
revenue. Other considerations, however, tend to favour benefit taxation
over contribution taxation, and, indeed, this is the tax design model
predominant in Table 6.1.

- Benefits taxation allows the application of the progressive tax rate
  schedule to take account of variability in investment performance
  and the form of withdrawal. This can be seen as more equitable than
  a contributions tax.
- With defined-contribution or accumulation pension plans, progressive benefit taxation would appear to entail more investment
  risk-sharing by the government than contribution taxation, beyond
  that implied by a social welfare safety net. Insurance against investment risk is difficult to procure in a DC context, and the social
  benefits associated with this risk-sharing could be significant.
- A third and more pragmatic consideration weighing in favour of
  benefits taxation, as opposed to contributions taxation, is that contributions are frequently made by employers. As Dilnot (1992) points
  out, such contributions are clearly a cost of earning income, and
  must therefore be deductible to the employer. In the case of DB
  schemes, imputed employee benefits will be unclear, and contribution taxation in the employer's hands will therefore be very difficult.
  If employee contributions are taxed, the likely result will be a simple
  financial one: tax-deductible employer contributions will replace
  taxable employee contributions.
- On the other hand, one might expect increasing movement towards
  taxation of contributions, with some anticipated relief of benefit
  taxation. This expectation stems from the observation that governments are under pressure to reduce deficits or increase surpluses on
  a current-year basis. Exactly this substitution was made in Australia
  in the late 1980s. This would seem to expose retirement saving
  schemes to an unacceptable degree of political risk, since, as the

current generation ages, the possibility of reintroducing a degree of benefit taxation emerges as a tempting proposition for government. A further argument against benefit taxation is one of tax arbitrage – the phenomenon that workers are in high marginal tax brackets throughout their working lives, but may be in lower marginal tax brackets after retirement. Benefits taxation will therefore be lower in present-value terms than contributions taxation, if both are taxed at the contributor's marginal tax rate. This point must be accepted as far as it goes. However, its importance can easily be overestimated. Where pension accumulations are available as lump sums, they are more often than not treated more generously than the personal income tax would allow, even when contributions are tax deductible.

Conclusion

Existing evidence suggests that capital income taxation inhibits economic growth by reducing saving and investment, to the extent that labour may be better off under a consumption tax regime than under a capital income tax regime. Although more controversial, there is also some evidence to suggest that poorer or less well-educated households will not undertake sufficient life-cycle saving to provide for contingencies in later life. This is seen to occur both through lack of foresight and lack of discipline.

In broad terms, the challenge of pension taxation design within an income-based tax structure is to fashion taxation (and transfer) policy that aligns domestic saving as closely as possibly with efficient self-provision levels, and at the same time provides adequate retirement income, while minimising distortions affecting the timing of retirement and asset choice. A number of specific implications follow.

The income tax structure, even if it exists only on a limited basis, provides the opportunity to encourage life-cycle, rather than short-term, saving and investment. An example is concessional taxation of owner-occupier housing, an asset less fungible than many other forms of wealth. In the same way, the concessional taxation of pension saving is in most cases contingent on preservation until late in the life cycle.

The two questions that arise are: how concessional should the taxation of pension saving be? At what point – contributions, earnings and benefits – should pension saving be taxed?

The limited evidence on the efficiency costs of inter-asset price distortion indicates that they are much more significant than has traditionally been thought. If owner-occupier housing receives expenditure tax treatment, then this suggests pension saving should be accorded similar tax treatment. This rules out the taxation of pension fund earnings. A fund earnings tax is probably a poor tax for other reasons as well: it is likely to significantly distort effective prices across financial assets offering returns in different forms, and it is likely to have a significant and adverse impact of its own on retirement timing.

The choice between contributions and benefit taxation is less clear cut but on balance, taxation of benefits is preferred. This is because it is easier to treat employer and employee contributions symmetrically; it reduces the political risk that future government will tax the retirement benefits of the baby-boom generation, after contributions have already been taxed; and there may be social benefit from government sharing the investment risk of individual contributors under a DC scheme.

More generally, political insulation of mandatory private retirement savings can be seriously compromised by arbitrary taxation. It follows that a pension tax regime which is integrated with the established broad-based taxes – usually a progressive income tax – is desirable, since it will reduce the political scope for arbitrary tax intervention.

Little research has been undertaken on pension fund taxation. In particular, the links between the financial planning literature and pension taxes do not appear to have been explored. In addition, the literature on the links between taxation and retirement timing, and portfolio choice, is sparse, and offers little firm guidance to policy-makers. Finally, limited attention has been paid to the specific question of whether income taxes should be encouraged at all in less developed economies (LDCs), and on the implications that the alternative – a direct expenditure tax regime – might have for pension taxation. This question assumes immediate importance because many LDCs are now considering or implementing pension reform, in some cases the private mandatory paradigm. All these issues will require urgent research attention as pensions, and their taxation, become more important globally.

Notes

1 In this chapter, we will use the terms 'retirement saving taxation' and 'pension taxation' interchangeably. In both cases, we refer to employment-linked retirement saving.
2 This cost is given various labels: 'efficiency cost', 'excess burden', 'welfare cost' and 'deadweight loss' are all used interchangeably. A well-known principle in public finance is that efficiency cost increases disproportionately with the tax that induces the price distortion (sometimes referred to as the Harberger l^2 rule). Compounding impacts can therefore

be expected to impose disproportionately high efficiency costs. This point is relevant to a number of choices affected by pension taxes.

3 It is important to note that the price distortion against future consumption from saving taxes carries no implication for saving behaviour. For uncompensated changes in tax and price, the direction of saving adjustment is ambiguous. The substitution effect of an increase in the price of future consumption, however, will necessarily imply lower saving. The efficiency cost of saving taxes derives from their impact on intertemporal consumption choice.

4 Australia's superannuation surcharge provides an example of an attempt to introduce individual differentiation within fund taxation. The extraordinary administrative complexity and cost that this incurs are detailed in Bateman and Piggott (1999b).

5 This view is supported by Atkinson et al. (1999), who find that there is little to distinguish the intra-generational equity impacts of the Australian TTT tax structure and the EET structure observed in most OECD countries.

6 Clark and Wolper (1997) review some of the literature regarding behavioural responses to changes in the tax treatment of pensions.

CHAPTER 7

Administrative Costs and Charges

Central to the debate over whether private mandating dominates public provision in second-pillar retirement support is the issue of administrative costs and charges. While public provision permits centralised administration and often incorporates old age social security administration with other programs such as unemployment insurance, competitive private service providers do not enjoy these advantages of scale and scope. As well, private mandatory retirement saving introduces (or expands the scope for) investment management costs. Any costs associated with private mandating will be reflected in administrative charges,[1] which will erode the rate of return that might otherwise be realised: expressed as a percentage of assets under management, even charges of 1 or 2% can make a major difference to retirement accumulations. Further, high administrative charges will reduce the credibility of reforms towards private mandatory retirement saving.

The economic analysis of administrative costs and charges for retirement saving is undeveloped.[2] There is broad agreement that public provision is less costly than private provision (although counter examples can always be found)[3] and that there are economies of scale in account administration and asset management. But we have little understanding of the impact of policy design, industry practices and regulatory arrangements. This chapter seeks to investigate the impact of these factors for administrative costs and charges. The emphasis here is on the accumulation phase of private mandatory retirement saving.

A formal analysis of administrative charges

Charges, like taxes, can be imposed on contributions, assets under management and/or benefits (see Kingston and Piggott 1993 for an analogous treatment of the taxation of retirement saving). The charges may be ongoing or one-off and applied at a flat or variable rate. A sensible comparison of administrative charges (whether between public and private arrangements or alternative private schemes) requires the standardisation of the metric under which they are calculated. Unless all charges are expressed as a percentage of contributions, or of benefits or of assets under management, it is difficult to gain any sense of their relative magnitudes.

We start with the simplifying assumption of variable (percentage) charges imposed on contributions or assets or benefits. And, as a further point of clarification, we consider contributions gross of administrative charges (as is the case in Australia), rather than net of charges (as is the case in Chile). (A similar approach in continuous time is taken in Diamond 1999b.) Consider mandatory private retirement saving by an individual over a period of T years. A contribution C is made at the beginning of each year, which earns a real rate of return of $r\%$ per annum. Assuming a percentage charge on contributions of β_C, and a discount rate R, which is assumed to be equal to the real rate of return r, the present value of the administrative charges over the T years of retirement saving, PVC_C, is given by:

$$PVC_C = \sum_{t=1}^{T} \frac{\beta_C C_t}{(1 + R)^t} \tag{7.1}$$

Similarly, if instead we assume a percentage charge on assets under management of β_A, the present value of administrative charges, PVC_A, is given by:

$$PVC_A = \sum_{t=1}^{T} \beta_A \left[\frac{\sum_{x=1}^{t} C_x (1 + r)^{x-t} (1 - \beta_A)^{x-t}}{(1 + R)^t} \right] \tag{7.2}$$

Finally, if we assume a percentage charge on the final accumulation (benefits) of β_B, the present value of the administrative charges, PVC_B, is given by:

$$PVC_B = \beta_B \frac{\sum_{t=1}^{T} C_t (1 + r)^{T-t}}{(1 + R)^T} \tag{7.3}$$

A number of results follow.

Firstly, if we set $PVC_A = PVC_B$

$$\sum_{t=1}^{T} \frac{\beta_C \, C_t}{(1+R)^t} = \beta_B \frac{\sum_{t=1}^{T} C_t (1+r)^{T-t}}{(1+R)^T} \tag{7.4}$$

and rearrange, we find that equation 7.4 reduces to $\beta_C = \beta_B$. This result implies that for a given present value of charges (and in the absence of taxes, or other withdrawals such as insurance premiums) a percentage charge on contributions of β_C is equivalent to a percentage charge on benefits equal to β_B and will lead to a decline in the retirement accumulation of β_C per cent, as compared to the no-tax case.

Further, if we set $PVC_C = PVC_A$ and rearrange, we can specify a relationship between β_C and β_A (and consequently β_B and β_A) as follows:

$$\beta_C = \beta_A \left\{ \sum_{t=1}^{T} \left[\frac{\sum_{x=1}^{t} C_x (1+r)^{x-t}(1-\beta_A)^{x-t}}{(1=R)^t} \right] \middle/ \sum_{t=1}^{T} \frac{C_t}{(1+R)^t} \right\} \tag{7.5}$$

The relationship between β_C and β_A thus depends on the accumulation period T, the pattern of contributions C and the real rate of return r.

These results can be clarified with numerical simulations. Using the above methodology we can derive values of β_C, β_A and β_B, which result in the same present value of administrative charges, or equivalently the same retirement accumulation, for a given accumulation period (T).

Table 7.1 illustrates the impact of alternative charge regimes of varying magnitudes over the accumulation phase of mandatory private retirement saving. Contribution periods of 20 and 40 years, and real rates of return of 5% and 10% are considered. We make the simplifying assumption that the charge rates are constant over the entire accumulation phase.

The essential message is that the relationship between alternative charge types and their impact on retirement accumulations varies by charge type, length of accumulation period and rate of return. For 20 years of continuous contributions (and an annual real rate of return of 5%), a 1% per annum assets charge would reduce the retirement accumulation by 11%. This is equivalent to an 11% contribution charge (or an 11% benefits charge). For 40 years of contributions, the 1% asset charge would reduce the retirement accumulation by 22.1% – equivalent to a 22.1% charge on contributions or benefits. Where the rate of return increases to 10%, a 1% assets charge over 40 years would equate to a contribution or benefits charge of 25.8%.

Table 7.1 Reduction in retirement accumulations due to administrative charges – impact of contribution period and rate of return[1]

	Charge as proportion of assets under management (%)	Equivalent[2] contribution or benefit charge (%)	Equivalent[2] contribution or benefit charge (%)
		$(r = 5\%)$	$(r = 10\%)$
20 years of	0.5	5.7	6.4
contributions	1.0	11.0	12.3
	2.0	20.7	22.9
	3.0	29.1	32.2
40 years of	0.5	11.8	13.9
contributions	1.0	22.1	25.8
	2.0	38.7	44.7
	3.0	51.2	58.4

1 The analysis assumes contributions of 9% of wages to a DC pension fund, real wages growth of 1% per annum, no taxes on contributions or fund earnings and no insurance premiums. Administrative charges are deducted from account balances.
2 The present value of administrative charges is equivalent for each charge regime.

Comparing charge regimes

A major difference between asset charges and contribution (and benefits) charges relates to transparency. The impact of a contribution or benefits charge on retirement accumulations is straightforward: a charge of x% of contributions or benefits will (in the absence of withdrawals such as taxation or insurance premiums) reduce the retirement accumulation by x%. But, for assets charges, the impact on retirement accumulations is a function of the charge rate, the accumulation period and the rate of return: the longer the contribution period and the higher the rate of return, the greater the impact of a given charge rate on the retirement accumulation. (Whitehouse 2000 discusses the robustness of the charge measures to changes in the assumptions.) Transparency would be further impeded where composite charge regimes were used.

A related difference is the time profile of asset charges compared with contribution charges. Figure 7.1 compares the dollar amount paid in asset charges and contribution charges over 40 years of retirement saving. The illustrative charge rates of 1% per annum of assets or 22.1% of contributions generate an equivalent present value of charges over the 40-year accumulation period.

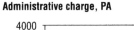

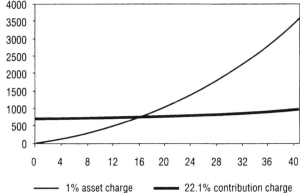

Figure 7.1 Time profile of administrative charges
Note: Simulation assumptions – as for Table 7.1 with a real rate of return of 5%.

While the present value of administrative charges is equivalent under both the contribution and asset charge regimes, there are quite different impacts on account balances in any given year: where mandatory contributions are set gross of charges (and consumption patterns where mandatory contributions are set net of charges). Under the given assumptions, a 1% per annum assets charge for 40 years is equivalent to a 22% contributions charge on every contribution. However, in year 5 the 1% assets charge is equivalent to 5.3% of the annual contribution; in year 25, 36% of the annual contribution; and in year 40, 74% of the annual contribution. It follows that contribution charges have a greater impact on those with a short contribution period, while asset charges have a greater impact the longer the contribution period (and therefore, the larger the asset base).

Consequently, the different charge types may have different impacts on retirement saving behaviour. For individuals, contribution charges – which are high as a proportion of assets in the formative years of retirement saving – may deter participation in the formal labour market (or lead them to collude with employers to gain exemption). Assets charges, which assume greater importance over time as the asset base grows, may act to bring forward the retirement decision (an analogy can be drawn with the impact of contribution and earning taxes; see Kingston and Piggott 1993). But, for the retirement saving providers, contribution charges allow set-up costs to be covered, while asset charges ensure a smooth flow of revenue.

This analysis illustrates the differing impacts over time of (front-loaded) contribution charges and (back-loaded) asset charges for individual retirement savers, and indicates that any comparison of retirement saving administrative charges should be made over the entire accumulation period, rather than at a point in time.

A taxonomy of administrative costs and charges

Administrative costs relate to the three main functions involved in the organisation and management of private mandatory retirement saving: the collection of contributions and the administration of the individual accounts, the investment of assets and the payment of benefits (a comprehensive listing of tasks involved in private retirement provision can be found in Diamond 1999a). Within each of these there may be marketing requirements.

Contributions may be collected directly from fund members, or through intermediaries such as employers, clearing houses or government agencies. Account administration involves the setting up and ongoing administration of individual accounts. This includes creating accounts, updating balances, managing records, organising withdrawals and transfers, deducting administration charges, insurance premiums and taxes, as well as communicating with fund members, complying with government requirements (for example, audits or actuarial assessments) and reporting to relevant government agencies.

Account administration marketing costs will arise where there is choice of financial intermediary and where functions are contracted out to specialist service providers. The amount of the marketing costs will depend on the target audience: individual employees, employers or trustees. Marketing costs could be minimised through limited or group choice, but this raises principal–agent issues.

The investment function involves the management of members' assets. Assets may be invested directly or through (active or passive) managed funds. As well, members may be offered portfolio choice. Investment marketing costs will arise to the extent that investment managers seek the business of the retirement saving organisation and will be exacerbated where individuals are offered choice, either of portfolio type or of a specific investment manager.

Finally, costs arise with the payment of benefits. For defined contributions in individual accounts a point of separation arises between the accumulation (retirement saving) and decumulation (retirement benefits) phase. Administrative charges will differ by the form of benefit allowed (and taken) and the organisation used to deliver these benefits.

The costs may be recouped by a variety of charge regimes. If charges were to reflect costs a likely scenario would be: a high entry fee to reflect start-up costs, an ongoing (possibly flat) account administration charge, an investment fee to reflect the costs of funds management and an exit fee. In practice, however, multiple charges are levied that may not reflect the profile of costs and, at any point in time, administrative costs and charges may differ. While costs and charges are likely to converge in the long run, the administrative charges facing retirement savers will reflect a range of additional factors including industry structure, institutional practices and the regulatory arrangements.

Industry structure and institutional practices

As discussed in Chapter 3, industry structure and institutional practice vary internationally. In Australia, Chile and many of the 'second-generation' reformers in Latin America, Denmark, Hong Kong, Hungary and The Netherlands the contributions are made directly to pension funds (known as superannuation funds in Australia, AFPs in some Latin American countries and pension funds elsewhere). The norm is for employee choice of pension fund, except in Australia where the policy requires employer choice of superannuation fund. In most cases the pension funds are 'open' to any person choosing to contribute, although in Australia, mandatory contributions are also made to 'closed' industry funds. However, Australian industry funds are increasingly becoming 'open' or public-offer funds. Specialist pension fund administrators are widely used in developed countries.

In the United Kingdom private retirement saving is characterised by its diversity. Workers can participate in private retirement saving through DB or DC occupational schemes, a personal pension provided on an individual or group basis, or a 'stakeholder' pension. Eligible arrangements therefore include employer and employee payment of contributions, 'closed' and 'open' pension funds, and contracting out to specialist pension fund administrators.

In a third group of countries a centralised agency collects and distributes contributions to the pension funds (Mexico, Argentina and Poland) or directly to investment managers (Sweden and Latvia). Under the Swedish arrangements, the public pension agency keeps all member records and aggregates individual contributions to make a single transfer to each mutual fund. One of the proposals for privatisation of US Social Security involves the government undertaking similar collection and administration functions (Diamond 1999a).

These differences in the organisation of retirement saving may affect administrative charges through their implications for choice (and there-

Table 7.2 Regulation of administrative charges – an international comparison[1]

Charge regulations	Country
No restrictions	Australia,[2] Hong Kong, United Kingdom (except stakeholder pensions)
Cross-subsidies to low-paid workers	Mexico
Limits on charge type	Argentina, Chile, Colombia, Peru, Hungary
Partial ceiling on charges	Poland
Variable ceiling on charges	Sweden
Fixed ceiling on charges	El Salvador, Kazakhstan, United Kingdom (stakeholder pensions)
Competitive bidding	Bolivia

1 Derived from Whitehouse (2000), Table 1.
2 Except on small-amount accounts (of less than $A1000) where the fees and charges are waived.

fore marketing costs), economies of scale, competitive practices and governance. Of particular importance is the governance of the institution responsible for managing and/or investing the retirement accumulations. Critical features are likely to include whether they operate in the public or private sector, whether they are profit-maximisers or non-profit organisations, and the composition of any board of trustees or directors.

Regulation of charges

Charges can be regulated by type and amount. Table 7.2 summarises international practice, which ranges from unregulated (Australia and Hong Kong), to considerable regulation (Sweden and Bolivia).

In Australia, administrative charges are determined freely and are generally a combination of flat-rate charges per account (and/or percentage contribution charges) and charges calculated as a percentage of assets under management. An exception is the 'charge waiver' offered to small-amount accounts (referred to as 'member protection' and ensures that administrative charges cannot reduce accounts below $A1000 – although amounts for taxes, losses and insurance can be deducted).

Until recently, charges in the United Kingdom have also been freely determined. However, for the newly introduced 'stakeholder' pensions, providers are restricted to assets charges and a ceiling of 1% of assets currently applies (Blake 2000b).

In Chile, asset management charges are banned: only charges on contributions and transfers are permitted. The 'second-generation'

Latin American reformers take differing approaches to charge regulation (see Queisser 1998 and Mitchell 1999). In Mexico charges must be approved by regulators (and must apply equally to all members), while in Colombia charges can only take the form of a percentage of contributions. Peru disallows flat-rate charges on contributions or assets under management, while Argentina allows flat-rate charges on contributions and entry fees, but no asset management fees.

Restrictions on charge amounts are increasingly used. Pension funds in Poland can levy proportional charges on both contributions and assets, but the asset-based charge is limited to 0.6% per year. Similarly, in Kazakhstan fees cannot exceed 1% of contributions plus 10% of the fund's investment return. In Sweden only mutual funds, which satisfy minimum charge requirements, are allowed to participate in the private mandatory retirement saving arrangements.[4]

Finally, when Bolivia introduced private mandatory retirement saving in 1997, asset management rights were auctioned off to two investment companies, chosen partly on their ability to minimise fees. In 1999 fees were 0.5% of wages (or 5% of incoming contributions) plus 0.23% of assets (over the accumulation phase of mandatory saving, this corresponds to 0.47% assets per year). However, there have been no marketing costs, as contributors were assigned to an investment company and have not been allowed to switch, and the assets are largely invested in government bonds (James et al. 1999).[5]

Comparing alternative regimes

The crucial issue is the extent to which administrative charges reduce retirement benefits. This is often difficult to determine at first glance. Charges can be imposed in a myriad of ways and total accumulation charges will be sensitive to the contribution period, rates of return and regulatory requirements. However, by applying a standard set of assumptions, the formal analysis derived earlier can be used to calculate a common metric to allow comparisons of quite different charge regimes.

Administrative costs and charges in Australia and Chile are considered first. This is an instructive comparison as it encompasses many points of difference between private mandatory retirement arrangements covering industry structure and governance, regulation of charges and policy design.

Estimating administrative charges in Australia

There are five broad types of superannuation fund in Australia: corporate, public, industry, retail and self-managed. Industry funds and

Table 7.3 Charging schedules for illustrative superannuation funds

Average industry fund	Illustrative master trust
Administration charge of $A47.84 per annum + Investment management fee of 0.3–0.7% of assets,	Contribution fee of up to 4.5% of each contribution + Member fee of up to $A42.36 to $A70.80 per annum + Asset administration fee of up to 0.95% of assets + Investment management fee of 0.4–1.08% of assets

Note: Estimates based on industry fund averages and illustrative master trust charges for 1998–99.

master trusts (a form of retail fund) are the most common destinations of the mandatory contributions and will be the focus of the analysis that follows (the Australian system is outlined in Appendix 1).

Charging schedules for the average industry fund and an illustrative master trust are summarised in Table 7.3 (a detailed discussion of the estimation of Australian charges is set out in Bateman and Valdes-Prieto 1999).

Industry funds are multi-employer funds originally established in the 1980s to accept contributions under award superannuation. They have adopted a fairly uniform charge regime, comprising flat-rate account management charges deducted from accounts and percentage investment management charges, deducted from returns. Some industry funds impose different account management charges for active and inactive accounts and for different contribution types. Few industry funds charge for exits, but with increasing portfolio choice, some funds have introduced switching charges. In 1998 annual administration charges for employer contributions ranged from $A16.64 to $A72.80 per account (the average annual charge for employer contributions, weighted by assets, was $A47.84 per account). A typical industry fund would spend around 80% of this on account administration (typically contracted out to a specialist administrator), around 15% on the running costs of the trustee and around 5% on marketing and member communications. Currently there are almost no direct marketing costs incurred by industry funds as they generally have a captive membership – due to their origins in award superannuation. However, as a result of recent policy developments in Australia, industry funds are increasingly becoming open (or public-offer funds) in order to expand their membership base.

Investment management charges are more difficult to determine, as reporting of aggregate investment fees is not required. Industry funds tend to use a variety of asset managers and fees vary between asset types. Anecdotal evidence suggests that the asset management charges for the largest industry funds in 1998 were of the order of 0.3 to 0.7% of assets under management.[6]

Master trusts are a form of retail superannuation fund. They are used by individuals, small employers who do not wish to establish company superannuation plans, and increasingly by large companies wishing to contract out of pre-existing corporate superannuation schemes. The administrative charges of master trusts are less uniform and there is considerable variation by plan size. Charges fall into two categories: product charges, and investment and fund charges. Product charges may include contribution charges, member charges, and transfer and terminating fees. Investment and fund charges refer to ongoing management charges, investment charges, switching charges, fund expenses, and trustee and custodian fees. The illustrative master trust used for this comparison is specifically designed for medium to large employers. Charges include a contributions fee of up to 4.5% of contributions, a flat-rate or member fee that reduces with plan size,[7] an annual asset administration fee of up to 0.95% of assets, and additional asset management charges for each investment option. These latter charges range from 0.4% per annum for an in-house capital secure fund to 1.08% per annum for an externally managed international share fund. There are no exit fees but switching charges apply to some investment options. Importantly, discounts are available for large plan and for very large schemes, where a tailored charging schedule would be negotiated – it is likely that these would eliminate the contribution charge and the annual asset management fees.

Cost comparisons – industry funds and master trusts

The charges identified in Table 7.3 reveal little about the impact of industry fund or master trusts administrative charges on retirement accumulations. However, if we assume that these charges apply over the entire accumulation period, we can use the formal analysis developed earlier to convert the disparate charging schedules to any of three comparable metrics. The results, summarised in Tables 7.4 and 7.5, indicate the wide range of accumulation charges associated with master trusts: for plans with few members and/or assets these are considerably higher than for industry funds.

Table 7.4 Industry funds – charges under alternative assumptions

Investment charges (% assets)	Decline in retirement accumulation (%)	Equivalent contribution charge (%)	Equivalent assets charge (%)
0.3	8.1	6.8	0.37
0.4	10.2	8.5	0.47
0.5	12.2	10.2	0.57
0.6	14.2	11.8	0.67
0.7	16.1	13.4	0.77

Note: Simulation assumptions – see Table 7.1. Australian superannuation taxes are included in these simulations. We assume a contributions tax of 15%, an effective earnings tax of 8% and an annual charge for insurance premia of $A67.60. Note that with the introduction of taxes and insurance premia, the equivalence between, β_C and β_B no longer holds.

The analysis of industry funds in Table 7.4 shows that, over the accumulation phase of private mandatory retirement provision, and for a typical range of investment charges (0.3 to 0.7% of assets), the reduction of retirement accumulations ranges from 8.1% to 16.1%. This equates to contribution charges in the range 6.8% to 13.4% of contributions and assets charges in the range 0.37% to 0.77% of assets under management.

The analysis of master trusts is summarised in Table 7.5. It is clear that total accumulation administrative charges differ markedly by plan size. For the small- to medium-size plans the overall impact of the current charge regime is to reduce the retirement accumulation by one-third (or twice the impact of the upper range of the average industry fund). However, this impact reduces the larger the plan (in terms of both members and assets). For large plans, the overall impact is a reduction in the retirement accumulation of about one-quarter. For very large plans the impact would be a reduction in the retirement accumulation of around one-fifth. Under the given assumptions this would be analogous to an industry fund with industry average account-management charges and investment charges of 0.9%.

However, it is becoming increasingly common for large companies to contract out their superannuation arrangements to master trusts. In these circumstances a schedule of fees and charges would be individually negotiated. In some circumstances the overall impact would be comparable to that of an average industry fund.

The analysis raises a number of issues. First, how can we account for this difference in charges? Second, can this difference be sustained? And third, what do these results imply for policy design? To answer the

Table 7.5 Representative master trust – charges under alternative assumptions[1]

	Decline in retirement accumulation (%)	Equivalent contribution charge (%)	Equivalent assets charge (%)
Small – medium plans (assets < \$A2 billion)			
< 100 members	33.4	27.7	1.81
> 1500 members	32.7	27.2	1.76
Large plans (assets \$A2–5 billion)			
< 100 members	26.4	22.0	1.35
> 1500 members	25.7	21.4	1.30
Very large plans[2] (assets > \$A5 billion)			
< 100 members	20.4	17.0	1.01
> 1500 members	19.6	16.4	0.96
Contracted-out corporate plans (typical negotiated charges)	8.8–14.8	7.3–12.3	0.4–0.7

1 Simulation assumptions – as for Table 7.1.
2 Charges are also lower where contributions are electronically transferred. For the very large plans with more than 1500 members, this translates to a reduction in the final benefit of 19.5% rather than 19.6%, an equivalent contribution charge of 16.2% and an equivalent assets charge of 0.95%.

first question one needs to consider some fundamental differences between industry funds and master trusts while the answer to the second will depend upon the evolution of retirement income policy and industry practice. The third question can be answered more constructively following consideration of the administrative charges of Chilean AFPs.

Estimating administrative charges in Chile

In Chile the private mandatory retirement saving takes place through Administratoras de Fondes de Pensiones (AFPs). AFPs were specifically introduced in 1981 for the management of private mandatory retirement savings. There are currently nine AFPs. The AFPs are limited liability corporations. Ownership and control are varied with some organised on an industry basis and others controlled by Chilean or international financial groups. All AFPs are 'open' to all employees (further details on mandatory private retirement provision in Chile can be found in Bateman and Valdes-Prieto 1999).

Table 7.6 Administrative charges of Chilean AFPs, December 1998

AFP	Charges subtracted from account Flat rate (peso)	Charges added to contribution – expressed as:		
		% salary	% total contribution	Market share (% members)
Aporta	480	2.3	17.76	0.40
Cuprum	0	2.09	16.47	7.01
Habitat	490	1.89	15.13	21.77
Magister	450	2.25	17.51	1.48
Planvital	1000	2.15	17.13	5.46
Proteccion	390	2.21	17.53	3.82
Provida	195	1.92	15.21	36.25
Santa Maria	490	1.99	15.81	15.58
Summa Bansander	385	2.07	16.27	8.22
Average	363	1.98	15.71	

Note: Total contribution refers to the mandatory contribution of 10% of wages plus the additional charge to cover costs plus insurance premiums.
Source: Derived from Table 9, Bateman and Valdes-Prieto (1999)

Charges are highly regulated. Asset charges are specifically disallowed (and prohibited since 1988), charges cannot be levied on inactive accounts and the same charge schedule must apply to all members. In fact, only two types of charges are allowed: charges on contributions, and a sales load charged when a worker transfers his or her account balance into the AFP. Administrative charges are calculated in advance by the AFPs and apply *in addition* to the mandatory contribution of 10% of earnings (insurance premia also apply *in addition* to the 10% mandatory contributions). When the AFP system commenced in 1981 the average fee was over 20% of contributions, but has gradually fallen since then. Charges for the nine AFPs existing in 1998 are summarised in Table 7.6.

In 1998 an average charge of 1.98% of salary applied *in addition* to the 10% mandatory contribution. As well, flat-rate charges of varying amounts were subtracted from accounts. In total, administrative charges averaged 16.8% of contributions.[8] Under reasonable assumptions (including no further reductions in charge amounts over time), this corresponds to an annual asset charge of 0.78%.

Comparing administrative charges in Australia and Chile

A comparison of the Australian and Chilean charges is reported in Table 7.7. The average AFP charge of 16.8% of contributions and 0.78% assets

Table 7.7 Total administrative charges – Chile and Australia[1]

Current charging schedule applied to the accumulation phase	Average industry fund	Illustrative master trusts	AFPs
% gross contribution[2]	8.1–16.1%	7.3–27.7%	16.8%
% assets under management	0.37–0.77%	0.41–1.81%	0.78%

1 Simulation assumptions: for Australia, see Table 7.3; for Chile we assume 40 years of contributions, a real rate of return falling from 7% per annum in the first 20 years to 5% per annum in the final 20 years (to reflect the transition from a developing economy) and real wages growth of 2% per annum.
2 We report % gross contribution as the Chilean charges are in addition to the mandatory contribution.

lies between the analogous contribution charges for the average industry funds and most of the representative master trust arrangements (except for very large plans and tailored corporate plans).[9] Importantly, an implication of the Chilean practice of applying charges *in addition* to the mandatory contribution is that charges reduce current consumption rather than retirement accumulations.

In the absence of empirical analysis, we speculate that the large differential in total administrative charges of Australian industry funds and master trusts and Chilean AFPs can be explained by a combination of differences in the organisation of the private mandatory retirement saving, governance, historical ethos and the regulation and disclosure of charges. The relevant differences are summarised in Table 7.8.

The organisation of private mandatory retirement saving

In Australia the mandatory retirement saving is organised around superannuation funds and in Chile through AFPs. Both of these are analogous to pension funds. In Australia, the nature of the mandate requires employer choice of fund. This, combined with the existence of longstanding employer superannuation practices, has meant little switching of accounts and, for industry funds – which have a captive membership (and therefore do not operate in the retail market for member accounts) – very low marketing costs. By comparison, master trusts operate in the retail market for member accounts: they must attract individuals and employers and therefore face higher marketing costs than industry funds. Master trusts, and increasingly industry funds, offer portfolio choice.

In Chile, the nature of the mandate is that employees choose AFPs and can switch freely between the nine AFPs. However, AFPs do not offer

Table 7.8 Retirement saving organisations in Australia and Chile

	Industry funds	Master trusts	AFPs
Characterisation	Industry superannuation fund	Retail superannuation fund	'Open' pension fund
Historical	Industrial relations, associated with support of labour unions for low-cost superannuation	Personal superannuation, sponsored by large financial conglomerates	Specifically introduced for private mandatory retirement saving
Nature of mandate	Employer choice of retirement saving organisation	Employer choice of retirement saving organisation	Employee choice of retirement saving organisation
Regulation and disclosure of charges	No restrictions except charge waiver for small-amount accounts Mandatory contribution set gross of charges	No restrictions except charge waiver for small-amount accounts Mandatory contribution set gross of charges	Restrictions on charge type Mandatory contribution set net of charges
Governance	Mutual – stakeholders are fund members Trustees – participating employees and employers, equal representation	Embedded in a corporate structure, stakeholders include shareholders Independent trustees	Embedded in corporate structure, stakeholders include shareholders Independent trustees
Services provided	Life and disability insurance, some portfolio choice, group discounts on home and business loans and health insurance, retirement planning advice	Life and disability insurance (tailored), choice of portfolio and investment manager, access to financial services provided by promoter of master trust	Life and disability insurance, phased withdrawals, agency for public (minimum) pension
Level of service	Moderate	High	Moderate
Market structure			
– member accounts	Captive (but increasingly open)	Retail	Retail
– asset management	Institutional	Institutional	Institutional
Marketing and distribution	Little marketing – historically captive membership No distribution network No commissions paid	Substantial marketing Wide distribution network Commissions paid	Substantial marketing Wide distribution network Commissions paid

portfolio choice and policy design (particularly the relative rate of return requirement) has led to all AFPs offering similar portfolios. Salespeople working on commission have facilitated excess switching by sharing their commissions, or providing gifts such as bicycles or mobile phones. These practices have led to huge AFP marketing costs (which in 1998 accounted for around 45% of total AFP costs), although regulations introduced in late 1997, which require requests for switching to be made in person, have significantly reduced switching. It is unclear how these differences will evolve as Australian policy moves towards greater employee choice of fund and industry funds increasingly seek members outside their traditional clientele.[10] As well, the core business of master trusts is gradually changing from individuals and small employers to large employers wishing to contract out corporate superannuation plans.

Governance

Another difference relates to fund governance. In the current context governance refers to both the form and philosophy of the entity responsible for the management and investment of the contributions. Industry superannuation funds are non-profit entities, set up with the sole objective of providing low-cost superannuation to workers covered by industrial awards. The funds were (and many still are) governed by boards of trustees with equal representatives of participating members and employers who are sympathetic to low-cost mandatory private retirement saving. While they continue to operate as 'closed' funds, the unique relationship between members, employers and trustees helps to address the agency issues that result from (the Australian policy of) employer choice of superannuation fund.

The governance of Australian master trusts and Chilean AFPs is quite different. Both are set up as 'open', or public-offer, arrangements with the promoter managing the fund as a business venture. In contrast to industry funds, master trusts and AFPs are essentially 'for profit' organisations, with the trustees (in the case of master trusts) or board members (in the case of AFPs) having no direct relationship with members. Under the Australian arrangements, the master trust form is less able to address the agency problems that arise with employer choice of superannuation fund.

Regulation

There are also important differences in the regulation and transparency of charges. While administrative charge types are regulated in Chile, they are considerably more transparent than in Australia. Most charges are calculated in advance and *added to* the mandatory contribution. With the exception of a charge waiver for small-amount accounts, Australia does not regulate charges. Disclosure of fees and charges is required only for 'open' (public-offer) superannuation funds: the requirement being disclosure of the type of charge and the periodic charge specification. There is no requirement that the composite impact of all charges be reported in a comparable format. 'Closed' industry funds are not required to disclose fees and charges, although many report weekly administration charges and/or annual asset fees in their annual reports.

Services

While it may be argued that the higher costs associated with master trusts reflect different services provided, it is unclear what is required beyond account administration, asset management and payment of benefits. Similar services are provided by industry funds, master trusts and AFPs. Thus far, however, master trusts have offered greater invest-ment choice (including choice of specific fund manager), and are generally associated with financial conglomerates, which can offer employers a complete package of financial services. It may also be argued that the higher costs are associated with better performance, but little can be said in the absence of comparable data (specifically risk-adjusted rates of return).

In the Australian environment, it is possible that master trusts thrive because they can utilise the distribution networks and marketing services of their promoters. By contrast, industry funds have no distribution network, do not pay commissions and, with an historically captive clien-tele, spend little on marketing. This has made it difficult for industry funds to attract members outside the traditional 'award' workers, but this is changing, as more industry funds become public-offer funds.

Other issues

These observations raise an important principal–agent issue. Under Australian legislation employers are responsible for fund choice, yet they have little incentive to choose the fund that will maximise net-of-charges returns. This issue is partly addressed in the case of industry funds that are characterised by participating trustees and an ethos of low-cost retirement saving. For master trusts, however, the additional feature of no employee trustee representation and commercial management leaves employees without representation in the determination of their retire-

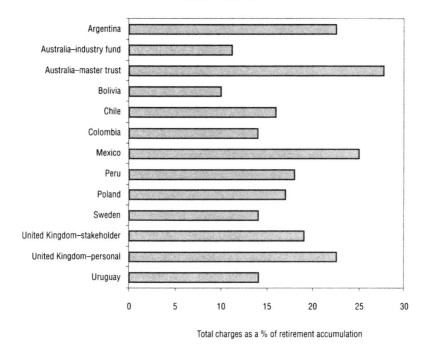

Figure 7.2 Total administrative charges – international experience
Source: Whitehouse (2000) Table 2, author's calculations

ment income interests. It is, however, unclear whether the unique governance characteristics of Australian industry funds can be maintained over the long term.

Other, more general, differences between Australia and Chile relate to set-up costs, coverage, access to economies of scale, and the level of economic development. Set-up costs were lower in Australia, which used the pre-existing institutional and regulatory framework. As well, the Australian arrangements exempt very low-income earners from the mandatory contributions and allow greater use of specialist service providers. More generally, the Australian economy and financial system are more developed.

International experience

The estimates of total accumulation administrative charges for Australia and Chile can be compared with similar estimates for a range of countries with private mandatory retirement savings. Figure 7.2 summarises the international experience.

Administrative charges are lowest in Bolivia, followed by Australia (industry funds), Colombia, Sweden and Uruguay. Administrative charges are highest in Argentina, Mexico, the United Kingdom (personal pensions) and for Australian master trusts.

As discussed in the case of Australia and Chile, we suggest that the differences in the organisation of private mandatory retirement saving, governance, transparency and the regulatory environment are probably the most important determinants of international differences in administrative charges.

Total administrative charges are higher where the retirement saving organisation operates in the retail market for member accounts; for example, Argentina, Mexico, the United Kingdom (personal pensions) and Australia (master trusts). These organisations are likely to have large marketing budgets as they seek to attract and retain members. However, marketing costs are nil in Bolivia, where workers are allocated to one of two pension funds, and minimal for 'closed' Australian industry funds.

However, even in an environment of employee fund choice and aggressive marketing, charges can be minimised through specific charge regulations. In Sweden, only mutual funds, which satisfy minimum charge requirements, are permitted to enter in the market for mandatory retirement savings. Another factor, which may minimise Swedish administrative charges, is the use of a clearing house to collect contributions and administer accounts. Costs, and therefore charges, can also be minimised through the use of clearing houses, although Mexico and Argentina must be outliers here.

Market structure is also important. While large numbers of pension funds and investment managers may enhance competition, there are significant economies of scale and scope in this industry (James et al. 1999; Mitchell 1998a).

Governance also differs internationally. The broad alternatives are 'for profit' or 'non-profit' entities and 'participating' or 'unrelated' trustees or board members. Australian industry funds are an example of 'non-profit' entities with participating trustees: the board of trustees comprises equal numbers of participating employees and employers, and the funds were established with the philosophy of providing low-cost retirement saving. Australian master trusts and the Chilean and 'second-generation' Latin American reformers are examples of the latter. Total accumulation charges are considerably lower for Australian industry funds.

Also relevant are transparency and disclosure of charges. In some Latin American countries – Chile, Colombia, El Salvador and Peru – charges are imposed on top of the mandatory contribution. This ensures that members are fully aware of the amount of the administrative charge, and that the mandatory contribution itself is not dissipated by charges. Under the analogous Australian arrangements the mandatory contribution of 9% is dissipated by the accumulation charges, insurance premia and taxes.

Transparency would also be achieved where there is full and meaningful disclosure of fees and charges. While this is currently not required in Australia, it would seem to be essential where some choice of retirement saving organisation is required.

Conclusion

We began by emphasising the analogy between taxes and charges for retirement accumulations and economic behaviour. At a formal level, the two are the same from the point of view of the individual. We then argued that sensible comparison of charges across policy designs and between alternative regimes requires the standardisation of the metric under which charges are calculated. Unless all charges are expressed as a percentage of contributions, or as a percentage of assets under management, or as a percentage of the final accumulation, it is difficult to gain any sense of their relative magnitudes.

The analysis and discussion suggest that administrative charges associated with private mandatory retirement saving are determined by a complex combination of industry structure, institutional practices, governance and regulatory requirements. This points to a number of stylised facts, which should be considered in the design of private mandatory retirement saving arrangements:

- There are considerable economies of scale and scope in account administration and asset management.[11]
- Transparency, through full (and standardised) disclosure, may contain administrative charges.
- Administrative charges may be moderated where governance of the retirement savings organisations reflects member interests (rather than profit-maximisation).
- Individual choice increases marketing costs but group choice introduces agency issues.
- Passive asset management is less costly than active management.

As well, the charge type is also important. Charges levied on contributions, assets or benefits will have differing impacts on the behaviour of both providers and fund members. Contribution charges, which will generate more up-front revenue than asset charges, may be preferred for immature systems with large set-up costs. But contribution charges will dissipate account balances in the early years of retirement saving and may deter participation. Further, while contribution charges may be easier for fund members to understand, they provide fund managers with income irrespective of performance.

By comparison, asset charges will generate more revenue as the scheme matures and may encourage providers to maximise fund returns. As back-loaded charges, their impact will be greater for older workers so they may encourage early withdrawal from the labour force. However, the impact of asset charges is likely to be less understood by fund members.

Notes

1 At the outset we noted the difference between charges and costs. Costs may be recouped by a variety of charge regimes that, in the short run, need not mirror actual costs.

2 There is a disparate mix of research covering costs and charges in Chile and Australia (see Bateman and Valdes-Prieto 1999), Mexico (Mitchell 1999) and the privatisation of US Social Security (see Mitchell 1998a, James et al. 1998, Diamond 1999a and b, James et al. 1999).

3 The measurement of public pension costs is likely to be deficient. However, private arrangements do offer the potential for higher returns, better service, more diverse products and significant economy-wide benefits.

4 The formula used to determine charges depends on the price charged for voluntary savings in the mutual fund, the value of the mandatory contributions attracted and the total value of mandatory pension assets managed.

5 However, this may change: switching was allowed from 2000 and new firms can enter the market after 2002.

6 A survey of public-offer industry funds showed a range of between 0.05% and 1.5% of assets (Rice Kachor 1999), and a wider survey of all industry funds indicated an average of 0.51% of assets (Hely 1999).

7 For plans with more than 1500 members it is $A42.36 per annum, reduced by $6 per annum for electronic transfers.

8 These official figures are complicated by the practice of commission-sharing by AFP salespeople, which reduces the 'effective' contribution rate. For example, 30% commission-sharing would reduce the effective contribution rate to 14%. As well, many agents provide gifts to entice workers to switch AFPs. Commission-sharing and gifts are ignored in this analysis.

9 Bateman and Valdes-Prieto (1999) report similar findings, using a slightly different methodology They consider a representative worker rather than a full working-life worker – where representative workers are assumed to face varying periods of unemployment and in Australia hold more than one mandatory retirement saving account. As well, they estimate single-year and total accumulation charges and present their results in purchasing power parity (PPP) US dollars.

10 The government supports employee choice of fund but cannot get the
   legislation passed by both Houses of Parliament. The proposed legislation
   will require employers to elect one of three models: limited choice of four
   funds, unlimited choice, or negotiating an agreed fund as part of a
   Workplace Agreement.
11 Mitchell (1998a) reports that in the United States, products aimed at the
   retail market are around three times as expensive as wholesale products.

CHAPTER 8

Conclusions

This book has provided an account of the most important economic and institutional aspects of structural pension reform. It has focused particularly on mandated private retirement saving schemes, in which employees or employers are required to contribute to a privately managed fund to help provide for the employee's retirement.

There is debate over whether this pension reform model is the best, or whether reforms moving policy in the direction of mandatory plans are desirable. We have canvassed this question and find ourselves sympathetic to this policy, especially where there is not a pre-existing second pillar. Much, however, depends on the detail of implementation. Further, no clear conclusion emerges over whether this will always be a worthwhile policy reform as a substitute for pre-existing social security structures.

In undertaking this project our primary aim was to study the role of institutional design features in implementing a mandatory retirement saving policy. We have documented that mandatory defined-contribution (DC)-based retirement saving is feasible. Examples include both *de novo* implementation, and full or partial replacement of public-defined contributions. Countries embracing this policy reform include examples from the developing countries of Asia, the transition economies, Latin America and OECD countries. Mandatory retirement saving reforms have taken several different paths, determined partly by pre-reform retirement arrangements, and partly by the specific imperatives that fuelled the reform process.

To an increasing degree, governments are resorting to mandation as the vehicle for delivering public services and transfers. Where a generation ago increased taxes provided a natural mechanism for funding public provision, this is no longer the case. Social security reform is a prime target for this change in the orientation of public policy. Population ageing, combined with likely disproportionate increases in non-functional longevity, implies dramatically increased public-sector obligations to the old in coming decades. These burgeoning outlays, combined with increasing pressure for a smaller public sector, have made this an attractive policy reform for governments.

Mandatory privately managed plans are generally of the defined-contribution type so rates of return are important, as is the management of investment risk in a life-long context. Governance must be carefully specified and administrative cost must be contained. Inter-cohort risk-sharing – a strong point of publicly provided defined benefits – must receive special attention. Because retirement insurance, including retirement income streams, are to be sold in the private market, adverse selection issues must be addressed.

This catalogue, extensive though it is, already assumes the existence of a robust legal and financial system, in which long-lived contracts spanning decades may be reasonably assured. In the absence of such infrastructure, it is difficult to see how a private mandatory retirement saving system can operate successfully. Some less-developed economies may not have sufficiently well-established financial markets to adequately support a retirement provision policy of this type.

The structure of contributions

An early issue in policy design relates to the institutional framework, as this has implications for governance, market structure and administrative costs and charges. A crucial question relates to the extent of intermediation between the contributor and the assets. International practice differs and the preferred approach is unclear.

In terms of contributions, preliminary questions include: what proportion of wages should total compulsory contributions be? Should this proportion be contingent on the contributor's age or pre-existing accumulation? (Switzerland provides an example of age-dependent contribution rates.)

Related policy issues include the legislative responsibility for, and the nature of, the contribution. Four interrelated policy specifications are involved here. Should the employer or employee be legally obligated to make the contribution? Should the law require only that a specified payment be made, or should the requirement be cast in terms of a net (of administrative charges and other outlays) payment? Who should select the financial institution responsible for investment? And how should administrative charges that may be levied on the account be regulated, if at all?

International practice varies. In Chile the employee is responsible for both payment and institution choice, the required payment is set net of administrative charges which may be levied on contributions only: this pattern has been replicated in the more recent mandatory policies appearing in Latin America. Also, in Chile compulsion ceases once the contributor is clear of potential reliance on the first pillar. In Australia, by contrast, the employer faces legal responsibility for contributory payment, and may select the financial intermediary maintaining the account. The contribution is defined gross of administrative charges, and there are no regulations on charge structure.

Suppose the contribution payment and the selection of institution are the legal obligations of the employer. Suppose further that the contribution is set gross of administrative charges. (This is roughly the case in Australia.) As a result, in the absence of complex trustee-type governance, no party to the transaction has any interest in controlling the size of administrative charges. The employee ends up paying these charges, in the form of reduced net contributions or reduced returns, but he or she has no say in the matter. The trustee structure of pension funds in Australia helps to mediate this difficulty.

Suppose, on the other hand, that the employee has legal responsibility for contribution payment and choice of financial institution, that the contribution is specified net of administrative charges, and that charges are regulated to apply to contributions only. (This is roughly the case in Chile.) As a result, competing institutions have an incentive to outlay large sums on marketing promotions, in order to attract employee accounts. Promotions may include gifts to employees who choose to switch between institutions. These charges are spread over both existing and new accounts, and increase the amount all employees must pay each period. Further, charges are regulated, and are therefore unlikely to accurately reflect the separate resource costs of administration and investment.

It is important that overall policy is internally consistent. It would appear to be sensible to have the contribution level specified net of administrative charges (and other outlays such as insurance premiums or taxes), but to make this meaningful, some control over charges is required, and this inevitably involves a mismatch between cost and charge. The idea that the agent responsible for paying the administrative charge should choose the financial institution is also appealing, but leaves open the scenario that if the employer is liable, he or she will choose a low-cost but low-quality provider.

One possible response to this issue, suggested by current UK proposals, is that some default level of service is specified, and associated administrative charges are payable by the agent legally responsible for

contribution payments. Additional services can be made available at an
additional charge, and these may be chosen and paid for by the
employee.

Investment strategies and portfolio regulation

Once the contribution structure has been established, the investment
environment must be determined. Should pension fund investments be
regulated and, if so, how? Should controls be placed on asset allocations? Should portfolio choice be available to pension fund members?
If pension guarantees are offered along with portfolio choice, households may be tempted to invest more in risky assets than they would
otherwise, thus inducing an increased contingent liability on the guar-
antor. This motivates investment regulation. How, then, do pension
fund regulations relate to accumulation or return guarantees?

Again, international practice varies. Civil law countries such as Chile
and Switzerland regulate asset allocation, either explicitly, or by requiring returns to meet some market benchmark. Both countries offer
guarantees on mandatory DC plans. This forces conservative allocations.
In common law countries such as Australia, by contrast, there is less
investment regulation, and while portfolio choice is not mandatory, it is
gradually becoming more available. There are no specific guarantees,
but the means-tested age pension does provide a retirement income
floor, which effectively underwrites pension accumulations for those
with limited assets other than their owner-occupied home.

There are some clear lessons from finance theory on the advantages
of providing individuals with choice of portfolio. Most households in
developed economies approach retirement with two major assets: their
owner-occupied residence, an undiversified asset with very particular
characteristics, and a pension with income replacement. Their human
capital inexorably runs down.

One of the major advantages of a mandatory DC-based retirement
saving policy is that it allows exposure to investment risk to be varied
across households, whose preferred exposure will depend on economic
and demographic circumstances, as well as underlying preferences. The
idea that financial wealth should be more heavily concentrated in safe
assets with age, advice frequently given by financial planners, can be
readily rationalised if the depreciating human capital stock is seen as
relatively safe. If households have limited control over their asset
allocation outside their pension fund, then welfare will be improved by
providing a range of portfolios within the pension fund. Preliminary
research suggests that the welfare gains afforded by such flexibility may

be very significant. It follows that policy designs which permit portfolio choice are to be preferred.

In developed economies, rapidly developing financial markets and international capital markets are providing new opportunities for spreading risk through diversification and the more widespread use of derivative instruments. As these markets develop further, allowing more refined specification of investment strategy, the appeal of DC-based privately administered retirement policies will increase.

The payout phase

Retirement provision policies may be seen as insurance against the various risks confronted by the elderly. Mandatory DC-type policies require separate stipulation of retirement payouts, and these entail a new set of policy decisions. Should life annuities be mandated? If so, should they be indexed, fully or partially, to inflation or to wages? Should there be a requirement to purchase annuities immediately on retirement, regardless of the prevailing annuity price? Could, or should, mechanisms be developed to spread annuity purchase over time to reduce the impact of annuity price variation on retirement incomes? In the case of an annuitant with dependants, should a reversionary annuity be required?

Annuities and annuity markets are under-researched. It is frequently observed that voluntary annuity markets are thin, even in countries, such as the United Kingdom, where there has been a long tradition of annuity purchase. Yet we have little evidence to support any particular view as to why this is so. Possible explanations include the loadings that have been found to be present in voluntary annuity markets, the existence of public transfers, the existence of a bequest motive, and the wish to retain control over capital to cope with unexpected uninsurable events.

International experience varies from broad insistence on mandatory non-indexed annuity purchase to the availability of lump-sum with-drawal. Given the dearth of research, and limited policy experience on these issues, few firm lessons can be drawn at this stage.

We are inclined to the view that some form of mandatory purchase of a retirement income product will be required, if this form of retirement provision is to deliver financial security in later life. Other-wise, the significant welfare gains from spreading longevity risk are unlikely to be realised because of adverse selection. But we conclude that there is no one preferred mandatory annuity design. Minimum criteria should ensure that adequate, if partial, insurance is provided, consistent with the size of the accumulation. Integration with the first pillar should ensure that affluent retirees are not able to inappropriately exploit first-pillar support.

Inflation insurance for annuitants is best underwritten by indexed securities. It would be sensible for governments to include long-duration indexed bonds as part of their debt issue to back inflation-insured annuities.

Pension taxation

Pension taxation design should fashion a tax (and transfer) policy that aligns domestic saving with efficient self-provision levels, and provides adequate retirement income, while minimising distortions affecting retirement timing and asset choice.

The two questions that then arise are: how concessional should the taxation of pension saving be? And at what point – contributions, earnings and benefits – should pension saving be taxed?

The limited evidence on the efficiency costs of inter-asset price distortion indicates that they are much more significant than has traditionally been thought. If owner-occupier housing receives expenditure tax treatment (as it usually does), then this suggests pension saving should be accorded similar tax treatment. This rules out the taxation of pension fund earnings. A fund earnings tax is probably a poor tax for other reasons as well: it is likely to significantly distort effective prices across financial assets offering returns in different forms, and it could promote premature retirement.

The choice between contributions and benefit taxation is less clear cut, because taxing of compulsory contributions is like taxing wages, but on balance, however, taxation of benefits may be preferable. This is because it treats employer and employee contributions more symmetrically, it reduces the political risk that future governments will tax the retirement benefits of the baby-boom generation (after contributions have already been taxed), and there may be social benefit from governments sharing the investment risk of individual contributors under a DC scheme. A benefit tax structure is the most common pension tax arrangement.

More generally, political insulation of mandatory private retirement savings – another major advantage of this policy paradigm – can be seriously compromised by arbitrary taxation. A pension tax regime that is integrated with the established broad-based taxes – usually a progressive income tax – will likely reduce the political scope for arbitrary tax intervention.

Limited attention has been paid to the specific question of whether income taxes should be encouraged at all in less-developed economies, and on the implications that the alternative – a direct expenditure tax regime – might have for pension taxation. This question assumes immediate importance because many LDCs are now considering private mandatory plans.

Broader considerations

If pension economics can be thought of as a disciplinary field, it is at best a hybrid. Analysis is drawn from the traditional fields of public finance, labour economics and the economics of finance, along with actuarial science. Progress has been made in each of these areas in understanding the impacts of mandatory retirement schemes on behaviour, in isolating the determinants of the retirement decision and in developing long-term investment strategies.

Much work remains to be done, however, in integrating these research programs so that a coherent body of research is available to inform and assess pension policy formulation and lifetime investment strategies, which must be designed with public programs in mind. Actuarial research largely ignores public transfers, although it does take account of the regulatory environment faced by insurance companies and administrative cost. Research by financial economists on investment strategies has typically ignored the existence and impact of social welfare safety nets and pension guarantees in optimising portfolio choice, although this question is now attracting research attention. The impacts of taxation are also frequently ignored. Most research on investment strategy ignores the question of labour supply, thereby implicitly assuming an exogenously determined retirement age. The specific characteristics of owner-occupier housing as a life-cycle asset, including its impact on remaining asset allocation, has seldom been studied, although work has been done on the development of insurance markets providing a hedge against real-estate risk.

Labour economists undertake an enormous amount of research into labour supply, but retirement timing, incorporating the influence of social security and pension rights, has been under-researched relative to pre-retirement labour supply. Little research has been undertaken on pension fund taxation.

Further, much of the research that has been carried out is based on US or UK policy structures and data sets. These research studies may have only limited relevance to other economies, especially those at earlier stages of development, where much pension reform activity is now located. Annuity mortality rates provide a good example of this. Almost everywhere outside the United States and the United Kingdom, annuitant mortality is estimated by taking UK or US annuitant mortality

tables and adjusting them in some way. Practitioners find that these
tables, suitably adjusted, 'seem to work', but much remains untested.
Differential patterns of mortality improvement, for example, will not be
captured using this approach, and this will only be discovered when
currently insured annuitants eventually die.

At this point the need for more research into pension issues is
evident.

Mandatory Retirement Saving in Australia

Formal retirement income provision in Australia can be traced back to occupational superannuation schemes first offered by banks and state governments in the nineteenth century. However, the year 1909 marked the beginning of a national retirement income policy with the introduction of a means-tested age pension. Since then retirement income provision has evolved into a multi-pillar arrangement comprising the age pension, occupational superannuation and other long-term saving through property, shares and managed funds. The 1990s saw the introduction of private mandatory retirement saving in the form of the Superannuation Guarantee. With the introduction of the Superannuation Guarantee, Australia joined a growing group of countries that centre their retirement income policy on private mandatory retirement saving.

Evolution of private mandating of retirement provision in Australia

Traditionally, Australia relied on its age pension (a universal, but means-tested, benefit payment) for retirement income provision. Entitlement is based on age, residency status, income and assets, but not on employment history. It is paid from general revenues. Tax concessions for voluntary superannuation were first introduced in 1915 and strengthened in 1936, but preservation was poor and coverage was low. As recent as the mid-1980s, only 30% of private-sector workers were covered by occupational superannuation.

Unlike most other developed countries, Australia never introduced policies to compel participation in a publicly provided employment or earnings-related retirement income scheme. Prior to the introduction of the Superannuation Guarantee, Australian retirement income policy comprised only two pillars: the means-tested age pension and voluntary retirement saving.

Australia's status as odd person out in this regard seems to have been more a matter of historical and political accident than of any consistent policy. It was always recognised that the age pension alone was not sufficient to fund adequate provision for the retired in a developed and rich society such as Australia's. Between 1913 and 1938, three unsuccessful attempts were made to introduce public earnings-related retirement income (social insurance) arrangements similar to those that were proving popular in Western Europe and the Americas. In 1938 Australia even got as far as passing the enabling legislation, but, with the coming of the Second World War, implementation was deferred indefinitely.

Nevertheless, occupational superannuation grew rapidly in the public sector in the years following the Second World War. However, it was less common in the private sector where it grew haphazardly, covering some occupations and not others, and providing markedly variable conditions and benefits. While the taxation arrangements were concessionary, the industry was largely unregulated and benefit standards were poor. As a result, even by the mid-1980s, less than 50% of full-time employees were covered by superannuation. Of this, private-sector coverage was only around 30%, and coverage of full-time females even lower at around 25%.

There was renewed interest in public earnings-related retirement income provision in the early 1970s when a commissioned study (see Hancock 1976) also recommended a scheme along the lines of those operating in most other OECD countries. However, this was disregarded by the government of the time in favour of greater support for voluntary superannuation. The trade union movement then carried the push for earnings-related retirement income provision with the emphasis moving away from publicly provided to multi-employer occupational arrangements.

When a Labor government was elected in March 1983, a major part of its economic strategy was a continuing contract with the union movement, the 'Accord', that survived through Labor's tenure of office. The Accord, along with Australia's then centralised wage determination system, contained the idea of building superannuation contributions into a national centralised wage decision. The idea became reality in 1986, when the Accord Mark II was agreed. A central element in that agreement was that while the increase in compensation to employees should be 6%, to keep pace with inflation, half of the increase would accrue in the form of a 3% employer superannuation contribution, to be paid into an individual account in an industry fund. This was known as productivity award superannuation.[1]

The introduction of productivity award superannuation in 1986 led to large increases in the coverage of occupational superannuation. Over the following three years, as individual industrial award agreements were negotiated and ratified under the umbrella of the 1986 national wage case decision, superannuation coverage increased markedly, particularly in the private sector and in industries dominated by women, part-time and casual workers. In retail trade, an industry representative of all of these groups, coverage grew from 24.6% in 1986 to 82% in 1993. Aggregate coverage nearly doubled from 40% to 79%.

However, award superannuation proved to be difficult and costly to enforce. In 1991 the Australian industrial court rejected an application, supported by both the government and the unions, for a further 3% increment. The government responded by introducing legislation requiring employers to make superannuation contributions to an approved fund on behalf of their employees. This policy commenced in 1992 and is now known as the Superannuation Guarantee.

Since the introduction of the Superannuation Guarantee, superannuation coverage has continued to grow, reaching 92% of employees in 1999 (a detailed discussion of the historical background can be found in Bateman and Piggott 1997 and 1998).

A chronology of Australian retirement policy is set out in the Annex on page 210.

Current retirement income provision in Australia

Current retirement income provision in Australia comprises three components (or pillars). The first pillar is a universal (but targeted) age pension financed from general revenues;[2] the second pillar is the slowly maturing private mandatory provision under the Superannuation Guarantee; and the third pillar is voluntary saving, including tax-preferred superannuation. The age pension provided under the first pillar is withdrawn where retirement income and assets provided under the other pillars exceed statutory thresholds.

Two aspects of the Australian arrangements are unusual when compared with other private mandatory arrangements. First, the first-pillar age pension operates as both the safety net and the second-pillar guarantee, and second, the first pillar is means-tested against all income and assets, rather than against private pension income only.

Each of the three pillars of retirement income provision, and the interaction between them, is discussed below.

First-pillar support – the age pension[3]

The age pension commenced in 1909. For most of the period since that time it has served as the social welfare safety net for the elderly and, in

Table A1.1 Features of the age pension[1]

Established	1909
Eligibility	Residency
	Age (males age 65, females age 61.5[2])
	Means-tested (income and assets)
Funding	General revenues
	PAYG
Amounts	Single rate – $A9529 per annum
	Married rate – $A7953.40 per annum
	(Subject to income and assets means tests)
	Age pension indexed to greater of growth of CPI and male average earnings.
Other benefits	Rent allowance, concessional pharmaceutical benefits, public transport, public utilities, and so on
Taxation	Pensioner tax rebate fully exempts full-rate age pensioners from income tax, partial exemption for part-rate pensioners
Means tests	*Income test*
	Pension withdrawn at the rate of 50c for each $A1 of private income in excess of a free area of $A51 per week (single rate), $A90 per week (married rate)
	Assets test
	Pension withdrawn by $A1.50 per week for every $A1000 of assets above thresholds:

	Single	Married
Home-owner	$A127 750	$A181 500
Non-home-owner	$A219 250	$A273 000

Thresholds and limits indexed to annual movements in the CPI

Part pension based on whichever test determines the lower rate of pension

1 These amounts are for February 2000.
2 The eligibility age for women was age 60. An increase to age 65 is being implemented during the period 1995 to 2014.

the absence of a compulsory earnings-related pillar, has provided a major source of retirement income for most retired people. In 2000 around 80% of the retired of eligible age received some age pension – of which around 66% were paid at the full rate (Department of Family and Community Services 2000). However, only 10% of these relied solely on the age pension.

The main features of the age pension are summarised in Table A1.1.

The age pension is payable to women aged 61.5 years and over, and to men aged 65 years and over (the eligibility age for women is being increased to age 65 by the year 2014). Claimants must also satisfy certain residency qualifications. The age pension is means-tested in accordance with either a person's income or assets – whichever determines the

Table A1.2 Minimum social security provision – single older person – in Australia and G7 countries in 1991, $A

	Australia	United States	Canada	France	Germany	United Kingdom	Italy
Level of benefits (PPP)	$A8805	$A6648	$A9462	$A7899	$A6201	$A6635	$A7434

Note: Precise estimates for Japan are not available, but the minimum value is below the G7 average. Purchasing power parity conversions were used.
Source: Whiteford (1995)

lower rate of pension. A higher rate of pension is payable to a single person than to each member of a married couple. The pension is automatically indexed twice yearly. Since 1997, indexation has been against the greater of the growth of the CPI and male total average earnings. Assistance received through the age pension is subject to personal income tax but a pensioner tax rebate is available, which fully exempts full-rate pensioners from income tax and provides partial exemption for part-rate pensioners.

In February 2000 the age pension amounts were $A9529 per annum for single people (around 25% average male earnings) and $A7953.40 per annum (around 20% average male earnings) for each of a married couple.

Recent policy has reflected an increased emphasis on targeting. Following a number of reviews over the 1980s and 1990s, the longstanding means-testing was endorsed and the administration simplified.[4]

Adequacy of the age pension

The government has legislated to maintain the single-rate age pension at a minimum of 25% of male total average weekly earnings (increases flow on to the married rate). As retirees solely reliant on the age pension pay no income tax, this translates to a net of tax replacement rate of 37%. Compared with other rich developed countries, these magnitudes are favourable for safety net payments, but fall far short of the payments promised under typical public employment-related pension schemes. As Table A1.2 indicates, in 1991 Canada was the only G7 nation with a higher minimum level of age benefit than Australia.

Means-testing has ensured that a high proportion of government transfers are received by the poorest aged, thereby generating significant redistribution (Bateman et al. 1994). It has also helped to keep the aggregate value of transfers modest.

Table A1.3 Features of the Australian Superannuation Guarantee

Commenced	1992
Contributions	9% earnings, paid by employer[1]
Funding	Fully funded
	Individual accounts
	Many private funds
	Few investment restrictions
Benefits	Defined contribution
	Fully vested, portable and preserved to age 55 (60 by 2025)
	No early withdrawals
	Choice of lump sum, pension, annuity with tax/transfer
Statutory coverage	All employees aged 18–65
	Earnings > $A450 month (14% average male earnings)[2]
	Self-employed not covered
Taxation	Employer contributions tax deductible
	Fund income (contributions and earnings) and benefits taxed at concessionary rates
Regulation	Prudent-man principle: no rate of return or asset requirements

1 The 9% employer contribution is being phased in over the period 1992–2002.
2 There is a proposal to make coverage optional for employees earning between $A450 (14% average male earnings) and $A900 a month (28% average male earnings).

Second-pillar support – the Superannuation Guarantee

The Superannuation Guarantee mandates employers to make superannuation contributions on behalf of their employees to superannuation funds of their choice. Employers that fail to do so are subject to the Superannuation Guarantee Charge, which comprises the shortfall in the minimum level of superannuation support *plus* interest *plus* an administrative cost component. It costs more to pay the Superannuation Guarantee Charge than the mandatory contribution, not least because this charge is not a deductible business expense, unlike the Superannuation Guarantee.

The superannuation contributions are placed in individual accounts in private superannuation funds and invested on behalf of the employees. Table A1.3 summarises the main features of the Superannuation Guarantee.

The arrangements apply to all employers and to almost all employees. Employees earning less than $A450 per month (around 14% of average male earnings) are specifically excluded. This decision was made largely on the grounds of high administration costs on small-amount accounts. As well, the government proposes to make contributions optional for employees earning between $A450 and $A900 per month (14–28% average male earnings).

The mandatory contributions are fully vested (that is, the member is fully entitled to all accrued benefits), fully preserved (that is, accrued benefits must remain in a fund until the statutory preservation age for access to benefits is reached), fully funded and must be paid into a complying superannuation fund, or a retirement savings account (RSA) offered by a financial institution. For public-sector employers, a government guarantee can substitute for full funding. DB schemes can count in meeting Superannuation Guarantee obligations provided an actuarial benefit certificate, specifying that the implicit level of superannuation support accords with the requirements, is obtained. Boards of trustees manage the superannuation funds.

The minimum level of superannuation support is being phased in, with the target of a 9% employer contribution to be reached by 2002.

Third-pillar support – voluntary retirement saving

Voluntary retirement saving comprises voluntary (or quasi-voluntary) occupational superannuation, personal superannuation and other forms of long-term saving through property, shares, managed investments and home-ownership. Voluntary occupational superannuation accounted for 62% of total superannuation contributions in 1998–99[5] with 43% of employees making voluntary or personal superannuation contributions at an average rate of 6% of earnings. Around 85% of current retirees own their home.

Integration of retirement income pillars

While the major source of income for most retirees is currently the age pension, this will change over coming decades as more Australians reach retirement with long periods of Superannuation Guarantee coverage.

Private retirement benefits

Retirement benefits accumulated under the Superannuation Guarantee and/or voluntary superannuation may be taken as a lump sum or an income stream upon reaching the preservation age, currently 55, increasing to age 60 over the period to 2025. Income streams are encouraged by tax and means-test incentives, but it is unclear whether

Table A1.4 Disbursement of lump-sum payment, November 1997

	Age at retirement from full-time work 65 and over (proportion of total lump-sum benefits)
Rolled over	25.9
Purchased immediate annuity	0.8
Invested	42.0
Paid off home	12.4
Bought motor vehicle	0.8
Cleared outstanding debts	5.9
Paid for holiday	6.7
Assisted family members	0
Undecided	1.9
Other	3.8

Source: ABS (1997) *Retirement and Retirement Intentions*, Australia, November, ABS Cat no. 6238.0, Table 12

these are affecting the long-term preference for lump-sum benefits (Bateman et al. 1993).

Currently around 75% of the value of retirement benefits are paid as lump sums, but benefits are generally small: the 1997 ABS *Retirement and Retirement Intentions* survey reports that, in the previous four years, around 50% of lump-sum retirement payments were less than $A60 000. However, the same survey indicated that lump sums are largely used for retirement purposes. Table A1.4, which sets out the disbursement of lump-sum payments for recent retirees, shows that most superannuation payments are invested, rolled over or used to pay off the family home.

Because superannuation accumulations do not have to be taken as a particular type of income stream, a range of retirement income stream products has evolved. There arc three main categories: superannuation pensions, traditional annuities and allocated pensions or annuities.

- Superannuation pensions are pensions paid by, or on behalf of, superannuation funds. These have traditionally been paid by DB schemes in the public and corporate sectors.
- Traditional annuities are offered by life insurance companies. Current products include fixed or indexed annuities for life or an agreed term. In the 12 months to June 1998, gross annuity sales totalled $A806 million, of which 16.6% were life annuities.
- Allocated pensions and allocated annuities (also known as phased withdrawals) are offered by a wide range of financial institutions.

Table A1.5 Retirement income streams – income and asset tests

Product type	Asset test	Income test
Life pension or annuity		
Life-expectancy pension or annuity	no	Income *less* full purchase price/life expectancy (or term)
Other term annuity > 5 years	yes	Income *less* full purchase price/term
Term annuity < 5 years		
Allocated pension or annuity (phased withdrawal)	yes	Deeming applies

Annual income payments are required to lie between defined minimum and maximum amounts.

Product design and demand have been driven by the differential tax and means-test arrangements applying to alternative types of income streams. Allocated products (phased withdrawals) have been the fastest growing segment of the market in recent years, but changes to the age pension means tests in September 1998 led to increased demand for life and life-expectancy products – in the 12 months to June 1998, gross sales of allocated products totalled $A4.3 billion, over five times that of traditional annuities.

Integration

The age pension means tests do not distinguish between voluntary and mandatory superannuation. However, they do distinguish between type of retirement benefit. Where a lump sum is taken and used to purchase financial assets, the capital value is assessed under the assets test and 'deemed' income is subject to the income test (a lump sum that is taken and dissipated is not counted under the means tests). Where a retirement income stream is purchased the means tests apply differentially, depending on the product type. The current rules are summarised in Table A1.5.

Life and life-expectancy products are given greatest preference, with exemption from the assets test and preferential income test treatment. Allocated products (phased withdrawals) and short-duration income streams are given least preference.

Future retirement benefits

Almost all employees are now covered by the Superannuation Guarantee; and many workers have additional voluntary superannuation

198   APPENDIX 1

coverage and improvements in vesting, portability and preservation. This means the composition of retirement income, and therefore the role of the public age pension as the major source of income in retirement, will change in future years.

This is illustrated in Figure A1.1, which shows the expected composition of net total (public and private) retirement income for a full working life of Superannuation Guarantee coverage.

Taxation and regulation

With the move towards greater reliance on private provision for retirement, the related areas of taxation and regulation have also been reformed.

Prior to 1983 superannuation benefited from a generous tax treatment: contributions were largely tax deductible, fund earnings were exempt from tax and only 5% of the value of a lump sum, the main form of retirement income, was included in taxable income. However, there was little industry regulation and the vesting, portability and preservation standards were poor.

Since the early 1980s the taxation of superannuation has been reshaped. Taxation of lump-sum benefits was introduced in 1983 and a tax on superannuation fund income (including both contributions and

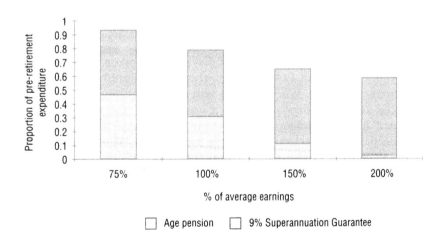

Figure A1.1 Future composition of retirement benefits
Note: We assume a single male worker on fixed-income levels between 75% and 200% of male average earnings. Voluntary saving is excluded and net of tax replacement rates are calculated as a percentage of pre-retirement expenditure.
Source: Bateman and Piggott (1997, p. 27)

investment income) in 1988. Taxation now applies at all three possible points: contributions, fund earnings and benefits. This contrasts with similar arrangements operating elsewhere in the world, which generally tax benefits only. Under the Australian arrangements, employer contributions are tax deductible (up to age-determined limits) but are taxed in the hands of the superannuation fund at a rate of 15%. In addition, a 15% superannuation surcharge applies to the contributions of high-income earners. Fund earnings are taxed at a statutory rate of 15%, which is reduced to the extent that income accrues in the form of dividends or capital gains. Full corporate tax imputation credits are available on dividend income that may be set off against tax on any income, including capital gains and taxable contributions, while capital gains tax is indexed to inflation. Retirement benefits are taxed as well, with the amount of taxation depending on the type of benefit and its size.

The 1980s also saw the introduction of a comprehensive regulatory framework for superannuation. As the Australian government does not have the constitutional power to make laws concerning superannuation *per se*, the taxation powers were utilised. Enforcement of the regulations was tied to tax concessions provided to superannuation funds: a superannuation fund that did not meet the regulatory requirements did not receive the tax concessions. An industry regulator was established (initially the Insurance and Superannuation Commission and from July 1999, the Australian Prudential Regulation Authority) and a set of operational standards for the industry was introduced. However, when the regulatory framework was strengthened in the 1990s greater enforcement powers were required. This time the enabling legislation was enacted under the Australian government's corporations and pensions power, in addition to the taxation power. This allowed the introduction of civil and criminal remedies against trustees who failed in their duties.

Prudential issues are largely left to superannuation fund trustees, who are personally liable to fund members for their decisions. Trustees are responsible for the management, operation and investments of superannuation funds. With the exception of a 5% of asset ceiling on in-house investments, and a 'no borrowing' rule, there are no asset requirements, nor is a minimum rate of return required.

The superannuation industry in Australia

The main institutions responsible for private mandatory retirement saving in Australia are superannuation funds (since 1997 other institutions have been allowed to offer retirement savings accounts (RSAs) as

Table A1.6 Characteristics of superannuation funds, September 2000

Types of fund	Assets ($A billion)	No. of funds	No. of accounts (millions)
Corporate	80	2 065	1.489
Industry	41	62	6.863
Retail	142	151	10.999
Public Sector	109	34	2.547
Small Funds	71	214 846	0.423
RSAs	3	na	na
Annuities, life office reserves etc.	47	na	na
All funds	489	217 158	22.321

Note: RSAs are included in retail funds.
Source: APRA Superannuation Trends, September 2000

an alternative). Superannuation funds operate as trusts and are managed by boards of trustees, which are generally required to comprise equal employee and employer representation. Other institutions such as banks, life insurance companies and investment managers have important roles as service providers.

There are five types of superannuation fund, each introduced in response to different historical and policy considerations. The public-sector superannuation funds appeared first in the nineteenth century, followed by corporate superannuation funds for white-collar workers. Retail funds were established by life insurance companies to promote personal superannuation, while the introduction of award superannuation in the 1980s followed by the Superannuation Guarantee in 1992 led to the introduction and rapid growth of industry superannuation funds and a variant of the retail fund – the master trust, which allows non-related individuals or companies to operate superannuation under a single trust deed. Finally, the mandatory coverage of small employers, combined with favourable tax treatment of superannuation, has led to the introduction and growth of small (self-managed) superannuation funds, which have five or less members and are generally established by a family owned company with family members as trustees.

In September 2000 there were 217 158 superannuation funds in Australia, comprising 214 846 'small' and 2312 'other' superannuation funds. The largest 100 superannuation funds account for around 65% of total superannuation assets (Clare and Connor 1999b).

All types of superannuation fund accept both mandatory and voluntary contributions, and any superannuation fund can apply to be established as an 'open' or public-offer fund.

Table A1.7 Asset allocation of Australian superannuation funds, September 2000

	Assets	
	$A billion	%
Cash and deposits	34	7
Loans and placements	23	5
Interest-bearing securities	90	19
Equities and units in trusts	205	42
Direct property	25	5
Overseas	97	20
Other	15	3
Total	489	

Source: APRA Superannuation Trends, September 2000

As stated above, RSAs have been introduced, which aim to provide a low-cost option for small contributions. RSAs are simple capital-guaranteed products offered by banks, building societies, credit unions and life insurance companies. They are owned and controlled by the superannuation members holding the accounts and are taxed and regulated like all other superannuation accounts. RSAs currently account for less than 1% of superannuation assets.

Assets and membership of the five superannuation fund types and RSAs are summarised in Table A1.6.

In practice, trustees delegate many tasks to service providers, including fund administrators, investment managers, asset consultants, custodians and other professionals such as lawyers, actuaries and marketing specialists. Industry estimates indicate that nearly 86% of industry funds, 70% of public-sector funds and around 60% of corporate funds use external fund administrators.

Superannuation assets

There has been a large increase in superannuation fund assets since the introduction of award superannuation and the Superannuation Guarantee. Measured as a percentage of GDP, total superannuation fund assets have grown from 2.8% in 1972, to 18.1% in 1986, to around 75% in 2000. Government estimates suggest that by the year 2020, superannuation fund assets could total around 116.5% of GDP (Tinnion and Rothman 1999).

In the absence of asset or rate of return restrictions, Australian superannuation funds tend to invest in a wide variety of assets with a

Table A1.8 Assessment of the Superannuation Guarantee – individual criteria

Coverage risk	Adequate for employees only
Replacement rate risk	Adequate for continuous contributions
Investment risk	Borne by retiree, but addressed through asset diversification
Longevity risk	Not covered – no mandatory purchase of indexed income streams, ineffective incentives
Inflation risk	Not covered – no mandatory purchase of lifetime income streams, ineffective incentives
Political risk	Accumulations are insulated from political risk, except for tax changes, but the public pension safety net remains exposed

mix of duration and risk-return characteristics. Less than 30% of assets are directly invested by superannuation funds: in December 1999, 39% of assets were invested by external investment managers and 31% in pooled superannuation funds.

The average asset allocations of Australian superannuation funds are set out in Table A1.7 on page 201.

An assessment of the Superannuation Guarantee

As Australian retirement income policy is in transition, any assessment of that policy must be contingent on the nature of future developments. Subject to this caveat, however, the Superannuation Guarantee performs favourably when assessed against both the individual and economy-wide criteria for the performance of retirement income arrangements (as discussed in Chapter 1; for a comprehensive discussion see Bateman and Piggott 1997 and 1998).

An assessment of the Superannuation Guarantee against the financial risks facing individuals in retirement is summarised in Table A1.8.

In a strict sense, the Superannuation Guarantee scores poorly in terms of the individual criteria, because of the lack of an income stream requirement. In particular, longevity and inflation risks are not addressed because of the failure to require a lifetime-indexed – or indeed any – income stream.

However, even if lifetime-indexed income streams were required, the Superannuation Guarantee on its own would only partially address many of the financial risks faced by an individual in retirement. In particular, the Superannuation Guarantee does not cover the self-employed (some 12% of the total labour force) and income replacement may be insufficient for non-standard workers.[6] As well, while Superannuation Guarantee accumulations rest in the private

Table A1.9 Assessment of Superannuation Guarantee – economy-wide criteria

Efficiency	Addresses dynamic inconsistency of preferences and price distortions, by compelling saving Does not address failure of annuities market

Equity	Enhances intergenerational neutrality
	Detrimental intra-generational impacts
	   – low-income earners forced to change intertemporal consumption stream
	   – tax concessions favour high-income earners

Administrative efficacy	Complex to administer Regulations prohibit charges on small-amount accounts

sector, and are therefore not part of the government budgetary process, they are not completely insulated from political risk. It is open to any government to increase tax rates on accumulations and/or benefits – as was the case with the introduction of the superannuation surcharge – or to make detrimental changes to the regulatory environment.

Many of these risks are, of course, mitigated by the interaction of the Superannuation Guarantee with the means-tested age pension.

Assessment of the Superannuation Guarantee against the economy-wide criteria of efficiency, equity and administrative efficacy is summarised in Table A1.9.

The Superannuation Guarantee is likely to lead to an improvement in economic efficiency. By compelling retirement saving, it addresses myopia (along with any dynamic inconsistency of preferences) and the inter-temporal price distortions arising from the income tax and the age pension. As well, it is likely to improve the composition of saving by reducing the emphasis on home-ownership. However, by failing to mandate retirement income streams the Superannuation Guarantee does little to address the issue of adverse selection in the annuities market.

The Superannuation Guarantee scores well on intergenerational equity. It compels those employees with the lifetime resources to help fund their own retirement; this would be expected to reduce calls on the means-tested age pension. This is confirmed in Bateman and Ablett (2000), who estimate a set of generational accounts for Australia. They find that the introduction of the Superannuation Guarantee has halved the generational imbalance in favour of current generations.

Within-generation distribution impacts, however, raise some concerns. First, if the Superannuation Guarantee is largely absorbed through slower wage growth, then the working poor may suffer more through reduced access to consumption today than they gain through increased retirement resources tomorrow. Second, superannuation tax concessions offer more of a tax break, relative to the comprehensive income tax, to the rich than the poor. Finally, the Superannuation Guarantee may be disadvantageous to non-standard workers, such as women – who have long periods out of the workforce, more part-time work and lower wages on average than men. Again, however, the means-tested age pension acts to reduce these inequities (equity issues and the Superannuation Guarantee are discussed in Bateman et al. 1994).

Due to the absence of a broadly accepted benchmark, the Superannuation Guarantee's rating on administrative efficacy is unclear. As a privately organised and funded form of retirement income provision it is likely to be more complex and more costly than public PAYG retirement income provision. However, while reported costs data may suggest that public arrangements are less costly, much public cost data are deficient. Private provision is likely to offer more choice, better governance and the potential for higher retirement benefits. These issues are addressed further in Chapter 7.

Finally, implementation of the Superannuation Guarantee was not problem-free. Of initial concern were the relatively high administrative charges placed on many accounts with small balances – inevitable in an immature system – and the proliferation of multiple accounts (there are around three superannuation accounts for every worker).

The government responded to the former with regulations limiting the fees charged on small-amount accounts.[7] The latter is being addressed through member education and changes in industry practice, which have simplified procedures for the transfer and amalgamation of superannuation accounts. However, an emerging problem is that of 'lost' accounts – the Australian Taxation Office estimates that there are about 2.5 million 'lost' accounts and $A2.4 billion held on behalf of superannuation fund members who are 'lost' to their fund.

Current evidence and projections

Preliminary evidence of the success of the Superannuation Guarantee has focused primarily on coverage and national saving.

Figure A1.2, reports trends in superannuation coverage.

Since 1986 superannuation coverage has increased markedly for all employees, particularly women.

Government estimates of the contribution to saving of a 9% Superannuation Guarantee is set out in Table A1.10.

The Superannuation Guarantee is projected to raise national saving by 1.2% of GDP by early in the twenty-first century and by around 3.6% of GDP by the year 2020. Private saving improves because of the

Table A1.10 The Superannuation Guarantee – contribution to national saving

	Public saving	Private saving	National saving
Financial year	(contribution as a % GDP)		
1992–93	−0.03	0.5	0.4
1995–96	−0.05	0.9	0.9
1999–00	−0.18	1.4	1.2
2004–05	−0.31	2.6	2.3
2009–10	−0.37	3.2	2.8
2014–15	−0.39	3.5	3.1
2019–20	−0.35	3.9	3.6

Note: Estimates assume implementation of policies announced in the 1996–97 and 1997–98 Budgets, with no increase in member contributions. Various saving-substitution rates are assumed, ranging from 5% for the first income decile to 50% for the tenth income decile.
Source: Gallagher (1997), Table 1

gradually increasing tax-preferred mandatory contribution, and the earnings thereon, net of saving substitution. However, over the period to 2020, public saving falls, as reductions in tax revenue exceed reductions in age pension outlays. This will, however, turn around in later

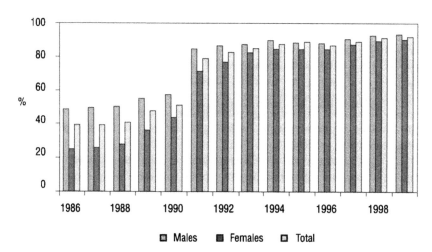

Figure A1.2 Trends in superannuation coverage of employees
Source: Employment Benefits Australia, ABS Cat. no. 6334.0; *Superannuation Australia,* ABS Cat. no. 6319.0; *Employee Earnings, Benefits and Trade Union Membership,* ABS Cat. no. 6310.0

Table A1.11 Households – net acquisition of financial assets[1]

	Bank deposits (%)	Life insurance, superannuation contributions (%)	Other[2] (%)
1970s	42	20	38
1980s	36	39	25
1990s	28	50	22

1 Includes unincorporated enterprises.
2 'Other' includes building society and credit union deposits, government securities, debentures, shares, unit trusts, and so on.
Source: Bateman and Piggott (1997)

years as the Superannuation Guarantee matures and the retired depend less on the age pension.

If these projections are correct, they reflect a major improvement in Australia's saving performance, which has been low by international standards. Net national saving currently stands at around 4.5% of GDP, so a 1.2 percentage point increase represents a 25% acceleration in net saving.

Certainly, the composition of households' financial asset saving flows has altered dramatically in the last decade. Table A1.11 reports the net acquisition of financial assets over the past three decades. Life insurance and superannuation contributions have increased from 20% of households' net acquisition of financial assets in the 1970s to 50% in the 1990s.

A final point on saving performance concerns the composition (or quality) of saving and investment. There are two main channels of tax-preferred saving in Australia: superannuation and owner-occupier housing. The latter is both treated more concessionally under the income tax and excluded from the age pension means test so, in the absence of compulsory superannuation, is likely to be chosen as the preferred personal saving vehicle.

A popular argument for introducing a mandatory and privately managed second pillar is that this policy will raise private or national saving. Preliminary evidence, however, is that pension reform has not raised national saving, with the exception of Chile (Samwick 2000). Countries that are switching to mandatory private provision are mostly replacing a public PAYG system. Indeed, in the year 2000 Australia was the only reformer to be in the process of replacing a wide-coverage public age pension – which is a universal and means-tested. (The other countries with wide-coverage public pensions were New Zealand, Iceland and South Korea.)

The Superannuation Guarantee may therefore contribute more to the efficient allocation of economic resources through its impact on the composition of saving and investment, than on aggregate saving performance. The reason is that, in Australia at least, wide-coverage pensions have encouraged a concentration of household wealth in residential real estate, at the expense of capital accumulation for the purpose of improving the productivity of the paid labour force. During the last third of the twentieth century, residential real estate came to occupy over half of Australian household net worth (excluding the present values of earnings and pension entitlements).

Since the mid-twentieth century, a striking feature of the typical Australian household's portfolio has been the increasing weight of dwelling assets, either owner-occupier or rented out. In 1960 the share of dwelling assets in the wealth of Australian households stood at 36%. By 1998 this share had risen to 55%, down from a peak of 59% hit in 1993 and again in 1995, yet still far ahead of superannuation's share in 1993; namely, 19%. This was also well ahead of comparable allocations by US households, where owner-occupied real-estate assets amounted to 33% of total household assets in 1992 (Poterba and Samwick 1997, Table 4.4).

Housing wealth in Australia has been a valuable aid to minimising tax liabilities while maximising eligibility for government-provided income streams. While mortgage interest payments on the principal place of residence are not deductible, the owner-occupied home is exempt from capital gains tax, and its actual value (as distinct from mere existence) is not taken into account for the purpose of means-testing of the age pension. Moreover, interest payments on rental property are fully tax deductible (as a business expense).

What problems remain and how can they be addressed?

Four broad areas of Australia's private mandatory retirement saving policy remain problematic. These include integration with the first-pillar age pension and retirement income streams, taxation, choice and adequacy.

Integration with the first-pillar age pension and retirement income streams

Perhaps the most difficult structural problem confronting the Superannuation Guarantee is its linkage with the first pillar – the age pension – and the related question of income stream choice in retirement. Lump-sum withdrawal of superannuation benefits is both permitted and widespread. This, combined with the disparity between the preservation age for superannuation benefits (currently 55, but increasing to 60) and the eligibility age for the age pension (61.5 for females, 65 for males), makes the integration of the Superannuation Guarantee with the age pension problematic. While most retirees dispose of their lump-sum benefits prudently, they have an incentive to do so in ways that maximise their age pension benefits (see Atkinson et al. 1996). This may involve reduced interest by workers in maximising investment returns and means-test avoidance for workers near the age pension threshold.

While current policy provides incentives through the age pension means tests to encourage the take-up of life and life-expectancy income streams, it is unclear whether these incentives will be effective over the long term. This was shown in Bateman et al. (1993), who found that the means test and tax incentives did little to encourage retirement income streams.

Taxation

Much avoidable complexity in the Australian taxation of retirement saving is introduced by maintaining three tax bases: contributions, earnings and benefits. All are taxed concessionally, so it is less the burden of tax than its complexity that is the difficulty here. However, the tax on earnings distorts net-of-tax returns, adversely affecting asset choice. In addition, earnings taxes probably further encourage early retirement, since it is when retirement is a viable option that the earnings tax bites most severely, reducing the lifetime reward for working another year. As well, contributions and earnings taxes are flat rate and therefore regressive. The superannuation surcharge, which attempts to make the contributions tax on superannuation funds progressive across fund members, has proved to be administratively complex and costly.

Further, the separation of superannuation tax rates from the personal tax rate schedule reduces the political insulation offered by private retirement provision. (For more detail on the superannuation surcharge see Bateman and Piggott 1999b. For a proposal for the simplification of superannuation taxation see Doyle et al. 1999.)

Choice

Choice in the Australian policy debate has two dimensions: choice of superannuation fund and choice of investment portfolio. Current policy reform has emphasised choice of superannuation fund (or retirement saving entity), but support for it is far from widespread. Draft legislation has been prepared and has been supported by the government in

Parliament, but the Australian upper house, the Senate, has so far rejected the proposal. As the current draft legislation stands, choice of fund must be offered to all employees receiving Superannuation Guarantee contributions except for those employed under state awards. Under the draft legislation employers will be able to meet their choice of fund obligation to employees by electing one of the three choice of fund models:

- limited choice of at least four funds that must consist of at least one public-offer fund and at least one RSA, and an industry fund and an in-house corporate fund if they exist under current arrangements; or
- unlimited choice, which requires employees to nominate their preferred fund; or
- negotiating a Certified Agreement or an Australian Workplace Agreement covering superannuation between employees and employers, or, alternatively, a fund proposed by an employee and agreed to by the employer, in writing.

There are arguments for and against greater choice. Choice of retirement saving organisation leads to greater marketing to individuals. In Chile (which allows employee choice of fund) this has proved expensive with marketing accounting for around 45% of total administrative costs. A second negative relates to the likely, if partial, breakdown of group life insurance arrangements. However, superannuation funds are increasingly offering portfolio choice with more than 50% of members able to choose their investment portfolio.

Irrespective of the choice of model pursued, it is vital that members are well informed and have access to easily understood comparative performance criteria. Therefore, government policy to facilitate greater investment choice should be complemented by appropriate disclosure rules and effective member education. These issues are currently under consideration following the release of the Government Consultation Paper *Financial Products, Service Providers and Markets – an Integrated Framework* (Corporate Law Economic Reform Program 1999).

Adequacy

While government estimates suggest that a 9% Superannuation Guarantee (plus the age pension) will deliver an adequate replacement rate for retirees with continuous workforce participation, this is no longer the norm – a proposal to allow the splitting of accrued superannuation benefits has been considered by the government (see Attorney-General's Department 1998; 1999). As well, under current policy design, taxation and administrative charges increasingly erode the mandatory contribution. This raises the issue of the adequacy of a mandatory contribution of 9% and whether the mandatory policy should be supplemented by incentives to make voluntary contributions.

Conclusion

This appendix has sought to explain the Australian version of private mandatory retirement saving – the Superannuation Guarantee – and to provide an assessment of the policy. In summary, the Superannuation Guarantee does well in the accumulations phase, because the mandatory contributions ensure full-fundedness and the private basis of the policy helps provide political insulation. In the benefits phase, the policy scores poorly, because retirement income streams are not mandatory. Given the historical right to take superannuation benefits as lump sums in Australia, mandating retirement income streams is politically difficult. In the long term, however, the success of the Superannuation Guarantee will depend upon the introduction of such a policy.

Annex: Chronology of retirement income policy in Australia

1908	Age pension introduced
1913	Conservative parties proposed contributory national superannuation
1914	Introduction of tax concessions for superannuation
1922	Commonwealth employees superannuation fund established
1928	Conservative government introduced National Insurance Bill – proposed national insurance scheme
1936	Service pension first paid. Tax concessions for lump sums introduced
1938	National Health and Pensions Insurance Bill passed – based on 1928 Bill
1943	Labor government establishes National Welfare Fund to fund social services
1945	Social services contribution established
1950	Social services contribution merged with personal tax system
1969	Age pension income test taper reduced from 100% to 50%
1973	Means tests abolished for persons aged over 75
1975	Means tests abolished for persons aged 70 to 74
1976	Assets test abolished for all persons
1978	Reintroduction of assets test for persons aged over 70
1983	Superannuation tax changes: lump-sum taxes introduced, increased tax deductibility for employees and the self-employed
1984	Rollover funds established. Tax concessions for annuities introduced
1985	Asset test reintroduced for all persons. Labor government and trade unions finalise Accord Mark II
1986	3% productivity award superannuation endorsed by Conciliation and Arbitration Commission

1987   Regulatory framework for superannuation introduced –
        Occupational Superannuation Supervision Act. Supervisory body
        established – the Insurance and Superannuation Commission
1988   Major reforms of superannuation taxation – introduction of 15%
        tax on superannuation income, reduction of lump-sum taxes, 15%
        annuity rebate introduced, increased tax deductibility for
        uncovered workers and self-employed, introduction of marginal
        Reasonable Benefit Limits (RBL) scales
1990   Age pension means tests liberalised for pensions and annuities.
        Introduction of tax rebates for superannuation contributions by
        low-coverage employees
1991   Industrial Relations Commission rejects further 3% productivity
        award superannuation. Government announces introduction of 9%
        Superannuation Guarantee to commence from July 1992
1992   Superannuation Guarantee commences
1993   Superannuation Industry Supervision Act passed
1994   Flat-rate Reasonable Benefit Limits replace marginal RBLs.
        Age-determined employer contribution limits introduced. Improved
        preservation. Increased eligibility for 15% annuity rebate.
        Commencement of phase-in of preservation age of 60
1995   Commencement of the phase-in of increase in the age pension age
        for women from age 60 to 65. The Labor government proposes to
        increase mandatory contributions to 15%
1996   Deeming applied to financial investments under the age pension
        income test
        Change of government. The 1996–97 Budget includes proposals to
        introduce RSAs, spouse contributions, superannuation surcharge
        and opt-out from Superannuation Guarantee for low-income earners
1997   RSAs established and superannuation surcharge introduced. The
        1997–98 Budget includes proposals to introduce employee choice
        of fund and replace previous government's proposed increased
        mandatory contribution rate with a 15% tax rebate for voluntary
        superannuation contributions (to a maximum of $A3000 per
        annum).
1998   Age pension means tests for retirement income streams revised.
        'A New Tax System' includes proposals to abolish 15% tax rebate
        and to change the age pension income test taper to 40%
1999   Government announces reforms of business taxation – includes
        proposals to reduce the capital gains tax rate for superannuation
        funds to 10% and to refund excess imputation credits
2000   Proposals announced in 'A New Tax System', implemented on
        1 July 2000

Notes

1 This agreement was subsequently ratified by the nation's industrial court,
  and survived a High Court challenge brought by the Confederation of

Australian Industry questioning its constitutionality (Dabscheck 1989, p. 99).

2 The Australian public age pension is universal to the extent that all residents of qualifying age are eligible, but targeted to the extent that it is subject to income and assets means tests.

3 In this discussion, we ignore the distinction between the age pension and the service pension, which is paid to ex-servicemen and women. The two pensions are very similar, except that the service pension is paid five years earlier.

4 Simplification related to the application of the income and assets to retirement income streams and the introduction of extended 'deeming' for financial assets. Under 'deeming', the income to be tested under the income test is determined by applying a statutory rate of return to the capital value of financial assets. The 1998/99 deeming rates are 3% for the first $A30 400 (single retiree)/$A50 600 (couple) and 5% for the remainder.

5 In other words the Superannuation Guarantee accounted for 38% of total superannuation contributions.

6 For example, Tinnion and Rothman (1999) show that a single male with a full working life of Superannuation Guarantee contributions out of average weekly earnings could expect a total net-of-tax replacement rate of 76% from private retirement income plus the age pension. This compares with a net-of-tax replacement rate of 37% from the age pension alone.

7 That is, the member protection rules which require that for superannuation accounts of less than $A1000, fund administration costs cannot exceed fund earnings. However, accounts can be debited for investment losses, contributions tax and insurance premiums.

International Comparisons of Private Mandatory Retirement Saving

Table A2.1 Characteristics of comprehensive private mandatory retirement saving – Chile, Switzerland and Australia

	Chile (AFP system)	**Switzerland** (BVG system)	**Australia** (Superannuation Guarantee)
Commencement	1981	1985	1992
Administration	AFPs (private companies)	Foundations (trusts)	Private superannuation funds (trusts)
Coverage	Employees	Employees	Employees
Contributions	10% employee plus around 3% for insurance and administration	Employer and employee, age and gender determined	9% employer
Financing	DC, accumulation, fully funded	DC and DB, fully (and partially) funded	DC, accumulation, fully funded
Payout age	65 (men); 60 (women)	65 (men); 62 (women)	55 (increasing to 60 by 2025)
Benefits	Indexed annuity and/or phased withdrawal, early withdrawal if benefits adequate	Annuity, lump sum if small accumulation, early withdrawal for home purchase	Lump sum, tax incentives to take income stream
Taxation	EET	EET	TTT (all concessionary)

Table A2.1 (cont.)

	Chile	Switzerland	Australia
Regulation	Maximum asset requirements, minimum relative rate of return	Maximum asset requirements, 4% nominal rate of return	Prudent-man principle
Actual asset allocations	Balanced	Mainly short term	Balanced
Government guarantee	Yes	Yes	No
Safety net (first pillar)	Minimum pension, assistance pension	Flat-rate public pensions, social assistance	Means-tested public pension
Other second pillar (publicly provided)	na	Earnings-related PAYG public pension	na
Transition	Recognition bonds	na	na

Source: Bateman (1998), Bateman and Valdes-Prieto (1999), Bateman and Piggott (1999a), Castillo (1993), Davis (1995), Diamond and Valdes-Prieto (1994), Edwards (1998), Hepp (1990; 1998), Queisser (1995; 1998)

Table A2.2 Characteristics of private retirement saving in Latin America

	Argentina	Bolivia	Colombia
Commencement	1994	1997	1994
Administration	AFJPs (private companies), centralised collection	AFPs (private companies)	AFPs (private companies), decentralised collection
Coverage	Voluntary, employees and self-employed	Mandatory, employees	Voluntary, employees
Contributions	7.5% employee plus insurance and admin. costs (about 3.5%)	10% employee + 2% insurance + 0.5% admin. costs	10% employee + insurance and admin. costs (3–3.5%)
Financing	DC, accumulation, fully funded, individual accounts	DC, accumulation, fully funded, individual accounts	DC, accumulation, fully funded, individual accounts
Payout age	65 (males); 60 (females)	65 (males and females), earlier for large accounts	62 (males); 57 (females), earlier for large accounts
Benefits	Indexed annuity or phased withdrawal, some lump sum if large accumulations	Annuity or phased withdrawal	Annuity or phased withdrawal, lump sum if large accumulation
Taxation	EET	EET	EET
Regulation	Maximum investment limits – but allows overseas assets and equities Minimum (relative) nominal rate of return	Investment limits: minimum govt transition bonds, at least 10% overseas	Investment restrictions: equities and foreign assets allowed, public debt max. of 50%
Actual asset allocations	Initially conservative 1997 – 46% govt bonds, 28% equities, 1% foreign assets	1997 – 95% equities	1997 – 20% govt securities, 44% bonds, 2.3% equities
Safety net (first pillar)	Minimum pension (after 30 years)	Universal public pension	Minimum pension (after 22 years)

Table A2.2 (cont.)

	Argentina	Bolivia	Colombia
Other second pillar (publicly provided)	Workers can opt to contribute to public PAYG DB system	Public PAYG DB plan closed	Option to stay in 'scaled down' public PAYG DB scheme or switch between
Transition	Compensatory pension	Compensatory pension	Recognition bonds

	Mexico	Peru	Uruguay
Commencement	1997	1993	1996
Administration	AFORES (private companies), centralised collections	AFPs (private companies)	AFAPs (private companies), centralised collection
Coverage	Private-sector workers	All workers	Mandatory above income threshold
Contributions	6.5% wages + (govt subsidy of 5.5% minimum wage + 4% wages for insurance, including health)	8% wages, increasing to 10% + insurance and admin. costs	15% wages above threshold + insurance and costs
Financing	DC, accumulation, fully funded	DC, accumulation, fully funded	DC, accumulation, fully funded
Payout age	65, earlier for large accounts	65, earlier for large accounts	60 (males); 55 (women, increasing to 60 by 2003)
Benefits	Phased withdrawal or annuity, limited lump-sum option	Phased withdrawal or annuity	Indexed annuity only
Taxation	EET	TET	EET
Regulation	Investment restrictions: minimum 65% in government bonds. No minimum rate of return requirement	Relative rate of return requirement abolished in 1997	Investment restrictions – minimum govt securities. Absolute real rate of return requirement

Actual asset allocations	1997 – 99% government bonds	1997 – 0.7% govt securities, 32% bonds, 34% equities	1997 – 80% govt securities, 18% deposits
Safety net (first pillar)	Minimum pension (after 25 years)	Minimum pension – law passed but not operating	Basic pension (after 35 years), advanced pension (age 70, after 15 years)
Other second pillar (publicly provided)	Public PAYG closed to new workers	Option to stay in 'scaled down' public PAYG DB scheme	Workers below income threshold can opt for public PAYG DB scheme
Transition	Public PAYG closed to new workers, lifetime switch close to retirement	Recognition bonds	No transition, public pension remains

Source: James (1997; 1998), Queisser (1995; 1998), Stanton and Whiteford (1998), Valdes-Prieto (1998)

Table A2.3 Characteristics of private mandatory retirement saving – other OECD countries

	United Kingdom (Contracted out SERPS)	Sweden (Premium pension system)
Commencement	1978, expanded in 1980s and 1990s	1995
Administration	Private pension funds and personal pension providers	Privately managed mutual funds
Coverage	Voluntary – over 70% employees in occupational schemes or with private pensions in late 1990s	Mandatory for all employees
Contributions	Minimum contributions must satisfy the minimum employer-provided pension (GMP) or the minimum contribution to a personal pension (GMC)	2.5% earnings
Financing	DC and DB funded	DC, fully funded
Payout age	65 (men): 60 (women)	From age 61
Benefits	Mainly pensions/ annuities, some lump sums	Annuity
Taxation	EET	ETT
Regulation	Trust law	Contributions made only to mutual funds that satisfy fee and reporting requirements
Actual asset allocations	Nearly 80% equities (in 1986)	Around 60% bonds; 35% equities (in 1986)
Safety net (first pillar)	Means-tested welfare	Means-tested guarantee pension
Other second pillar (publicly provided)	Public PAYG earnings-related pensions – only for those who have not contracted out of public pensions	Public earnings-related notional DC PAYG (contribution 16% earnings)
Transition	na	Buffer funds accumulated

	Denmark (Labour market pensions)	The Netherlands
Commencement	1993	1957
Administration	Pension funds and insurance companies	Pension funds and insurance companies
Coverage	Collective bargaining covering 80% of workers	Compulsory where collective bargaining, covers 90% workers
Contributions	5–15%	variable
Financing	DC, funded	DB, funded
Payout age	60	65
Benefits	Lump sum and annuity	Life annuity
Taxation	ETT	EET
Regulation	Regulations on asset allocation – at least 60% assets in low-risk investments, guaranteed rate of return on pension contracts	Prudent-person concept applies
Actual asset allocations	65% bonds (1994)	63% bonds; 26% equities (1995)
Safety net (first pillar)	Yes	Yes
Other second pillar (publicly provided)	Flat rate plus small earnings-related public pensions	Flat rate, depends upon household composition
Transition	na	na

Source: Blake (2000b), Bovenberg (1994), Budd and Campbell (1998), Davis (1999b), Herbertsson et al. (2000), Laboul (1998), Kalisch and Aman (1998), OECD (1998a; 1999), Sundén (1998), Whitehouse (1998)

Table A2.4 Characteristics of private mandatory retirement saving – transition economies

	Poland	Latvia	Hungary
Commencement	1999	proposed	1998
Administration	Pension funds	One or several private asset managers	Mutual benefit funds
Coverage	Employed and self-employed. All new entrants	Mandatory for workers under 30	Mandatory for new workers, voluntary for others
Contributions	9% net of contributions (shared between employee and employer)	7% (rising from 2% initially)	8% employee contributions
Financing	Pension fund (employee choice)	DC, accumulation, fully funded	DC, accumulation, fully funded
Pensionable age	60 (females); 65 (males)	55 (females); 60 (males)	62
Benefits	Mandatory annuity	Mandatory annuity	Life annuity and lump sum
Taxation	EET	EET	EET
Regulation	Investment limits: for example, 40% shares, 5% foreign securities, 10% central bank bonds Relative rate of return guarantee	Investment rules: government-guaranteed securities of Latvia, other Baltic states, G10, EU countries. No rate of return requirement	Restrictions on internal asset management, relative rate of return requirement
Actual asset allocations	Bonds 80% (1999)		Mainly bills and bonds, equities < 1%
Safety net	Guaranteed minimum pension	Minimum pension	Means-tested social assistance
Other second pillar (publicly provided)	Public earnings-related notional DC PAYG (9% contribution)	Public earnings-related notional DC PAYG	Contribution of 22% to pre-existing public PAYG scheme
Transition	Reducing public pension benefits, funds from privatisation	na	Tax financing + parametric changes to system

Source: Chlon, Gora and Rutkowski (1999), Fox and Palmer (1999), Palacios and Rocha (1998)

Table A2.5 Characteristics of private mandatory retirement saving – Hong Kong

Commencement	2000
Administration	Private mandatory provident funds – company schemes or master trusts
Coverage	All employees and self-employed aged 18–65
Contributions	5% wages (employee) + 5% wages (employer) Voluntary contributions allowed
Financing	DC, accumulation, fully funded
Pensionable age	60
Benefits	Lump sum Fully preserved and portable
Taxation	EEE
Regulation	Prudent-man principle, subject to some regulations; for example, maximum 70% assets with foreign currency exposure
Actual asset allocations	na
Safety net (first pillar)	Social assistance
Other second pillar (publicly provided)	na
Transition	na

Source: Sin and MacArthur (2000)

APPENDIX 3

An Introduction to Options

Options confer the right but not obligation to buy or sell an asset, on prespecified terms. Options have been around since ancient times; the following quotation from Aristotle's *Politics* appears in more than one exposition of investments:

> Thales used a financial device which, though it was ascribed to his skill as a philosopher, is really open to anybody. The story is as follows: people had been saying to Thales that philosophy was useless, as it had left him a poor man. But he, deducing from his knowledge of the stars that there would be a good crop of olives, while it was still winter raised a little capital and used it to pay deposits on all the oil-presses in Miletus and Chios, thus securing an option on their hire. This cost him only a small sum, as there were no other bidders. Then the time of the olive-harvest came and as there was a sudden and simultaneous demand for oil-presses, he hired them out at any price he liked to ask. He made a lot of money and so demonstrated that it is easy for philosophers to be rich, if they want to; but that is not their object in life. (Aristotle, *The Politics*, Trans. T.A. Sinclair, Penguin Books, Harmondsworth, 1962, p. 48.)

The two main kinds of options are the *call option*, which confers the right to buy an asset, and the *put option*, which confers the right to sell. In either case the price charged for the option is known as its *premium*. Taking an option is like taking out an insurance policy. Hence the use of insurance terminology, such as 'premium' and 'writer'.

The right to exercise the option is sometimes confined to a single future date, in which case the option is said to be of the *European* variety. The alternative is an *American*-style option, which entitles the holder to exercise at any time up to the expiry date. Exchange traded options tend to be the American type. Because the American feature gives the option-taker more flexibility, an American option will always cost at least as much as a European one that is identical in other respects.

Embedded options are latent within a particular asset (real or financial) without having been stripped out and traded separately. Many decisions involve option-like flexibility aspects. For example, the *life-cycle model of retirement* (Chapter 2) sees the worker as holding an embedded American-style real option; namely, the right to exchange a future stream of wages for a future stream of retirement-conditioned benefits together with freedom from the disutility of work. Also relevant to pension economics are *basket* financial options to buy or sell an entire portfolio of securities. Numerous basket-option products are actively traded, and these are useful for the diversified portfolios that underlie the investment strategy of most pension schemes outside the self-managed sector.

Even the three-pillars doctrine (Chapter 1) can be interpreted as an options-based pension plan. Specifically, let L stand for the present value of a household's claim on the national retirement income system, and let π_i (i = 1, 2, 3) be the present value of the household's ith-pillar entitlement. According to the World Bank and others, retirement income policy should be designed so as to ensure:

$$L = \max(\pi_1, \pi_2 + \pi_3)$$

where π_1 is positive for all households, yet less than the sum of π_2 and π_3 in the case of most households.

The preset price at which the option-taker can buy or sell the security is the *strike* or *exercise* price. Whenever the strike price of a call is greater than the current market price of the underlying asset, or the strike price of a put is less than the current market price of the underlying asset, then the option in question is *out-of-the-money*. Whenever the strike price of a call is less than the current market price of the underlying security, or the strike price of a put is greater than the current market price of the underlying security, the option in question is *in-the-money*.

An in-the-money option has *intrinsic value* defined by the dollar amount the option-taker could net by exercising immediately. However, option premia are almost invariably higher than intrinsic values. The reason is *time value*, which is the price worth paying for the possibility that at some time between the purchase date and expiry date, news arrives about the underlying asset, thereby changing its price in a way that drives your option into (or further into) the money. In this way, we can decompose premium costs as follows:

Option premium = intrinsic value + time value

Time value decays as the expiry date draws closer.

Profit profiles

Profit profiles portray the relationship between the value of the underlying asset and the profits or losses incurred by option buyers and sellers
(see Figure A3.1). In Figures A3.1(a) and A3.1(b) the horizontal axis
shows possible values of the price of the underlying asset. The vertical
axis shows profits or losses incurred by an option buyer. The diagonal
lines have slopes of plus 45 degrees and minus 45 degrees respectively.

In Figure A3.1(a) the call premium is C, and the exercise price is S.
If at the exercise date the price of the underlying asset is less than S,
the call has finished out of the money and is worthless; the buyer has
lost $\$C$. If at the exercise date, the price of the underlying asset is $S+C$
then the option has finished sufficiently in-the-money for the premium
to be recouped. For prices higher than $S+C$, the option exercise will
realise positive net profits for the buyer.

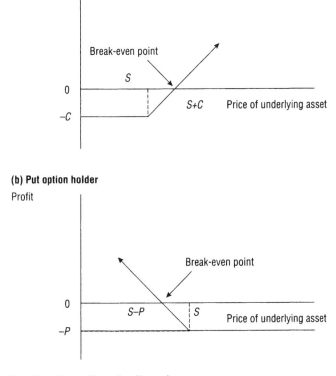

Figure A3.1 Profit profiles of calls and puts

In Figure A3.1(b) the put premium is P and the exercise price is again S. If at the exercise date the price of the underlying asset is more than S, the put has finished out-of-the-money and is worthless; the buyer has lost P. If at the exercise date the price of the underlying asset is less than $S–P$ then option exercise will realise positive net profits for the buyer.

Option valuation

Until the 1970s it was generally thought that accurate valuation of options would require knowledge of both the average degree of risk aversion of market participants and the expected return to the underlying asset. Black and Scholes (1973) demonstrated that options could be valued without attempting to measure either of these notoriously elusive magnitudes. Rather, under fairly mild assumptions, and abstracting from the complication of a dividend flow from the underlying asset, there were five factors affecting option premia:

- volatility of returns to the underlying asset
- price of the underlying asset at the time that the option is purchased
- strike price
- time to expiry
- interest rate applicable over the time to expiry.

Put options, for example, will be expensive to the extent that volatility is high, the price of the underlying asset is low, the strike price is high, the time to expiry is long and the interest rate is low.

References

Aaron, H. (1997), 'Privatizing Social Security: A Bad Idea whose Time will Never Come', *The Brookings Review*, vol. 15, no. 3, Summer 1997, pp. 16–23.

——(1999), 'Social Security: Tune It Up, Don't Trade It In', in H. Aaron and J. Shoven, *Should the United States Privatize Social Security?*, MIT Press, Cambridge, MA.

Aaron, H. and Shoven, J. (1999), *Should the United States Privatize Social Security?*, edited and with an introduction by B. Friedman, MIT Press, Cambridge, MA.

Advisory Council on Social Security (1997), *Final Report of the 1994–96 Advisory Council on Social Security*, Social Security Administration, Washington DC.

Agulnik, P. (1999), 'The Proposed State Second Pension', *Fiscal Studies*, vol. 20, no. 4, pp. 409–21.

Asher, M. (1999), *The Pension System in Singapore*, Pension Reform Primer Series, Social Protection Discussion Paper No. 9919, The World Bank, Washington DC.

ASX Index office *www.asx.com.au.*

Atkinson, M., Creedy, J. and Knox, D. (1996), 'Alternative Retirement Income Strategies: A Cohort Analysis of Lifetime Redistribution', *Economic Record*, vol. 72, no. 217, pp. 97–106.

——(1999), 'Some Implications of Changing the Tax Basis for Pension Funds', *Fiscal Studies*, vol. 20, no. 2, pp. 189–203.

Attorney-General's Department (1998), *Superannuation and Family Law: A Position Paper*, May 1998, Australian Government Publishing Service, Canberra.

——(1999), *Property and Family Law – Options for Change*, March 1999, Australian Government Publishing Service, Canberra.

Australian Bureau of Statistics (1992), *Retirement and Retirement Intentions in Australia*, ABS Cat. no. 6238.0, Australian Government Publishing Service, Canberra.

——(1997a), *Retirement and Retirement Intentions*, ABS Cat. no. 6238.0, November 1997, Australian Government Publishing Service, Canberra.

——(1997b), *Superannuation Australia*, ABS Cat. no. 6319.0, Australian Government Publishing Service, Canberra.

——(1998a), *Australian Demographic Statistics*, Cat. no. 3101.0, Australian Government Publishing Service, Canberra.

——(1998b), *Year Book Australia 1998*, Australian Government Publishing Service, Canberra.

——(1999), *Australian System of National Accounts 1997–98*, ABS Cat. no. 5204.0, Australian Government Publishing Service, Canberra.

——*Employee Earnings, Benefits and Trade Union Membership*, ABS no. 6310.0 (various issues), Australian Government Publishing Service, Canberra.

——*Employment Benefits Australia*, Cat. no. 6334.0 (various issues), Australian Government Publishing Service, Canberra.

——*Consumer Price Index*, Cat. no. 6401.1, (various issues), Australian Government Publishing Service, Canberra.

Australian Prudential Regulation Authority (APRA) Superannuation Trends, June quarter 2000, www.apra.gov.au.

——(2001), *Superannuation Trends*, September 2000.

Baekgaard, H. (1998), *The Distribution of Household Wealth in Australia: 1986 and 1993*, Discussion Paper No. 34, National Centre for Social and Economic Modelling, University of Canberra.

Baeza Valdes, S. and Burger-Torres, R. (1995), 'Calidad de las Pensiones del Sistema Privado Chileno', in S. Baeza Valdes and F. Margozzini (eds), *Quince Anos Despues: Una Mirada al Sistema Privado de Pensiones*, Centro de Estudios Publicos, Santiago.

Banks, J., Blundell, R. and Tanner, S. (1998), 'Is There a Retirement-Savings Puzzle?', *American Economic Review*, vol. 88, no. 4, September, pp. 769–88.

Barrientos, A. (1998), *Pension Reform in Latin America*, Ashgate Publishing Ltd, Aldershot, England.

Bateman, H. (1997), 'Risk Management Issues for Mandatory Private Retirement Provision: Roles for Options', *Australian Journal of Management*, vol. 22, no. 2, December 1997, pp. 175–97.

——(1998), *Three Essays on the Economics of Mandatory Private Retirement Saving*, PhD thesis, University of New South Wales, Australia.

Bateman, H. and Ablett, J. (2000), 'Compulsory Superannuation and Australian Generational Accounts', *Economic Analysis and Policy*, vol. 30, no. 1, March, pp. 33–46.

Bateman, H., Doyle, S. and Piggott, J. (1999), 'Private Mandatory Retirement Provision: Design and Implementation Challenges', paper presented to the Social Security Conference, Institute for Economic Research, University of Tokyo, September 1999.

Bateman, H., Frisch J., Kingston G. and Piggott, J. (1991), 'Demographics, Retirement Saving, and Superannuation Policy: An Australian Perspective', in P. Stemp (ed.), *Saving and Policy: Proceedings of a Conference*, Centre for Economic Policy Research, Australian National University, Canberra, pp. 193–227.

Bateman, H., Kingston, G. and Piggott, J. (1993), 'Taxes, Retirement Transfers and Annuities', *The Economic Record*, vol. 69, no. 206, September 1993, pp. 274–84.

——(1994), 'The Equity Implications of Mandated Funded Pension Schemes', in J. Creedy (ed.) *Taxation, Poverty and Income Distribution*, Edward Elgar, England, pp. 163–74.

Bateman, H. and Piggott, J. (1992), 'The Superannuation Guarantee Charge: What Do We Know About Its Aggregate Impact?', in *Economic and Social*

Consequences of Australia's Ageing Population – Preparing for the Twenty-first Century, EPAC Background Paper no. 23: 41–52.

——(1997), *Private Pensions in OECD Countries – Australia*, Labour Market and Social Policy Occasional Papers, no. 23, OECD, Paris.

——(1998), 'Mandatory Retirement Saving in Australia', *Annals of Public and Cooperative Economics*, vol. 69, no. 4, December 1998, pp. 547–69.

——(1999a), 'Mandating Retirement Provision: The Australian Experience', *Geneva Papers on Risk and Insurance*, vol. 24, no. 1, January 1999, pp. 93–113.

——(1999b), *The Costs of the Superannuation Surcharge*, CEDA Information Paper No. 66, October 1999, Committee for Economic Development of Australia, Sydney.

Bateman, H. and Valdes-Prieto S. (1999), *The Mandatory Private Old Age Income Schemes of Australia and Chile: A Comparison*, Research Paper no. 13, Retirement Economics Group, University of New South Wales, Sydney.

Bernheim, D. (1994), *Do Households Appreciate their Financial Vulnerabilities?*, mimeo, Princeton University.

Bernheim, D. and Scholz, J. (1993), 'Private Saving and Public Policy', *Tax Policy and the Economy*, vol. 7, pp. 73–110.

Bernheim, D., Skinner J. and Weinberg, S. (1997), *What Accounts for the Variation in Retirement Wealth Among US Households?*, Working Paper 6227, National Bureau of Economic Research, Cambridge, MA.

Black, F. and Litterman, R. (1992), *Global Asset Allocation and the Home Bias*, mimeo, Goldman Sachs.

Black, F. and Scholes, M. (1973), 'The Pricing of Options and Corporate Liabilities', *Journal of Political Economy*, vol. 81, no. 3, pp. 637–59.

Blake, D. (1995), *Pension Schemes and Pension Funds in the United Kingdom*, Clarendon Press, Oxford.

——(1997), 'Pension Choices and Pension Policy in the United Kingdom', in S. Valdes-Prieto (ed.), *The Economics of Pensions: Principles, Policies and International Experience*, Cambridge University Press, Cambridge.

——(1999a), *Financial System Requirements for Successful Pension Reform*, Pensions Institute Discussion Paper PI–9906, January, Pensions Institute, Birkbeck College, London.

——(1999b), 'Annuity Markets: Problems and Solutions', *Geneva Papers on Risk and Insurance: Issues and Practice*, vol. 24, no. 3, July 1999, pp. 358–75.

——(1999c), 'Annuities in Pension Plans', text of talk for World Bank Annuities Workshop, 7–8 June.

——(2000a), 'The United Kingdom: Examining the Switch from Low Public Pensions to High-Cost Private Pensions', in M.S. Feldstein and H. Siebert (eds), *Coping With the Pension Crisis – Where Does Europe Stand?* University of Chicago Press, presented at the National Bureau of Economic Research, Kiel Institute Conference on 'Coping with the Pension crisis – Where does Europe Stand?', Berlin March 2000 and forthcoming.

——(2000b), *Two Decades of Pension Reform in the UK: What are the Implications for Occupational Pension Schemes?*, Pensions Institute Discussion Paper PI–2004, March, Pensions Institute, Birkbeck College, London.

——(2000c), 'Does It Matter What Type of Pension Scheme You Have?', *Economic Journal*, vol. 110, February 2000, pp. F46–F81.

Blake, D. and Timmerman, A. (1999), *Mutual Fund Performance: Evidence from the UK*, Pensions Institute Discussion Paper PI–9903, Pensions Institute, Birkbeck College, London.

Blinder, A.S. and Rosen, H.S. (1985), 'Notches', *American Economic Review*, vol. 75, no. 4, September 1985, pp. 736–47.

Blöndal, S. and Scarpetta, S. (1998), 'Retire Early, Stay at Work?', *OECD Observer*, No. 212, June/July 1998, pp. 15–19.

Bodie, Z. (1990a), 'Pension Funds and Financial Innovation', *Financial Management*, vol. 19, no. 3, Autumn, pp. 11–22.

——(1990b), 'Pensions as Retirement Income Insurance', *Journal of Economic Literature*, vol. 38, pp. 28–49.

——(1990c), 'Inflation insurance', *Journal of Risk and Insurance*, vol. 57, no. 4, pp. 634–45.

Bodie, Z. and Crane, D.B. (1997), 'Personal Investing: Advice, Theory and Evidence', *Financial Analysts Journal*, vol. 53, no. 6, November–December 1997, pp. 13–23.

——(1999), 'The Design and Production of New Retirement Saving Products', *Journal of Portfolio Management*, vol. 25, no. 2, Winter 1999, pp. 77–82.

Bodie, Z., Merton, R.C. and Samuelson, W.F. (1992), 'Labor Supply Flexibility and Portfolio Choice in a Life Cycle Model', *Journal of Economic Dynamics and Control*, vol. 16, no. 3–4, July–October 1992, pp. 427–49.

Bodie, Z., Mitchell, O.S. and Turner, J. (eds) (1996), *Securing Employer-based Pensions: An International Perspective*, Pensions Research Council, University of Pennsylvania Press, Philadelphia.

Bohn, H. (1998), *Risk Sharing in a Stochastic Overlapping Generations Economy*, mimeo, University of California at Santa Barbara.

Boskin, M., Kotlikoff, L. and Shoven, J. (1988), 'Personal Security Accounts: A Proposal for Fundamental Social Security Reform', in S. Wachter (ed.), *Social Security and Private Pensions: Providing for Retirement in the Twenty-first Century*, Lexington Books, USA, pp. 179–206.

Bovenberg, A.L. (1994), *The Economics of Pensions: The Case of The Netherlands*, Papers and Proceedings 9401, Research Centre for Economic Policy, Erasmus University, Rotterdam.

Brennan, M.J. and Cao, H.H. (1997), 'International Portfolio Investment Flows', *Journal of Finance*, vol. 52, no. 5, December 1997, pp. 1851–80.

Brown, C. (1993), *Tax Expenditures and Measuring the Long-term Costs and Benefits of Retirement Income Policy*, Retirement Income Modelling Task Force Conference Paper no. 93/1, Canberra, July.

Brown, J., Mitchell, O. S. and Poterba, J. (1999), *The Role of Real Annuities and Indexed Bonds in an Individual Accounts Retirement Program*, Working Paper 7005, National Bureau of Economic Research, Cambridge, MA.

Brugiavini, A. (1993), 'Uncertainty Resolution and the Timing of Annuity Purchases', *Journal of Public Economics*, vol. 50, no. 1, January 1993, pp. 31–62.

Budd, A. and Campbell, N. (1998), 'The Roles of the Public and Private Sectors in the UK Pension System', in M. Feldstein (ed.), *Privatizing Social Security*, National Bureau of Economic Research Project Report, University of Chicago, Chicago, pp. 99–127.

Burbidge, J.B. and Robb, A.L. (1980), 'Pensions and Retirement Behavior', *Canadian Journal of Economics*, vol. 13, pp. 421–37.

Campbell, J.Y. (2000), 'Asset Pricing at the Millennium', *Journal of Finance*, vol. 55, no. 4, August 2000, pp. 1515–67.

Campbell, J.Y., Cocco, J., Gomes, F. and Maenhout, P. (1999), *Investing Retirement*

Wealth: A Life-Cycle Model, Working Paper No. 7029, National Bureau of Economic Research, Cambridge, MA.

Campbell, J.Y. and Viceira, L. (1999), 'Who Should Buy Long-term Bonds?', Working Paper No. 6801, National Bureau of Economic Research, Cambridge, MA.

Carroll, C.D. (1997), 'Buffer-Stock Saving and the Life Cycle/Permanent Income Hypothesis', *Quarterly Journal of Economics*, vol. 112, no. 1, February 1997, pp. 1–55.

Carroll, C.D. and Summers, L.H. (1991), 'Consumption Growth Parallels Income Growth: Some New Evidence', in R.D. Berheim and J.B. Shoven (eds), *National Saving and Economic Performance*, A National Bureau of Economic Research Project Report, University of Chicago Press, Chicago, pp. 305–43.

Castillo, R.B. (1993), 'Analysis of a National Private Pension Scheme: The Case of Chile – Comments', *International Labour Review*, vol. 123, no. 3, pp. 407–16.

Chan, S. and Huff Stevens, A. (1999), *Job Loss and Retirement Behavior of Older Men*, Working Paper No. 6920, National Bureau of Economic Research, Cambridge, MA.

Chand, S. and Jaeger, A. (1996), *Aging Populations and Public Pension Schemes*, Occasional Paper No. 147, International Monetary Fund, Washington DC.

Chlon, A., Gora, M. and Rutkowski, M. (1999), *Shaping Pension Reform in Poland: Security Through Diversity*, Pension Reform Primer Series, Social Protection Discussion Paper No. 9923, August 1999, The World Bank, Washington DC.

Clare, R. and Connor, D. (1999a), *Superannuation Tax Concessions – Recent Trends and Levels*, ASFA Research Centre, April 1999.

——(1999b), *The Superannuation Market in Australia*, paper presented to the Seventh Annual Colloquium of Superannuation Researchers, Melbourne, July.

Clark, R. and Wolper, E. (1997), 'Pension Tax Expenditures: Magnitude, Distribution and Economic Effects', in S. Schieber and J. Shoven (eds), *Public Policy Toward Pensions*, MIT Press, Cambridge, MA.

Commonwealth Treasury of Australia (1998), *Economic Roundup*, Summer 1998, Australian Government Publishing Service, Canberra.

——(1999), *Economic Roundup*, Summer 1999, Australian Government Publishing Service, Canberra.

Cooper, I. and Kaplanis, E. (1994), 'Home Bias in Equity Portfolios, Inflation Hedging, and International Capital Market Equilibrium', *Review of Financial Studies*, vol. 7, no. 1, Spring 1994, pp. 45–60.

Corporate Law Economic Reform Program (1999), *Financial Products, Service Providers and Markets – An Integrated Framework*, Australian Government Publishing Service, Canberra.

Costa, D. (1998), *The Evolution of Retirement: An American Economic History, 1880–1990*, NBER Series on Long-term Factors in Economic Development, University of Chicago Press, Chicago.

Dabscheck, B. (1989), *Australian Industrial Relations in the 1980s,* Oxford University Press, Melbourne.

Davis, E.P. (1995), *Pension Funds: Retirement-income Security and Capital Markets, an International Perspective*, Clarendon Press, Oxford.

——(1998), 'Regulation of Pension Fund Assets', in *Institutional Investors in the New Financial Landscape*, OECD, Paris.

——(1999a), *Linkages between Pension Reform and Financial Sector Development,*

Pensions Institute Discussion Paper PI–9909, Pensions Institute, Birkbeck College, London.

——(1999b), *Investment of Mandatory Funded Pension Schemes*, Pensions Institute Discussion Paper PI–9908, Pensions Institute, Birkbeck College, London.

——(2000), *Pension Funds, Financial Intermediation and the New Financial Landscape*, Pensions Institute Discussion Paper PI–2010, Pensions Institute, Birkbeck College, London.

Davis, S. and Willen, P. (2000), *Occupation-level Income Shocks and Asset Returns': Their Covariance and and Implications for Portfolio Choice*, Working Paper No. 7905, National Bureau of Economic Research, Cambridge, MA.

Demarco, G. and Rofman, R. (1999), *Implementing a Pension Reform: Practical Problems and Solutions*, mimeo, The World Bank, Washington DC.

Department of Family and Community Services (2000), *Annual Report 1999–2000*, AGPS, Canberra.

Department of Social Security (1984), *Population, Pension Costs and Pensioners' Incomes*, mimeo, London.

——(1998), *A New Contract for Welfare: Partnership in Pensions*, Cm. 4179, The Stationery Office, London.

Diamond, P. (1977), 'A Framework for Social Security Analysis', *Journal of Public Economics*, vol. 8, no. 3, December 1977, pp. 211–24.

——(1993), *Privatization of Social Security: Lessons from Chile*, Working Paper No. 4510, National Bureau of Economic Research, October 1993, Cambridge, MA.

——(1996), 'Proposals to Restructure Social Security', *Journal of Economic Perspectives*, vol. 10, no. 3, Summer 1996, pp. 67–88.

——(1997), 'Insulation of Pensions from Political Risk' in S. Valdes-Prieto (ed.), *The Economics of Pensions: Principles, Policies and International Experience*, Cambridge University Press, pp. 33–57.

——(ed.) (1999a), *Issues in Privatizing Social Security*, Report of an Expert Panel of the National Academy of Social Insurance, MIT Press, Cambridge, Massachusetts.

——(1999b), *Administrative Costs and Equilibrium Charges with Individual Accounts*, Working Paper No. 7050, National Bureau of Economic Research, Cambridge, MA.

Diamond, P. and Valdes-Prieto, S. (1994), 'Social Security Reforms', in B. Bosworth, R. Dornbusch and R. Laban (eds), *The Chilean Economy: Policy Lessons and Challenges*, Brookings Institution, Washington DC, pp. 257–320.

Dilnot, A. (1992), 'Taxation and Private Pensions: Costs and Consequences', in *Private Pensions and Public Policy*, OECD, Paris.

——(1996), 'The Taxation of Private Pensions', in Z. Bodie, O.S. Mitchell and J. Turner (eds), *Securing Employer-based Pensions: An International Perspective*, Pensions Research Council, University of Pennsylvania Press, Philadelphia.

Dilnot, A. and Johnson, P. G. (1993a), *The Taxation of Private Pensions*, Institute for Fiscal Studies, London.

——(1993b), 'Tax Expenditures: The Case of Occupational Pensions', *Fiscal Studies*, vol. 14, no. 1, February 1993, pp. 42–56.

Dilnot, A., Disney, R., Johnson, P. and Whitehouse, E. (1994), *Pensions Policy in the UK. An Economic Analysis*, Institute for Fiscal Studies, London.

Disney, R. (1995), 'Occupational Pension Schemes: Prospects and Reforms in the UK', *Fiscal Studies*, vol. 16, no. 3, August 1995, pp. 19–39.

——(1996), *Can we Afford to Grow Older? A Perspective on the Economics of Aging*, MIT Press, Cambridge, MA and London.

——(1999), *Notional Accounts as Pension Reform Strategy: An Evaluation*, Pension Reform Primer Series, Social Protection Discussion Paper No. 9928, December 1999, The World Bank, Washington DC.

——(2000) 'Crises in Public Pension Programmes in OECD: What Are the Reform Options?', *Economic Journal*, vol. 110, no. 461, February 2000, pp. F1–23.

Disney, R., Emmerson, C. and Tanner, S. (1999), *Partnership in Pensions: An Assessment*, Commentary No. 78, March 1999, Institute for Fiscal Studies, London.

Disney, R. and Whitehouse, E. (1999), *Pension Plans and Retirement Incentives*, Pension Reform Primer Series, Social Protection Discussion Paper No. 9924, September, The World Bank, Washington DC.

Dixon, J. (1982), 'Provident Funds in the Third World: A Cross-national Review', *Public Administration and Development*, vol. 2, pp. 325–44.

Doyle, S., Kingston, G. and Piggott, J. (1999), 'Taxing Super', *Australian Economic Review*, vol. 32, no. 3, September, pp. 207–18.

Doyle, S. and Piggott, J. (1998), 'Mandatory Annuity Design: A Preliminary Study', paper prepared for the Society of Actuaries Conference 'Retirement Needs Framework', Florida, December.

——(1999), 'Retirement Payouts in a Mandatory Annuity Market', paper presented to the University of Munich Welfare State Workshop, Venice International University, San Servolo, July 2000.

Edey, M. and Britten-Jones, M. (1990), 'Saving and Investment', in S. Grenville (ed.), *The Australian Macroeconomy in the 1980s*, Reserve Bank of Australia, Sydney.

Edwards, S. (1998), 'The Chilean Pension Reform: A Pioneering Program', in M. Feldstein (ed.), *Privatizing Social Security*, National Bureau of Economic Research, University of Chicago Press, Chicago, pp. 33–62.

Emmerson, C. and Tanner S. (1999), *The Government's Proposals for Stakeholder Pensions*, IFS Briefing Note 1/99, October, Institute for Fiscal Studies, London.

Engen, E., Gale, W. and Scholz, J. (1996), 'The Illusory Effects of Saving Incentives on Saving', *Journal of Economic Perspectives*, vol. 10, no. 4, pp. 113–38.

English Life Tables (1909), 'English Life Tables No. 6', *Journal of the Institute of Actuaries*, vol. 43.

Feldstein, M. (1976), 'Social Security and Saving: The Extended Life-cycle Theory', *American Economic Review*, vol. 66, no. 2, May, pp. 77–86.

——(1996), 'The Missing Piece in Policy Analysis: Social Security Reform', *American Economic Review*, vol. 68, no. 2, May, pp. 1–14.

——(1997), 'Transition to a Fully Funded Pension System: Five Economic Issues', Working Paper No. 6149, National Bureau of Economic Research, August, Cambridge, MA.

——(ed.) (1998), *Privatizing Social Security*, National Bureau of Economic Research Project Report, University of Chicago, Chicago.

Feldstein, M. and Ranguelova, E. (2000), *Accumulated Pension Collars: A Market Approach to Reducing the Risk of Investment-based Social Security Reform*, Working Paper No. 7861, National Bureau of Economic Research, Cambridge, MA.

Feldstein, M. and Samwick, A. (1997), *The Economics of Prefunding Social Security and Medicare Benefits*, National Bureau of Economic Research Working Paper No. 6055, June.

——(1998), 'The Transition Path in Privatizing Social Security', in M. Feldstein (ed), *Privatizing Social Security*, University of Chicago Press, Chicago.

Fields, G.S. and Mitchell, O.S. (1984), *Retirement, Pensions, and Social Security*, The MIT Press, Cambridge, MA.

Finkelstein, A. and Poterba, J. (1999), *Selection Effects in the Market for Individual Annuities: New evidence from the United Kingdom*, mimeo, Massachusetts Institute of Technology.

FitzGerald, V.W. (1993), *National Saving: A Report to the Treasurer*, Australian Government Publishing Service, Canberra.

Formica, A. and Kingston, G. (1991), 'Inflation Insurance for Australian Annuitants', *Australian Journal of Management*, vol. 16, no. 2, December, pp. 145–64.

Foster, R.A. (1996), *Australian Economic Statistics 1949–50 to 1994–95*, Reserve Bank of Australia, Sydney.

Fox, L. and Palmer, E. (1999), *Latvian Pension Reform*, Pension Reform Primer Series, Social Protection Discussion Paper No. 9922, September, The World Bank, Washington DC.

——(2000), New Approaches to Multi-Pillar Pension Systems: What in the World is Going On?, Paper presented for the World Bank Conference, 'New Ideas About Old Age Security', September 1999.

Friedman, B.M. and Warshawsky, M.J. (1990), 'The Cost of Annuities: Implications for Saving Behaviour and Bequest', *Quarterly Journal of Economics*, vol. 105, no. 1, February 1990, pp. 135–54.

Friedman, M. (1957), *A Theory of the Consumption Function*, National Bureau of Economic Research, Princeton, .

Gallagher, P. (1997), *Assessing the National Savings Effect of the Government's Superannuation Policies: Some Examples of the New RIMGROUP National Savings Methodology*, Retirement Income Modelling Task Force, Paper presented to the Fifth Colloquium of Superannuation Researchers, University of Melbourne, July.

Gordon, M., Mitchell, O.S. and Twinney, M. (eds.) (1997), *Positioning Pensions for the Twenty-first Century*, Pensions Research Council, University of Pennsylvania Press, Philadelphia.

Gordon, R. and Varian, H. (1988), 'Intergenerational Risk Sharing', *Journal of Public Economics*, vol. 37, no. 2, November 1988, pp. 185–202.

Gourinchas, P.-O. and Parker, J. (1999), *Consumption over the Life Cycle*, Working Paper No. 7271, National Bureau of Economic Research, Cambridge, MA.

Gruber, J. and Wise, D. (eds) (1999), *Social Security Programs and Retirement around the World*, National Bureau of Economic Research Project Report, University of Chicago, Chicago.

Hall, R.E. (1978), 'Stochastic Implications of the Life Cycle – Permanent Income Hypothesis: Theory and Evidence', *Journal of Political Economy*, vol. 86, no. 6, December, pp. 971–87.

Hamermesh, D. (1985), 'Expectations, Life Expectancy, and Economic Behaviour', *Quarterly Journal of Economics*, vol. 10, no. 2, May, pp. 389–408.

Hamilton, B. and Whalley, J. (1985), 'Tax Treatment of Housing in a Dynamic Sequenced General Equilibrium Model', *Journal of Public Economics*, vol. 27, no. 2, July 1985, pp. 157–75.

Hamilton, J.H. (1987), 'Taxation, Saving and Portfolio Choice in a Continuous Time Model', *Public Finance*, vol. 42, no. 2, pp. 264–84.

Hancock, K.J. (1976), *National Superannuation Committee of Inquiry – Final Report*, Australian Government Publishing Service, Canberra.

Hannah, L. (1986), *Inventing Retirement: The Development of Occupational Pensions in Britain*, Cambridge University Press, London.

Hathaway, N. (1992), 'Super Reserving Policies', paper presented to the Second Annual Colloquium of Superannuation Researchers, University of Melbourne, (7 and 8 July).

Hayashi, F., Altonji, J. and Kotlikoff, L. (1996), 'Risk-sharing between and within Families', *Econometrica*, vol. 64, no. 2, March 1996, pp. 261–94.

Heaton, J. and Lucas, D. (2000), 'Portfolio Choice and Asset Prices: The Importance of Entrepreneurial Risk', *Journal of Finance*, vol. 50, no. 3, June 2000, pp. 1163–98.

Hely, S. (1999), 'Good Returns Set the Scene for Funds' Growth', *Superfunds: The Journal of the Association of Superannuation and Provident Funds of Australia*, no. 222, March, pp. 20–9.

Hemming, R. and Kay, J. (1982), 'The Costs of the State Earnings-related Pension Scheme', *Economic Journal*, vol. 92, no. 366, June, pp. 300–19.

Hepp, S. (1990), *The Swiss Pension Funds: An Emerging New Investment Force*, Paul-Haupt, Berne.

——(1998), 'Mandatory Occupational Pension Schemes in Switzerland: The First Ten Years', *Annals of Public and Cooperative Economics*, vol. 69, no. 4, December, pp. 533–45.

Herbertsson, T.T., Orszag, J.H. and Orszag, P. R. (2000), *Retirement in the Nordic Countries: Prospects and Proposals for Reform*, report prepared for the Nordic Council of Ministers, Report 2000–19, Centre for Pensions and Social Insurance, London, http://www.pensions-research.org/papers.

Holzmann, R. (1997), 'Pension Reform, Financial Market Development and Economic Growth: Preliminary Evidence from Chile', *IMF Staff Papers*, vol. 44, no. 2, pp. 149–78.

Hsieh, S.-J., Chen, A. and Ferris, A. (1994), 'The Valuation of PBGC Insurance Premiums Using an Option Pricing Model', *Journal of Financial and Quantitative Analysis*, vol. 29, no. 1, March 1994, pp. 89–99.

Hubbard, R. and Skinner, J. (1996), 'Assessing the Effectiveness of Saving Incentives', *Journal of Economic Perspectives*, vol. 10, no. 4, pp. 73–90.

Hurd, M. (1990), 'Research on the Elderly: Economic Status, Retirement, and Consumption and Saving', *Journal of Economic Literature*, vol. 28, no. 2, June 1990, pp. 565–67.

Hurd, M. and McGarry, K. (1995), *The Predictive Validity of Subjective Probabilities of Survival*, Working Paper No. 6193, National Bureau of Economic Research, Cambridge, MA.

Iglesias, A. and Palacios, R. (2000), *Managing Public Pension Reserves, Part 1: Evidence from the International Experience*, Pension Reform Primer Series, Social Protection Discussion Paper No. 0003, January 2000, The World Bank, Washington DC.

Intech *www.Intech.com.au.*

Ippolito, R. (1990), *An Economic Appraisal of Pension Tax Policy in the United States*, Pension Research Council, University of Pennsylvania Press, Philadelphia.

James, E. (1997), *New Systems for Old Age Security: Theory, Practice and Empirical*

Evidence, Policy Research Working Paper No. 1766, The World Bank, Washington DC.

——(1998), 'The Political Economy of Social Security Reform: A Cross-country Review', *Annals of Public and Cooperative Economics*, vol. 69, no. 4, December 1998, pp. 451–82.

James, E., Ferrier, G., Smalhout, J. and Vittas, D. (1998), 'Mutual Funds and Institutional Investments – What is the Most Efficient Way to Set up Individual Accounts in a Social Security System?', paper presented to the NBER Conference on Social Security, 4 December.

James, E., Smalhout, J. and Vittas, D. (1999), 'Administrative Costs and the Organization of Individual Account Systems: A Comparative Perspective', paper presented to the World Bank Conference 'New Ideas About Old Age Security', September.

James, E. and Vittas, D. (1999), *Annuity Markets in Comparative Perspective: Do Consumers get their Money's Worth?*, mimeo, The World Bank, Washington DC.

Johnson, P. (1992), 'The Taxation of Occupational and Private Pensions in Western Europe', in Mortensen, J. (ed.), *The Future of Pensions in the European Community*, Brasseys, UK, pp. 133–50.

Johnson, P. and Stears, G. (1996), 'Should the Basic State Pension be a Contributory Benefit', *Fiscal Studies*, vol. 17, no. 1, February 1996, pp. 105–12.

Kalisch, D. and Aman, T. (1998), *Retirement Income Systems: The Reform Process Across OECD Countries*, OECD Ageing Working Paper AWP3.4, OECD, Paris.

Kingston, G. (1995), 'The Foreign Currency Loans Affair: An Economist's Perspective', *Australian Economic Papers*, vol. 34, no. 64, June, pp. 31–49.

——(2000), 'Efficient Timing of Retirement', *Review of Economic Dynamics*, vol. 3, pp. 831–40.

Kingston, G., Bateman, H. and Piggott, J. (1992), 'Customised Investment Strategies for Accumulations Superannuation', in K. Davis and I. Harper (eds), *Superannuation and the Australian Financial System*, Allen and Unwin, pp. 139–56.

Kingston, G. and Piggott, J. (1993), 'A Ricardian Equivalence Theorem for the Taxation of Pension Funds', *Economics Letters*, vol. 42, no. 4, pp. 399–403.

——(1999), 'The Geometry of Life Annuities', *Manchester School*, vol. 67, no. 2, March 1999, pp. 187–91.

Knox D. (1991), *Tax, Super and the Age Pension: The Issues of Cost, Equity and Incentives*, Research Study No. 14, Australian Tax Research Foundation, Sydney.

——(1993), 'Taxing Superannuation in Australia: Costs and Benefits of the Alternatives', *Australian Tax Forum*, vol. 10, no. 1, pp. 39–74.

Kohli, M., Rein R., Guillemard A.-M. and Van Gunsteren H. (eds) (1991), *Time for Retirement: Comparative Studies of Early Exit from the Labour Force*, Cambridge University Press, Cambridge.

Kotlikoff, L. (1992), *Generational Accounting*, The Free Press, New York.

——(1996a), 'Privatization of Social Security: How It Works and Why It Matters', in J. Poterba (ed.), *Tax Policy and the Economy*, Vol. 10, MIT Press, Cambridge, Massachusetts.

——(1996b), *Simulating the Privatization of Social Security in General Equilibrium*, Working Paper No. 5776, September, National Bureau of Economic Research, Cambridge, MA.

Kotlikoff, L. and Sachs, J. (1997), 'Privatizing Social Security: It's High Time to Privatize', *The Brookings Review*, vol. 15, no. 3, Summer 1997, pp. 16–23.

Kotlikoff, L., Smetters, K. and Walliser, J. (1998), *Social Security, Privatization and Progressivity*, Working Paper No. 6428, February, National Bureau of Economic Research, Cambridge, MA.

Kotlikoff, L. and Spivak, A. (1981), 'The Family as an Incomplete Annuities Market', *Journal of Political Economy*, vol. 89, no. 2, April, pp. 372–91.

Kuhn, P. and Davies, J. (1987), *Social Security, Longevity, and Moral Hazard*, University of Western Ontario Department of Economics Research Report, no. 8706, April.

Laboul, A. (1998), *Private Pension Systems: Regulatory Policies*, OECD Aging Working Paper AWP2.2, OECD, Paris.

Laibson, D. (1996), *Hyperbolic Discount Functions, Undersaving and Savings Policy*, Working Paper No. 5635, June, National Bureau of Economic Research, Cambridge, MA.

Laibson, D., Repetto, A. and Tobacman, J. (1998), 'Self-control and Saving for Retirement', *Brookings Papers on Economic Activity*, January–June 1998, pp. 91–172.

Lazear, E.P. (1979), 'Why Is There Mandatory Retirement?', *Journal of Political Economy*, vol. 87, no. 6, December 1979, pp. 1261–84.

——(1986), 'Retirement from the Labor Force', in O. Ashenfelter and R. Layard (eds), *Handbook of Labour Economics*, North-Holland, Amsterdam.

Leckey, A. (1999), 'Cash-balance Pensions Anger Older Workers', *Chicago Tribune*, 26 June, Section 2, p. 1.

Lumsdaine, R., Stock, J. and Wise, D. (1997), 'Retirement Incentives: The Interaction between Employer-provided Pensions, Social Security, and Retiree Health Benefits', in M. Hurd and N. Yashiro (eds), *The Economics of Aging in the United States and Japan*, University of Chicago Press, Chicago.

Mankiw, N.G., Romer, D. and Weil, D.N. (1992), 'A Contribution to the Empirics of Economic Growth', *Quarterly Journal of Economics*, vol. 107, no. 2, May, pp. 407–37.

McGarry, K. and Schoeni, R. (1998), *Social Security, Economic Growth, and the Rise in Independence of Elderly Widows in the 20th Century*, Working Paper No. 6511, April, National Bureau of Economic Research, Cambridge, MA.

Meade, J.E. (1978), *The Structure and Reform of Direct Taxation*, Allen and Unwin for the Institute for Fiscal Studies, London.

Merrilees, W.J. (1982), 'The Mass Exodus of Older Males from the Labour Force: An Exploratory Analysis', *Australian Bulletin of Labour*, vol. 8, no. 2, March 1982, pp. 81–94.

Merton, R.C. (1969), 'Lifetime Portfolio Selection Under Uncertainty: The Continuous Time Case', *Review of Economics and Statistics*, vol. 51, no. 3, August, pp. 247–57.

——(1971), 'Optimum Consumption and Portfolio Rules in a Continuous-time Model', *Journal of Economic Theory*, vol. 3, no. 4, December 1971, pp. 373–413.

Merton, R.C., Bodie, Z. and Marcus, A. (1987), 'Pension Plan Integration as Insurance against Social Security Risk', in Z. Bodie, J. Shoven and D. Wise (eds), *Issues in Pension Economics*, National Bureau of Economic Research Project Report series, University of Chicago Press.

Mitchell, O.S. (1998a), 'Administrative Costs in Public and Private Retirement

Systems', in M. Feldstein (ed.), *Privatizing Social Security*, NBER, US, pp. 403–52.

——(1998b), *Building an Environment for Pension Reform in Developing Countries*, Social Protection Discussion Paper No. 9803, January, The World Bank, Washington DC.

——(1999), *Evaluating Administrative Costs in Mexico's AFORES Pension System*, Working Paper No. 99–1, Pensions Research Council, Wharton School, University of Pennsylvania.

Mitchell, O.S. and Bodie, Z. (2000), 'A Framework for Analyzing and Managing Retirement Risks', Working Paper No. 2000–4, June, Pensions Research Council, forthcoming in O.S. Mitchell, Z. Bodie, B. Hammond and S. Zeldes (eds) (2001), *Financial Innovations for Retirement Income*, Pensions Research Council, Wharton School, University of Pennsylvania.

Mitchell, O.S. and Fields, G. (1984), 'The Economics of Retirement Behavior', *Journal of Labor Economics*, vol. 2, no. 1, January, pp. 84–105.

Mitchell, O.S. and Hsin Ping Lung (1997), 'Public Sector Pensions and Performance', in S. Valdes-Prieto (ed.), *The Economics of Pensions: Principles, Policies and International Experience*, Cambridge University Press, Cambridge.

Mitchell, O.S., Myers, R. and Young, H. (eds) (1999a), *Prospects for Social Security Reform*, Pensions Research Council, University of Pennsylvania Press, Philadelphia.

——(eds) (1999b), 'An Overview of the Issues' in O.S. Mitchell et al. (eds), *Prospects for Social Security Reform*, Pensions Research Council, University of Pennsylvania Press, Philadelphia.

Mitchell O.S., Poterba, J. and Warshawsky, M. (1997), *New Evidence on the Money's Worth of Individual Annuities*, Working Paper No. 6002, National Bureau of Economic Research, Cambridge, MA.

Mitchell, O., Poterba, J., Warshawsky, M. and Brown, J. (1999), 'New Evidence on the Money's Worth of Individual Annuities', *American Economic Review*, vol. 89, no. 5, December, pp. 1299–318.

Mitchell, O.S. and Zeldes, S. (1996), 'Social Security Privatization: A Structure for Analysis', *American Economic Review*, vol. 86, no. 2, May, pp. 363–7.

Modigliani, F. and Brumberg, R. (1954), 'Utility Analysis and the Consumption Function: An Interpretation of Cross-section Data', in K.K. Kurihara (ed.), *Post-Keynesian Economics*, Rutgers University Press, New Brunswick, N.J. pp. 388–436.

Murthi, M., Orszag, J.M. and Orszag P. R. (1999), 'Administrative Costs under a Decentralised Approach to Individual Accounts: Lessons from the United Kingdom', paper presented to the World Bank Conference 'New Ideas About Old Age Security', September.

Nalebuff, B. and Zekhauser, R. (1985), 'Pensions and the Retirement Decision', in David A. Wise (ed.), *Pensions, Labor and Individual Choice*, University of Chicago Press, Chicago, pp. 283–316.

OECD (1994), *Taxation and Household Saving*, Paris.

——(1997), *Private Pensions in OECD Countries: The United Kingdom*, Labour Market and Social Policy Occasional Paper No. 21, Paris.

——(1998a), *Maintaining Prosperity in an Ageing Society*, Paris.

——(1998b), *Institutional Investors Statistical Yearbook*, Paris.

——(1999), 'Occupational Private Pension Systems', *Financial Market Trends*, No. 73, June.

——(2000), *Private Pension Systems and Policy Issues No. 1*, Paris.

——*Labour Force Statistics*, various issues, Paris.

Office of the Australian Government Actuary (1995), *Australian Life Tables 1990–92*, Australian Government Publishing Service, Canberra.

Orszag, P. and Stiglitz, J., 'Rethinking Pension Reform: Ten Myths About Social Security Systems', in R. Holzmann and J. Stiglitz, (eds), *New Ideas About Old Age Security*, The World Bank, 2001.

Outreville, J. (1996), 'Life Insurance Markets in Developing Countries', *Journal of Risk and Insurance*, vol. 63, no. 2, June, pp. 263–78.

Owens, J. and Whitehouse, E. (1996), 'Tax Reform for the 21st Century', *International Bulletin of Fiscal Documentation*, vol. 50, no. 11–12, November–December, pp. 538–47.

Palacios, R. and Pallarès-Miralles, M. (1998), *International Patterns of Pension Provision, Mimeo*, World Bank.

——(2000), *International Patterns of Pension Provision*, Pension Reform Primer Series, Social Protection Discussion Paper No. 0009, The World Bank, Washington DC.

Palacios, R. and Rocha, R. (1998), *The Hungarian System in Transition*, Pension Reform Primer Series, Social Protection Discussion Paper No. 9805, April, The World Bank, Washington DC.

Philipson, T. and Becker, G. (1998), 'Old-age Longevity and Mortality-contingent Claims', *Journal of Political Economy*, vol. 106, no. 3, June, pp. 551–73.

Piggott, J. (1997), *Taxation and Pensions, Designs for Retirement Saving*, Research Report prepared for the Social Protection Division, The World Bank, Washington DC.

Piggott, J. and Doyle, S. (1998), *Annuitising Mandated Retirement Accumulations: A Primer*, paper prepared for the Social Protection Department, The World Bank, Washington DC.

Poterba, J. (ed.) (1993), *Public Policies and Household Saving*, National Bureau of Economic Research, University of Chicago Press, Chicago.

——(1997a), 'The Growth of 401(k) Plans: Evidence and Implications', in S. Schieber and J. Shoven (eds), *Public Policy Toward Pensions*, MIT Press, Cambridge, MA.

——(1997b), *The History of Annuities in the United States*, Working Paper No. 6001, April, National Bureau of Economic Research, Cambridge, MA.

Poterba, J., and Samwick, A. (1997), *Household Portfolio Allocation Over the Life Cycle*, Working Paper No. 6185, September, National Bureau of Economic Research, Cambridge, MA.

Poterba, J., Venti, S. and Wise, D. (1996), 'How Retirement Saving Programs Increase Saving', *Journal of Economic Perspectives*, vol. 10, no. 4, pp. 91–112.

——(1998a), '401(k) Plans and Future Patterns of Retirement Saving', *American Economic Review*, vol. 88, no. 2, May, pp. 179–84.

——(1998b), 'Personal Retirement Savings Programs and Asset Accumulation: Reconciling the Evidence', in D. Wise (ed.), *Frontiers in the Economics of Aging*, University of Chicago Press, Chicago.

——(1998c), 'Implications of Rising Personal Retirement Saving', in D. Wise (ed.), *Frontiers in the Economics of Aging*, Chicago, University of Chicago Press.

——(2000), 'Saver Behaviour and 401(k) Retirement Wealth', *American Economic Review*, vol. 90, no. 2, May, pp. 297–302.

Poterba, J. and Warshawsky, M. (1999), *The Costs of Annuitizing Retirement Payouts from Individual Accounts*, Working Paper 6918, National Bureau of Economic Research, Cambridge, MA.

Purcal, T.S. (1996), *Optimal Portfolio Selection and Financial Planning*, Retirement Economics Group Research Paper No. 4, University of New South Wales, Sydney.

Queisser, M. (1995), 'Chile and Beyond: The Second-generation Pension Reforms in Latin America', *International Social Security Review*, vol. 48, pp. 23–40.

——(1998), *The Second-generation Pension Reforms in Latin America*, OECD Ageing Working Paper AWP 5.4, Paris.

Quinn, J.F. (2000), 'New Paths to Retirement', in O.S. Mitchell, P.B. Hammond and A.M. Rappaport (eds), *Forecasting Retirement Needs and Retirement Wealth*, Pensions Research Council, University of Pennsylvania Press, Philadelphia, pp. 13–32.

Randall, J., Higgins, R. and Goddard, L. (1996), *Superannuation* (Deloitte Touche Tohmatsu), Australian Tax Practice, North Ryde, Sydney.

Rice Kachor (1999), *Master Trust Analysis*, Rice Kachor Research, Sydney.

Rofman, R. and Demarco, G. (1999), *Collecting and Transferring Pension Contributions*, Pension Reform Primer Series, Social Protection Discussion Paper No. 9907, February, The World Bank, Washington DC.

Samuelson, P. (1987), 'Comment', in Z. Bodie and J. Shoven (eds), *Financial Aspects of the United States Pension System*, University of Chicago Press: 276–87.

Samuelson, P. A. (1989), 'A Case at Last for Age-phased Reduction in Equity', *Proceedings of the National Academy of Sciences*, vol. 86, pp. 9048–51.

Samwick, A. (1998a), *New Evidence on Pensions, Social Security, and the Timing of Retirement*, Working Paper No. 6534, April, National Bureau of Economic Research, Cambridge, MA.

——(1998b), 'New Evidence on Pensions, Social Security and the Timing of Retirement', *Journal of Public Economics*, vol. 70, no. 2, November, pp. 207–36.

——(2000), 'Is Pension Reform Conducive to Higher Saving?', *Review of Economics and Statistics*, vol. 82, no. 2, May, pp. 264–72.

Samwick, A. and Skinner, J. (1998), *How Will Defined Contribution Pension Plans Affect Retirement Income?*, Working Paper No. 6645, June, National Bureau of Economic Research, Cambridge, MA.

Schmidt-Hebbel, K. and Serven, L. (1997), *Saving across the World: Puzzles and Policies*, Discussion Paper No. 354, The World Bank, Washington DC.

Schwarz, A. and Demigüc-Kunt, A. (1999), *Taking Stock of Pension Reforms Around the World*, Social Protection Discussion Paper No. 9917, The World Bank, Washington DC.

Senate Select Committee on Superannuation (1995), *Member Investment Choice*, Parliament House, Canberra.

Shah, H. (1998), 'Towards Better Regulation of Private Pension Funds', in *Promoting Pension Reform: A Critical Assessment of the Policy Agenda*, Proceedings of the APEC Regional Forum on Pension Reform, Cancun, Mexico, 4–6 February, Asian Development Bank, Manila, pp. 120–72.

Shiller, R. (1993), *Macro Markets: Creating Institutions for Managing Society's Largest Economic Risks*, Oxford University Press, Oxford.

Shoven, J. (1999), 'Social Security Reform: Two Tiers are Better than One', in H. Aaron and J. Shoven, *Should the United States Privatize Social Security?*, MIT Press, Cambridge, MA.

Sin, Y. and MacArthur, I. (2000), 'Country Profile for Hong Kong' in R. Holzmann, I. MacArthur and Y. Sin, *Pensions in East Asia and the Pacific: Challenges and Opportunities*, Social Protection Discussion Paper No. 0014, June, The World Bank, Washington DC.

Srinivas, P.S., Whitehouse, E. and Yermo, J. (2000), *Regulating Private Pension Funds' Structure, Performance and Investments: Cross-country Evidence*, Pension Reform Primer Series, Social Protection Discussion Paper, July, The World Bank, Washington DC.

Stanton, D. and Whiteford, P. (1998), *Pension Systems and Policy in the APEC Economies: Vol. 2; Pension Systems and Policy – Discussion Papers*, paper prepared for the Asian Development Bank.

Stock, J.H. and Wise, D.A. (1990), 'Pensions, the Option Value of Work, and Retirement', *Econometrica*, vol. 58, no. 5, September, pp. 1151–80.

Stulz, R.M. (1996), 'Rethinking Risk Management', *Bank of America Journal of Applied Corporate Finance*, vol. 9, no. 3, Fall, pp. 8–24.

Sundaresan, S. and Zapatero, F. (1997), 'Valuation, Optimal Asset Allocation and Retirement Incentives of Pension Plans', *Review of Financial Studies*, vol. 10, no. 3, pp. 631–60.

Sundén, A. (1998), 'The Swedish NDC Pension Reform', *Annals of Public and Co-operative Economics*, vol. 69, no. 4, December, pp. 571–83.

——(2000), *How Will Sweden's New Pension System Work*, Issues in Brief no. 3, Centre for Retirement Research, Boston College.

Surrey, S.S. (1973), *Pathways to Tax Reform: The Concept of Tax Expenditure*, Harvard University Press, Cambridge.

Thaler, R.H., Tversky, A., Kahneman D. and Schwartz, A. (1997), 'The Effect of Myopia and Loss Aversion on Risk Taking: An Experimental Test', *Quarterly Journal of Economics*, vol. 112, no. 2, May, pp. 647–61.

Tinnion, J. and Rothman, G. (1999), *Retirement Income Adequacy and the Emerging Superannuation System – New Estimates*, Retirement Income Modelling Unit, The Treasury, paper presented to the Seventh Colloquium of Superannuation Researchers, The University of Melbourne, July.

United Nations, *Demographic Yearbook*, vols 1 (1948) and 48 (1996), Dept. of Economic and Social Affairs, Statistical Office, New York.

United States Treasury (1977), *Blueprints for Basic Tax Reform*, US Government Printing Office, Washington DC.

Useem, M. and Mitchell, O.S. (2000), 'Holders of the Purse Strings: Governance and Performance of Public Retirement Systems', *Social Science Quarterly*, vol. 81, no. 2, June, pp. 491–506.

Valdes-Prieto, S. (1994), 'Administrative Charges in Pensions in Chile, Malaysia, Zambia, and the United States', Policy Research Working Paper 1372, The World Bank, Washington DC.

——(1998), 'The Private Sector in Social Security: Latin American Lessons for APEC', in *Promoting Pension Reform: A Critical Assessment of the Policy Agenda*, Proceedings of the APEC Regional Forum on Pension Reform, Cancun, Mexico, 4–6 February, Asian Development Bank, Manila, pp. 43–73.

Viceira, L. (2001), 'Optimal Portfolio Choice for Long-horizon Investors with Nontradeable Labor Income', *Journal of Finance* vol. 56, no. 2, April, pp. 433–70.

Walliser, J. (1997a), *Understanding Adverse Selection in the Annuities Market and the Impact of Privatising Social Security*, Technical Paper 1997–4, Congressional Budget Office, Washington DC.

——(1997b), *Privatising Social Security While Limiting Adverse Selection in Annuities Markets*, Technical Paper 1997–5, Congressional Budget Office, Washington DC.

——(2000), 'Adverse Selection in the Annuities Market and the Impact of Privatising Social Security', *Scandinavian Journal of Economics*, vol. 102, no. 3, September, pp. 373–93.

Whiteford, P. (1995), *The Use of Replacement Rates in International Comparisons of Benefit Systems*, Discussion Paper No. 54, Social Policy Research Centre, University of New South Wales.

Whitehouse, E. (1998), *Pension Reform in Britain*, Pension Reform Primer Series, Social Protection Discussion Paper no. 9810, June, The World Bank, Washington DC.

——(1999), *The Tax Treatment of Funded Pensions*, Pension Reform Primer Series, Social Protection Discussion Paper no. 9910, April, The World Bank, Washington DC.

——(2000), *Administrative Charges for Funded Pensions: An International Comparison and Assessment*, Pension Reform Primer Series, Social Protection Discussion Paper No. 0016, June, The World Bank, Washington DC.

Wise, D. (ed.) (1998), *Frontiers in the Economics of Aging*, National Bureau of Economic Research Project Report, University of Chicago, Chicago.

Wood, J. (1997), 'A Simple Model for Pricing Imputation Tax Credits under Australia's Dividend Imputation Tax System', *Pacific Basin Finance Journal*, vol. 5, no. 4, September, pp. 465–80.

World Bank (1994a), *Averting the Old Age Crisis: Policies to Protect the Old and Promote Growth*, Oxford University Press, New York.

——(1994b), *World Population Projections*, The World Bank, Washington DC.

Index

Accord, 190

account administrative charges, 71, 158, 163, 167, 182

account-keeping, 64, 65

accrued entitlements, 77, 209

accumulation access, 60–2

accumulation amount, 52–3, 56, 70, 71, 72

accumulation period, 160, 161, 162, 163, 168

accumulation phase, 52–3, 76, 125, 160, 161, 163, 182–4

accumulation policies, 2, 21, 39

accumulation schemes *see* defined-contributions schemes

accumulations, 16, 160, 161, 168–9, 170, 172, 202–3

active fund management, 86–7, 163

actuarial fairness, 12, 25*n*, 43–4, 104, 123, 124, 125, 130

actuaries, 94

administration costs/charges, 16, 19–20, 52, 53, 57, 59, 63–4, 66, 71–2, 73, 126, 158–80, 182, 183–4, 187, 195, 204, 208, 209–10, 212*n*, 214, 215

administrative efficiency, 53, 57

adverse selection, 9, 25*n*, 43, 79, 100, 120–4, 125, 130, 132*n*, 182, 185, 203

Afghanistan, 6

AFORES, 216

AFPs, 54–5, 57, 59, 60, 61, 64, 65, 68, 69, 70, 164, 170–1, 172, 173, 174, 175, 179*n*, 213–14, 215

Africa, 4, 5, 6

age and investment risk, 87–90

age pension *see* social security payments

age-phasing, 88–90, 91–2

aged dependency ratio, 6

ageing population, 1, 3, 5–7, 16, 18, 51, 153, 155, 182

aggregate saving and tax, 144–5

allocated products *see* asset allocation; phased withdrawals

American Express Company, 39–40

American style options, 222

annuities, 19, 100, 102–33, 185, 194, 196, 203, 213, 215, 216, 218, 219 *see also* life annuities

annuity demand, 124–5

annuity design, 102–11, 126, 128

annuity-issuer regulation, 111, 112

annuity market failure, 104, 120–6

annuity mortality rates, 187–8

annuity pricing, 104, 110–11, 120–1, 123–4, 125, 185

annuity risk rate, 110, 112, 126

Argentina, 14, 15, 51, 56, 60, 65, 67, 69, 70, 115–16, 141, 164, 165, 166, 176, 177, 215–16

Asia, 4, 5, 6, 181

assessment criteria, 20–3

asset allocation, 53, 54, 58–9, 66, 77, 85, 87, 90, 91–2, 97–8, 140, 144,

76, 77, 100, 102–30, 134–5, 139–49,
151–2, 158–80, 182, 184, 185, 186,
189–90, 194–220
mandatory public schemes, 2–3, 4, 8,
9–10, 11–12, 13, 15, 21–2, 29, 58–9,
60, 61, 77, 145, 158, 189, 190, 191–
3
mandatory schemes, 1, 3, 4, 7, 8, 10,
12, 13–15, 51, 181–2, 185–6, 187
market failure, 9–10, 12, 22, 25n, 104,
120–6, 136
market forces, 4
market risk, 81
market structure, 54
mass retirements, 27–9, 33
master trusts, 55, 58, 167, 168, 169–70,
172, 173, 174, 175–6, 177, 200, 221
means-testing, 8, 9, 29, 101, 117, 118,
184, 189, 190, 191, 192–3, 197, 203,
206, 207, 208, 212n, 214, 218, 220
medical technology, 7
member education, 52, 72
men
    accumulation access, 60–2
    age pension, 208
    annuity price variation, 110, 111
    education, 79
    labour force participation rates,
    27, 28, 29, 30, 147
    life expectancy of, 132n
    longevity, 42
    mass retirements, 27–9
    payout/preservation age, 213, 214,
    216, 218
    population ageing, 6
    purchasing power erosion, 108
    retirement age, 27–30, 37, 38, 39,
    192
    social security, 28, 30
    superannuation coverage, 205
    wages, 31, 32, 79
Mexico, 14, 15, 51, 56, 59, 61, 63, 65,
67, 69, 70, 115–16, 140, 164, 165,
166, 176, 177, 216
Mitchell, O.S., 38, 148
momentum investors, 86
moral hazard, 25n, 43, 71, 79, 122,
133n
mortality tables, 122, 123
multi-employer funds, 167 *see also*
industry superannuation/funds

mutual funds, 55, 56, 65, 66, 68, 166,
173, 177, 218
myopia, 22, 96–8, 203

national saving, 16–17, 204, 205, 206
net contributions approach, 63–4, 71
Netherlands, The 29, 33, 51–2, 66, 67,
140, 164, 219
New Zealand, 29, 33, 140, 153, 206
nominal annuities, 109, 111, 113, 123,
127, 128, 129, 133n
Northern America, 4, 5, 6, 7
Norway, 28–9, 33, 140

occupational schemes, 8, 18, 55, 73,
118, 119, 150, 164, 189, 190, 195,
218
Oceania, 4, 5
OECD countries, 13, 18, 28, 29, 31, 32,
33, 42, 51–2, 54, 55, 57–8, 101, 134,
140, 147, 181, 190, 218–19
open funds, 164, 173, 174, 175, 179n,
200, 209
option valuation, 225
options, 92–8, 106, 222–5
out-of-the-money put options, 92, 222
owner-occupier housing, 136, 145,
149–50, 153, 184, 186, 187, 195,
203, 206, 207 *see also* housing assets

Palacios, R., 1, 2, 14, 58
parametric reform, 11–12, 13, 25n
passive fund management, 86–7, 163
paternalism, 9
PAYG schemes, 2–3, 4, 8, 9, 11, 13,
15–16, 17, 18, 19, 21, 55, 59, 63,
113, 115, 149, 150, 151, 214, 215,
216, 217, 218, 220
payout/pensionable age, 213, 214,
216, 218, 219 *see also* retirement
age
payout phase, 185–6
Pension Benefit Guarantee Corporation, 95
pension fund assets, 15, 94, 146–7,
149, 154
pension funds, 54, 55, 56, 58–9, 61, 83,
112, 153–4, 164, 166, 172, 177,
213–20, 222 *see also* AFPs; managed
funds; mandatory schemes; mutual
funds; superannuation

For EU product safety concerns, contact us at Calle de José Abascal, 56–1°,
28003 Madrid, Spain or eugpsr@cambridge.org

www.ingramcontent.com/pod-product-compliance
Ingram Content Group UK Ltd.
Pitfield, Milton Keynes, MK11 3LW, UK
UKHW012155180425
457623UK00007B/40